Under the Maple Leaf

UNDER THE
MAPLE LEAF

THE REMARKABLE STORY OF FOUR CANADIAN VOLUNTEERS WHO FLEW
WITH BOMBER COMMAND DURING THE SECOND WORLD WAR

KENNETH B. COTHLIFF

Published in 2015 by Fighting High Ltd
www.fightinghigh.com

Copyright © Fighting High Ltd, 2015
Copyright text © Kenneth B. Cothliff, 2015

The rights of Kenneth B. Cothliff to be identified as the author of this book are asserted in accordance with the Copyright, Patents and Designs Act 1988.

The print publication is protected by copyright. Prior to any prohibited reproduction, storage in a retrieval system, distribution or transmission in any form or by any means, electronic, mechanical, recording or otherwise, permission should be obtained from the publisher.

The ePublication is protected by copyright and must not be copied, reproduced, transferred, distributed, leased, licensed or publicly performed or used in any way except as specifically permitted in writing by the publisher, as allowed under the terms and conditions under which it was purchased, or as strictly permitted by applicable copyright law. Any unauthorised distribution or use of this text may be a direct infringement of the author's and the publisher's rights and those responsible may be liable in law accordingly.

British Library Cataloguing-in-Publication data. A CIP record for this title is available from the British Library.

ISBN – 13: 978-0993212918

Typeset in Adobe Minion 11/17pt
by Alex Szabo-Haslam, www.truthstudio.co.uk

Printed and bound in China by Toppan Leefung.
Front cover design by www.truthstudio.co.uk

Dedication

Dedicated to Mrs Christina Gracie, and the Gracie family, who wholly accepted me into their lives in 1978, and without whom this book could not have been completed.

Contents

Prologue

Part I: Goldfish
1	Training in BCATP	1
2	Overseas to Britain	10
3	Bison Squadron	21

Part II: Evader
4	From Mining to Flying	55
5	Operations with the 'Lions'	67
6	Nuremberg	75
7	With the Maquis	86

Part III: Pathfinder
8	The Boy from Victoria	120
9	Tirpitz and the Ruhr	129
10	Pathfinder Force	135

Part IV: Scotty
11	The Young Volunteer	159
12	Iroquois Squadron	167
13	Alouettes and a Date with Destiny	171

Appendix — 184
Glossary — 186
Index — 189

Prologue

The stories in this book encompass the wartime experiences of four Second World War bomber crew. All of them were Canadian, and volunteers. There was no mandatory conscription in Canada, so the choice to serve their country and the Commonwealth was theirs alone. Although the basic accounts of their wartime lives in the air force were similar, their personal circumstances were very different, and all came from varying backgrounds. Three of these men survived the risky existence of being wartime aircrew – when the chance of getting past five operations was fairly slim – and returned home, but were radically changed for ever.

Much of the information has come from personal conversations or diaries and although, at the time of writing, three are no longer with us, they were known to the author as friends, and in one case, family. Bill 'Scotty' Gracie's story is a very personal one for me and was the catalyst for writing this book – he was my father. Born just a week after he was killed on operations, in August 1944, and then being put up for adoption by my birth mother, I never knew who my natural father was until 1977, when British adoption laws were changed. Having had an interest in aviation history since my teenage years, and having been given the tantalising clue that my birth father was a Canadian by my adoptive parents, Hilda and Malcolm Cothliff, I was keen to find out who I really was. But that is a long story in itself; suffice it to say for this work, I established contact with my birth family in Canada, and my mother in Wallasey, Merseyside. The Gracie family, and Mrs Christina Gracie – Bill's mother, and my grandmother – took me into their circle, and I maintain close links with them to this day.

Pathfinder 'ace', Reg Lane, joined Bomber Command relatively early and was in action by the autumn of 1941. He rose from NCO pilot to three-star general (air vice marshal) in the post-war RCAF, eventually retiring in the 1970s. Jim Moffat, the 'Evader' after twelve operations, ended his combat career fighting on the European mainland with the brave Resistance fighters. In Steve Puskas's story, I have taken advantage of his comprehensive diaries and unpublished writings to detail the full account of his training experiences in the British Commonwealth Air Training Plan (BCATP), shared by many Commonwealth and British aircrew, and an organisation unique in the annals of military history.

There are many special people to thank for their cooperation in putting this book together. The late Reg Lane and his dear late wife Barbara have allowed me exhaustive access to their family records; John Lane copied his father's log book, and Susan and David Lane helped with memories and access to Reg's sister Barbara. Their family have been friends to my late wife, Doreen, and I for many years, and the times Reg stayed with us filled in many aspects of his wartime life.

Jim Moffat has given me much advice, and I am deeply indebted to his sister, Mary Thomas, who has allowed me to use her biography of Jim, *Behind Enemy Lines*, as a basis for his story. Her book was published locally only in Canada, and I hope this publication will give the wider readership an insight into Jim's bravery. Marie Puskas provided me with a copy of her husband Stephen's unpublished wartime biography. Steve had told me he would have liked it to be published, but never got the opportunity. His notes gave a detailed account of his time in the BCATP, and I felt this was a narrative that Reg, Jim, Steve and many Bomber Command aircrew shared, and would help in the readers' understanding of Bomber Command, and especially 6 (RCAF) Group operations.

Bill's story, as well as being a personal one I felt I needed to tell, typifies the sacrifice given by more than 55,000 Bomber Command aircrew during the dark days of the Second World War, and is now symbolised by the magnificent memorial in London's Green Park.

Many thanks are due to the Gracie family, and grandma Christina in particular, who gave me all the documentation and letters. Bill's brothers – David in Bill's home town of Peterborough, Ontario, and Thomas, who passed away in 2011 – have been so supportive in allowing me to pry into their memories and family photographs, and I am grateful to them having passed me the family photograph album.

Not least, I owe a great deal of indebtedness to my late parents, Hilda and Malcolm. They made sure I always knew I was adopted. They gave me a secure and loving family home, and many good opportunities, and told me I was special as I was a 'chosen one', thereby removing any stigma of adoption. Sadly Hilda passed away in 1967, and never knew of my research, but Malcolm did meet Uncle Thomas and his wife Betty during one of their visits to the UK in the 1980s. He also took great interest in the tales of my three visits to Canada, before he passed on in 1988.

It has really been great fun putting all of this down on paper. I could not have done it without the support of my present wife, Julie, who has been with me on many of my trips, both to France, Canada and the Bomber Command Memorial unveiling in London in 2012. Others who helped include my dear friend, David Lee, former Deputy Director of IWM Duxford, who gave me much guidance; Canadian 6 (RCAF) Group historian and 6 Group webmaster, Richard Koval, who has helped with research in Canada and copied numerous documents and photographs from his extensive collection; Wing Commander (Retired) Alan Mawby, curator of the Museum Room at RAF Linton-on-Ouse, where so much of Reg's story took place; Mrs Barbara Hewitt, who has allowed the painting 'Thank You Canada' by her late husband John Rayson, G.Av.A, to be used; Karl Kjarsgaard, Bomber Command Museum, Nanton, Alberta; and finally a special thanks to Geoff Wood of Tholthorpe for his support in the early days of my research, and introductions to so many people over the years, including those who knew Bill in service.

I hope this book is enjoyed by all those who read it, and possibly inspires anyone interested in family research, as well as any adoptee out there, to look into their history. Let us hope the sacrifice and courage of the men and women of Bomber Command is never forgotten.

Ken Cothliff
Rawdon, Leeds
May 2015

UNDER THE
MAPLE LEAF

PART I
GOLDFISH

Steve Puskas (centre).

Part I: Goldfish

1. Training in BCATP

As the Handley Page Halifax bomber hit the waves of the cold North Sea, off the Scottish coast, it bounced once then rested back on the swell. The front nose fairing was 'stove in' and Steve Puskas found himself pinned in the pilot's seat by the rushing waves. He struggled to undo his harness, gulping in the seawater. The escape hatch over his head was locked, so his only option was to try further aft in the fuselage. He really thought his time had come, as he struggled to get out of the slowly sinking aircraft. It had been just over two years since he had volunteered for the Royal Canadian Air Force.

It has been said that first impressions are the most lasting, and certainly for nineteen-year-old Steve that was true. He never forgot waking up that first morning after arriving at the No. 1 RCAF Manning Depot in Toronto, having come from his home in Hamilton, Ontario, the previous day. He was conscious of unfamiliar noises. He opened his eyes to see a pair of lady's panties, obviously used, right in front of his eyes. The look on his face prompted gales of laughter from his new-found friends and 'inmates'. It was the way of things for men who had little knowledge of each other when they were grouped together in barracks. Pranks such as this eased the difficulties of their new lives.

Stephen Puskas was born in Czechoslovakia in June 1922 of Czech parentage; his father had worked on a large estate in an area called 'Mala Paloma', close to the Austrian border before emigrating to Canada and working his way across the country in the early 1920s. Steve and his mother joined him in their new family home in 1927 in the 'steel city' of Hamilton, Ontario, at the western end of Lake Ontario. On leaving school, Steve worked locally at Westinghouse Electric as a draughtsman while he waited for his call-up papers. In the meantime – pursuing his long-held interest in aviation – he engaged in lessons at Hamilton Flying Club, at nearby Mount Hope airfield, today home of the Canadian Warplane Heritage collection. His thought was to learn the complexities of flying, and to make sure he could master the 'art' before joining up. His experience might do him some good with the RCAF selection board. He took the aircrew medical and waited impatiently for his papers to come through. On 14 January 1942, along with four others, he made his way to the RCAF Manning Depot at the Exhibition Centre down by the Lake Ontario waterfront in Toronto, for the inevitable 'kitting out' and medicals.

The Manning Depot was housed in a huge area into which thousands of bunks, two-high, had been crammed. So numerous were they that one could easily lose their way back in the middle of the night after a visit to the bathroom. It was a world of queuing for food, clothing, bedding, pay, medicals, haircuts, or even a washbasin to shave and wash in. There were young men from all over Canada who were first strangers and soon intimates, and those whose personal habits were a bit 'rustic' or un-appealing. You just had to get used to it. The major factor for Steve – and indeed all the recruits – was the total absence of privacy, and the lack of space to think one's own thoughts. This was so different from his sheltered upbringing at home.

He had joined up with Albert Young, another chap he had known from Westinghouse, and they became inseparable. After a week confined to barracks, they were allowed out into Toronto, to get their ill-fitting uniforms put into decent shape, and explore the big city. They were only paid $41 a month and it did not go far. Steve and Albert often hitch-hiked back to Hamilton, where Albert had a girlfriend, and would try and get back before 'lights out'. One day it did not work out, and they found themselves outside the guarded area. They went over to the Salvation Army stand for a coffee, and merged in with guards on their rest – some of whom were their friends – and marched back in with them, sneaking off to their beds before they were found out.

Such was the way of life for the raw recruits. Smoking became normal, as it was an excuse for a 'break'. Steve and his chum also devised a plan to get out of the monotonous route marches, by volunteering to go to the Ryerson Technical Institute and be 'guinea pigs' for their decompression tests. 'Never complain,' was the advice given to him. Those who did, usually got no compassion, and ended up on kitchen duties. On one occasion one of the sparrows that lived in the high ceiling of the mess hall, relieved itself on Steve's plate, just as an inspecting officer came by. He asked Steve, 'Why aren't you eating your meal?' Steve replied, 'I like more potatoes with my meat, so I'm hoping to get some more.' The officer snorted, and moved on, and Steve had avoided an unwanted penalty.

When they had finished the basic training, many such as Steve were shipped out to various locations for 'guard duty' or 'tarmac duty', as the system was not yet ready for the next stage of their instruction. These were euphemisms for airfield labouring; anything to keep them busy and out of the way. Steve's move was to No. 5 Service Flying Training School (SFTS) at Brantford to become an airfield guard. Guarding from what they did not know – the enemy was thousands of miles away across the Atlantic. But after a medical called a 'short arm' inspection to check they were still healthy and had not contracted anything – after all, many, including Steve, had been into Toronto in the evenings, still only teenagers but trying to be men! – they packed all their gear, and the bus picked them up. At Brantford they met the men they were to replace, many of US citizenship, older, and who had volunteered to join the RCAF and fight with the British, and quite honestly were rather fed up with all this inactivity. Guard duty was four hours on duty and four hours off, and they were allocated a guard post on the top of a hangar, with spotlight, rifle and a few rounds of ammunition. Steve said, 'We never saw any "subversives", but did spot a few amorous activities.' On the second day three of them had to guard the crash site of an Avro Anson. The RCAF crews had just cut airmen's bodies out of the wreck, leaving the sweet sickly odour of death behind. It turned out an instructor had taken a couple of friends on a pleasure flight. It was a smell that Steve would never forget, and was a lesson learned about showing off in an aeroplane. Steve was detailed for the funeral parade.

By spring 1943 they were on their way to No. 6 Initial Training School (ITS), back at Ryerson Technical Institute, where they were to have ground school teaching them the basics of the theory of flight, meteorology, navigation, etc., with homework every day. A lot of collusion with your chums could help with the examinations. Nobody wanted to fail these tests; they were the first major hurdle in becoming aircrew. At the same time, they were told by a long-serving warrant officer about the 'hazards' of life in the city. There were always girls hovering around their billets, which were not far from a local street. Health failings could also jeopardise your flying chances. Still being innocent in many ways, the youngsters learned of all sorts of hidden dangers, including 'crabs'. These tiny mites could cause serious itching, and one of the students asked for help from the WO. 'Pour some whisky on your crotch, and that will get them drunk,' he was told, 'then put some sand on them, at which point they will stone one another to death!' Great hilarity again.

However, most of the time was spent studying maths, navigation, flying theory, meteorology and air force administration, as well as hours spent in the 'Link Trainer'. This latter piece of equipment was a very early form of flight simulator, in which the student climbed into a replica cockpit attached to electrical apparatus mounted on a table that represented the ground. The idea was to get a 'feel' of the aircraft and an aptitude for trusting the instruments. It was the bane of many students, but it was this and the exams that 'washed out' students from pilot training. Steve's friend, Albert Young, was 'washed out' and was sent to navigation school. Steve did well, though, and the proud day came at the end of his time at the ITS when he, along with the others, were awarded the propeller insignia of leading aircraftman, and the much coveted white flash of the aircrew trainee for his RCAF forage cap.

After a leave during which he travelled down to the USA to meet relatives, the next move was to No. 9 Elementary Flying Training School (EFTS), at St Catharines, just north of Niagara Falls. Soon decisions would have to be made about single-engined (fighter) or multi-engined (bomber) types. Sadly his friend Albert could not be with him; eyesight problems had meant his transfer to a navigator's course. Steve was really happy at this base, run on behalf of the RCAF by the local flying club: 'It was the happiest I was ever at during my time in the forces.' The instructors were civilians wearing a similar but darker uniform than the RCAF, and Steve had an American named Morgan as his assigned tutor. Morgan was as miserable as anyone could be; he had only joined up for free flying coaching, and had a job lined up back in the USA with United Air Lines. His attitude on the continuation training of his students was relaxed indeed.

Steve started flying on 18 August 1942, in a DH-82C Canadian-built Tiger Moth, No. 3943, powered by a Menasco engine. The Canadian Moths were different to their British-built counterparts, having modified cowlings and brakes, and raked forward undercarriage to reduce the threat of 'nose-over' on braking. In addition, metal struts were fitted. The most obvious variation was the covered sliding cockpit canopy, to give some protection from the cold in winter. As Steve had flying experience he was told the minimum number of hours he could get away with before soloing was five. He went solo in seven on 7 September in Moth No. 1297, and his first cross-country exercise in No. 8905 followed on 30 September.

On 21 September he had experienced his first forced landing, in Tiger Moth No. 8890, when, after doing some aerobatics with other students, he was heading back to one of their 'away airfields', St Kitts. As he emerged from cloud the propeller stopped. Steve tried to restart, using the prescribed procedure of a dive. At about 1,500 feet the engine gave a couple of coughs and ceased again, so he decided the safest course of action was to find a field to land in. The taught procedure was to pick a field and stick with it, but as he approached his selection he noticed some overhead power lines, so he swung the aircraft round into another field, only to discover – to his alarm – there was a tree in the middle of it. Just missing its branches, he found he was heading towards a gully, so he ground-looped the aircraft, luckily without damage to the airframe. As he sat in the cockpit gathering his wits about him he noticed a farmer leaning on a fence. The farmer said he 'would swing the prop'. Caution took hold and Steve said he had to report to his base, so he was directed to a farmhouse with a telephone, and luck was on his side again: he was inside the solo flying boundary for his 'base' airfield. By the time he got back to the aircraft, the 'locals' were all over it, and he had to retrieve his helmet from some enthusiastic children. When the station personnel arrived, the mechanic said that the carburettor had been set too lean. As a result, the chief flying instructor (CFI) flew the aircraft back to base.

It was while he was at St Catharines that one of the senior students flew his Tiger Moth under the 'Rainbow Bridge' that crossed the Niagara gorge, just downstream of the falls. There were plenty of dangerous air currents from the river there, and it was extremely hazardous. It took a lot of nerve to attempt it and, according to Steve, 'It gave him a hell of a fright.' However, the identity number of the aircraft had been taken and by the time the student got back there was a reception committee waiting for him. The authorities were reasonably relaxed about some fooling around, but this was too far, almost suicidal. His penalty was twenty-eight days in the cells and he was 'washed out'.

Later that summer, the first of the RAF trainees under the British Commonwealth Air Training Plan (BCATP) arrived from the UK. This was a scheme devised by the Canadian prime minister, William McKenzie-King, for Canada to contribute to the Commonwealth dominion's war effort, without the huge losses that Canada had suffered in the First World War. Those losses were still deep in the psyche of the Canadian people, and one of the reasons there was no conscription in Canada. In fact the RAF already had some airfields in operation in Alberta. The British representatives in Canada, led by Lord Riversdale in October 1939, envisaged twelve Elementary Flying Training Schools (EFTS), twenty-five Advanced Service Flying Training Schools (ASFTS), fifteen Air Observer Schools (AOS), fifteen Bombing and Gunnery Schools (B&GS), as well as three Air Navigation Schools (ANS) and one Wireless Training School (WTS), a huge commitment by any standards. However, the 'patronising' attitude of the British did not auger well for the conference in Ottawa, and the plan nearly 'stumbled at the first hurdle'. In the end Lord Balfour, the British Parliamentary Under Secretary, was under instructions from Winston Churchill to make it work. He and McKenzie-King figured out a deal, and so was born one of the most successful aviation training organisations the world has ever seen. St Catharines came into existence on 14 October 1941, and continued for just over three years.

Initially the British trainees took time to acclimatise to the Canadian way of doing things. It seemed to the young Canadians these chaps from across the sea all lived in castles and big houses, and they took their meals differently. At the school they all ate cafeteria style, and took as much as they wanted; something that was 'alien' to the British after the rationing at home. It appeared a brawl would occasionally break out over the seating. Nothing serious to scrap over, but the Canadians felt the British airmen should abide by their rules, and believed their attitude was initially wrong. It took time for things to settle down.

On 9 October 1942, Steve was 'signed off' and was ready for the next stage of his training. Most of the young pilots wanted to go on to single-engined instruction on Harvard, or Yale (a Harvard with fixed undercarriage) monoplane trainers. They had heard of the exploits of the RAF during the Battle of Britain and the lure of flying fighters was strong in many. Steve had an idea he would like to continue flying whenever the war finished and become a civilian pilot, and so immediately opted for multi-engined

TRAINING IN BCATP   7

coaching on Avro Anson trainers. He looked forward to moving to No. 5 SFTS at Brantford, Ontario, not that far from his home, and where he had been on guard duty in the early days.

Many of the local women at St Kitts organised a reception centre in the town where the young homesick men could enjoy some female company. Even a regular Saturday dance took place in the town. The Canadians often left these facilities to the British. After all, these poor boys were far from home and many had their families living through the bombing in the UK. Steve could understand their need for social contact. Steve took the opportunity of his post-course leave to head to New York with his chum, Harry Snyder, who was continuing on to Brantford with him. It was an eye-opening experience.

Returning to Canada, they transferred to No. 5 SFTS, where they re-established themselves in familiar surroundings at Brantford, and 28 October saw Steve's first familiarisation flight. The aircraft they were using at this time were the British-built Avro Anson Mk I with Cheetah IX engines, soon to be supplemented with the Canadian-built Mk II version, with a ply fuselage and American 330hp Jacobs engine. Much later the RCAF had the all-ply Mk V, with the 'greenhouse' windows replaced by circular portholes, and powered by the Pratt & Whitney Wasp Junior R985. These later models soldiered on in the RCAF until the late 1950s. The Anson was a stable training aircraft, ideal for multi-engined and navigation training, and many of the early ones had been retired from RAF use where they had been used for coastal patrols, and as light bombers, and shipped over to Canada to get the BCATP scheme quickly off the starting blocks.

Steve's primary tutor was Pilot Officer Van Adel, who had just qualified as an instructor. Newly married he told Steve he was his first pupil, and turned out to be understandably very cautious. Steve soloed in Anson No. 6931 on 4 November. The next stage was cross-country navigation and training, both solo and with another pilot on long flights. This was often quite boring; not so bad for Steve and his compatriots in Ontario, but especially so for student pilots in Saskatchewan and the flat lands where the countryside had few recognisable features. It was easy to lose concentration sometimes, and the toll on the aircraft could be heavy, especially in the busy confines of the airspace around the airfield. On one occasion at Brantford, an Anson piloted by a student on Steve's course came down and literally bounced on top of another. The lower aircraft had the tail torn off, causing it to loop and crash alongside the runway. The top Anson hit the ground, landing on its starboard wing. Such was the robust nature of the aircraft that fortunately nobody was killed, although one student had his front teeth knocked out by the control column.

Steve, too, had a close shave early on the course, on 6 November, when he was told to report to the flight line for a test with Flight Lieutenant Smith, one of the much feared examiners. Anson No. 6951 was on the apron with the engines turning, with Smith inside the cockpit. 'Should I go through the ground check?' asked Steve. 'No need, I've done it', was the reply. So he climbed into the pilot's seat and started to inspect the controls, part of the very basic routine when taking charge of an aircraft. 'Ailerons – OK. Elevators – OK. Flaps – OK.' But the rudder was stiff. Steve suggested, 'I should check the rudder', but Smith said, 'It should be all right.' Steve went to look anyway, and there on the rudder was the red wooden clamp, firmly fixed in position. He returned to the cockpit with the evidence; 'It was still on!' Silence – no apology, just, 'Well, carry on.' Even examiners were not infallible.

Towards the end of January 1943, they were joined on the flight by a new instructor, Warrant Officer Bringloe. There was a story that he had been a tutor on Harvards, and had crashed while doing some unauthorised aerobatics, killing his pupil. One of the students in Steve's flight, Russ Baer, told them in the billet one evening that Bringloe and he had looped and rolled an Anson during a flight. This was greeted with some scepticism. A few days later Russ, along with American, C. Haines-Finnell, decided to loop their aircraft. During the upstage of the manoeuvre the Anson had stalled upside down. After many frantic moves on the control column, its equilibrium was regained and it was two very chastened student pilots who carefully flew back to Brantford. That evening, as the aircraft was pushed back into the hangar, a wing dropped a bit, something it should not do. The main spar had broken. After much grilling, the flight commander, Flying Officer Guest, was no nearer to finding the answer, so a line was drawn under the matter.

On 23 February Steve had his 'wings check', including forced-landing procedure, and that was followed by his 'instrument check' with Guest a couple of days later, both of which he passed. His final selection interview then took place, during which Steve was a little forthright, even though he had been told to express his opinions truthfully. Steve had said: 'Why do we have to wash aircraft and push them around? Other flights do not have to do that.' Flying Officer Bitz did not want to hear that. 'Better men than you and I have washed aircraft', was his reply. It had not gone down too well, and at the end of the course during the 'rumble party', after a few beers Flying Officer Van Adel strode up and told Steve that he thought he would have had a commission if it had not been for that exchange. They parted in a not too friendly state.

The last flight to complete his hours came on 15 March. With Warrant Officer Bringloe in Anson No. 7288, he took the aircraft up to 10,000 feet. As they levelled off Bringloe asked: 'Did you know you can loop and slow roll an Anson?' 'I've heard about that, but don't believe it,' responded Steve. 'Follow me through,' indicated Bringloe, and he proceeded to put the aircraft through the manoeuvres. As they went over the top, Steve looked back to see the tailplane flutter a little! Then Bringloe said, 'You do it.' With some trepidation, Steve did. That was his last service school flight, and one he would never forget.

By the end of the course at No. 5 SFTS, Steve had totalled 224 hours and 50 minutes, considerably more than pilots in the UK, especially at the beginning of the war. It was time for the Wings Parade, when their pilot's wings were pinned on their uniform, and they could remove the white flash on their caps. Their families were present; Steve's parents came over from Hamilton, with sister Mary and some of his school friends, the parade being held in one of the hangars. Afterwards, their American friend, C. Haines-Finnell, had his family from New York throw a big party at the Royal Connaught Hotel in Hamilton. They rented a suite of rooms in the hotel and the booze kept coming all night. There were shortages, and they had no permits, so it can only be guessed that the 'bootleggers' did a roaring trade that night. Then it was embarkation leave, and for Steve the anticipation of an overseas posting, as he had volunteered to go abroad.

Part I: Goldfish

2. Overseas to Britain

Taking the train from Hamilton to Toronto, then on to the Mont Royal Hotel in Montreal, Steve had arranged to meet up with some of his friends from Brantford, including Russ Baer, and Charles Haines-Finnell. There they were, and the party had already started. So it continued across Canada to the 'Maritime Provinces' and Halifax, Nova Scotia. When they arrived at Halifax, they were broke, hungry and tired. They were shown to No. 17 Depot to await a vessel. Here time was spent on interminable kit inspections to ensure they had all they needed, and then boring parades. If you lost an item of kit, you had to buy a new one. One chap's raincoat went missing and he reported it to the service police. He was told, 'What do you want me to do about it? Get a replacement the same way you lost yours!' One morning they were told to parade with full kit, to be ready to leave. Rumour went around they were off to New York and a passage on the *Queen Mary*. Much to their surprise the train stopped at Moncton, New Brunswick, about 100 miles to the west, where they were told to disembark and march to No. 31 Personnel Reception Depot (PRD), an RAF holding unit. The place was dire, and the food especially so; many of the men, including Steve, went into town to the local restaurants for food. Discipline started to break down, and parades were missed. The camp staff could not cope with all their complaints. It was difficult to believe this was still Canada. Eventually a waitress at a restaurant told them they would be departing soon; so much for security! That night the gates were closed and locked.

The following morning, Steve and the others boarded a train, but instead of heading to New York, they travelled back to Halifax to a large vessel at the docks; there was another parade, then it was up the gangplank to board the *Empress of Scotland*, a Canadian Pacific liner turned troopship. These ships were fast by the standards of the day, so it set sail alone, rather than in convoy, making a swift passage even in its consistent zigzagging to deter any U-boat attack.

The Canadian NCOs were led down into the bowels of the ship where there was a room full of tiered bunks, and each man was allowed a space of about 7 feet x 30 inches x 30 inches into which one had to fit yourself and all your kit. It seemed to Steve to be a seething mass of bodies with, in the corner, a foul-smelling toilet that spilled over in rough weather. Food was taken in a mess with long wooden tables and benches, and the main meal was often 'utility' sausages and mash, dumped in bulk on the table. These sausages were said to consist of 50% bread, 20% meat and 30% sawdust. When one was hungry they tasted all right. While walking around the deck, Steve discovered some of his contacts from his time at Brantford, including the first chap to be 'washed out', a fellow named Zellen, who was now sporting an air gunner's brevet, and a commission, so he had a cabin. The irony was not lost on Steve.

After about seven days, land was spotted; it was Northern Ireland and they were greeted by an RAF Anson, with turret flashing an Aldis lamp at the ship. A day or so later, they berthed at Liverpool, and were greeted with the strange sight of barrage balloons.

After disembarking they boarded a train at the dockside to take them to the aircrew reception centre at Bournemouth, the town a holiday resort on the south coast. The majority of the local hotels had been turned over to accommodation for the incoming Commonwealth aircrew. After a few nights the young Canadians were greeted by a broadcast on the radio of German propaganda with 'Lord Haw-Haw' saying: 'Welcome all you Canadians. Wait until Saturday and we'll show you something.' But nothing actually happened that Saturday night. The sirens did go off occasionally, and the more long-standing residents told the newcomers, 'Don't worry they are on their way inland.' One day, though, aircraft did bomb and strafe the town. It was all very exciting, and even made the poor food they were getting more palatable. However, a lot of time was spent on route marches and running along the seafront to keep their minds active.

Steve did get a chance to acquaint himself with English life, taking a train to Nottingham to stay with some relatives of his friend, Jim Bolton. It was Steve's first opportunity to experience how the English were living under rationing, and it was very different from home. Their host was quite devout, and the day started with a religious broadcast on the radio. But realising his young guests might want to explore, he took them on to the city, and to the famous local pub, 'Ye Olde Trip to Jerusalem', carved into a rocky outcrop under Nottingham Castle, and reputed to be the oldest in the UK, dating from AD 1189. They also tried rowing on the River Trent. Before long it was back to Bournemouth. It was about this time Steve met a girl called Peggy, spending evenings with her and her friends and his chums. With Peggy he visited her family at home during his service, and Steve kept in contact, not only during the war but afterwards throughout his life. It was socialising with these English people that gave relief from the boredom of service existence, and the distance from home, and made things more bearable. It was also about now he got used to English tepid 'bitter' beer, so different from that in Canada, and it took time to acquire the taste. He also kept up a little 'flying' practice on a locally based Link Trainer.

In June 1943 they went before a selection board to decide their future postings and were asked what aircraft they would like to fly. Steve said, 'Mosquitoes.' He was questioned: 'Could you cope with the night flying in England, which is more difficult than in Canada?' 'Don't think there would be a problem,' Steve confidently replied. One officer quizzed: 'What would be your second choice?' 'Mitchells!' They dismissed Steve and he marched out, feeling it had been a good interview. However, pilots were needed for the 'heavies' of Bomber Command; that was where the biggest losses were. So almost all the fellows were sent on courses for four-engined bombers, including Steve, and his first posting was to No. 15 (P) Advanced Flying Unit at Ramsbury.

Four and a half miles east of Marlborough, Wiltshire, Ramsbury was used to train pilots from the BCATP unused to the European climate. Normally a pilot would spend about six weeks there flying the Airspeed Oxford, but Steve's stay was relatively short, and three weeks and forty-three flying hours (mostly in daylight) later he was off to his next posting at RAF Cranage on the Cheshire plain, just north of Crewe. Cranage was built as a training station, to house No. 2 School of Air Navigation, but its location south of Liverpool and Manchester meant it was on the routes of the German bombers on their way to attack the industrial and port areas of Lancashire, and had been the base for Defiant and Hurricane fighters. By the time Steve arrived it was home to No. 1531 Squadron Beam Approach Training. This was used to tutor pilots in the use of instruments on approach to landing, and Steve found the course – which was mostly flown in 'blind' conditions in Airspeed Oxfords – really enjoyable. By 4 August he was at No. 18 Advanced Flying Unit at RAF Snitterfield, north of Stratford-upon-Avon, in the Midlands, for night-flying instruction. It was difficult in the blacked-out conditions of England. Identifying the Morse letters flashed out by the 'Pundit Lights' on the airfields was important, and a big help when returning from an operation. One night Steve and his instructor saw a raid in progress on the university town of Oxford.

The pilots also used to take turns at the runway control caravan at the airfield, giving a green or red signal with the Aldis lamp to landing aircraft. On one occasion, while Steve was fidgeting with a flare gun used for emergencies, it went off – the flare crossed the front of a landing Oxford, scaring the pilot, who staggered around for another circuit. Nobody in charge appeared to notice, much to Steve's relief, and a lesson was learned – don't play with guns!

On one solo he encountered heavy cloud and decided to fly on instruments above it. After a while Steve became worried he was lost. Eventually the clouds broke and he found himself over the sea. Reversing course, and this time staying below the cloud, he had landfall, and spotted an airfield. Landing there, he was told he was at RAF Locking, on the Somerset coast near Weston-super-Mare. He then took off and returned safely to base. Map reading and weather conditions were so different to the vast areas of Canada, and it was proving difficult; it was a major concern to him. Among other things to contend with were barrage balloons. One took the life of a member of their group when his Oxford aircraft got caught by it and was brought down. Another got shot at by a convoy off the south coast; the Navy tended to shoot first, and identify later!

Having heard that one of his friends, Albert Young, was at No. 24 Operational Training Unit (OTU) at Honeybourne, Steve decided, while on leave in London, to try and get a posting there. He stopped in at the RCAF's European headquarters in Lincoln's Inn Fields, in the city centre, and asked for a transfer, hoping to get crewed up with Albert. He was told in no uncertain terms that it was an impossible request. 'What kind of mess would the RCAF be in if they made postings on such arrangements?' he was told. Steve went away dejected, 'After all,' he thought, 'I was not asking for much.'

When the next posting came through it was indeed to RAF Honeybourne and No. 24 Operational Training Unit, as he had hoped. Located near Stratford, the unit was equipped with the elderly Armstrong Whitworth Whitley Vs.

Six of Steve's group were posted there. His comrades were not impressed: 'Don't you know the Whitley is known as the flying coffin?' But Steve didn't care, as now it might be possible to crew up with Albert after all.

On the way to Honeybourne they had to use a slow local train, which was late arriving. Steve's colleagues were still giving him a hard time: 'Hey Puskas, why don't you ask the station master when the train is due?' The station master was a tall, imperious-looking chap with a smart uniform, 'scrambled egg' braid on his cap, and a rolled-up flag and whistle on a chain; obviously a man of some importance. 'Hey Mac!' Steve called, 'When is the train due?' The official glanced at Steve haughtily and replied tersely: 'I beg your pardon, my name is not Mac', much to the great amusement of the Canadians who rocked with laughter.

After settling in, Steve looked up his old friend, Albert, but he was in the base hospital recovering from a crash on take-off. It was nothing too serious, so Steve went to his flight commander to ask if they could be crewed together. Sadly no luck; the commander was quite adamant. Albert Young was three weeks ahead of Steve, and as such would complete the course before him. The RAF would not budge on the matter.

Now came the strange time when the crews were teamed up. All bomber crews went through this stage, and all remember it as a difficult time. In Steve's case five pilots and navigators were put into a room, and told to get on with it. Of the crew, most of the navigators were officers and pilots were NCO sergeants, and after introductions they were expected to sort themselves out. Steve approached one chap, but was rebuffed as he preferred another pilot, 'Doc' Murray. Steve was 'miffed', and in the end it came down to the two left and, by process of elimination, Steve and Flying Officer James 'Jasper' Still formed an alliance. Eventually the two men bonded together and became good friends. The same sequence happened with the bomb aimers, except that Sergeant Ted Bowles got on with Steve immediately. Ted's attitude at the meeting gave Steve the confidence that he knew his job. Next, Steve asked a tall, lanky easy-going gunner, Sergeant Alvin Williams, to be one of his gunners, and he agreed. Alvin knew of another gunner who was not crewed up yet, and Sergeant Wilf Faulkner joined forces in the rear position. Wilf gave all the impression of being a 'farm boy', but he had an accurate eye, as was proved later, and knew his guns well. Last to sign up was their wireless operator/air gunner, Sergeant Wilson. For now that was the full crew for a twin-engined Whitley; later they would need to add a flight engineer for a four-engined bomber.

It was now 24 September, and the next few weeks saw them lumbering around the countryside in the elderly Whitley, visiting bombing ranges, having fighter affiliation attacks by RAAF Kittyhawks, and participating in lots of cross-country flights.

Steve's third flight at Honeybourne was alone with his crew, a quick trip of some 40 minutes. In order for the airmen to get on well together it was decided that new crews would have a 'get acquainted party', to be held in the sergeant's mess (NCOs were not allowed in officers' quarters). With the Canadians, there were always difficulties between officers and NCOs. The RAF hierarchy did not go down well with the easy-going 'colonials'. After a few 'beery' competitions, including many 'boilermakers' (a glass of whisky in a pint of beer), Steve saw sandwiches being laid out in another room. 'Good idea,' thought Steve. 'Spam sandwiches will soak up the booze.' He strode through to get some, when an officer pulled him to one side and said the tray was to be left there, and the men were to collect their own food. When Steve told his crew they were angry, and Wilf went into the room and grabbed the officer by his shirt and tie, and asked if he was the one who said his pilot could not have the plate of food. 'Oh no', was the reply. 'Good,' said Wilf and picked up the tray. The following day the CFI called Steve into his office and instructed him on etiquette: 'That gunner of yours has a bad temper. You know he grabbed the wrong chap?'

The men were coached on the proper behaviour with officers: pilots were in command in their aircraft, but on the ground, officers should be given due accord, and saluted. Steve was not too happy about this, and in a crew meeting together, Steve told Jasper that nobody in the crew should call him 'Sir'. He felt the team aspect was more important. Flying Officer Still agreed: 'It's all right by me.' However, he did not mingle with the rest of the crew as much. But they slept in the same hut, ate, and even went on leave together.

Steve's opinion of the Whitley V was that it was 'a dreadful contraption': slow and ungainly and always looking like it was flying downwards, the rear gunner being higher that the pilot. The trim constantly had to be adjusted, and during fighter affiliation its lack of manoeuvrability was painfully obvious. On their first night-time cross-country on 16 October, they were briefed to locate an island off the Welsh coast and photograph it. Wilbur Wilson was told to drop a photo-flash flare to light the sky. It took ages to ignite, and then went off too close to the aircraft. On their return to base, Steve asked Wilbur what had happened. Apparently he had pulled the pin to activate it, then it had jammed in the flare chute. After bashing it with his flying boot it eventually dropped, exploding immediately under the aircraft. Another close shave and a lesson learned.

Getting used to the cumbersome kit was another lesson. Their parachutes had a strap that hung down until they got in the aircraft, when it was then engaged to the release clasp. This strap was suspended between their legs as they travelled to the aircraft, usually on a truck. One day Steve's strap got caught on the tailgate and was pulled upwards, causing excruciating agony for him as his 'family jewels' were crushed. It was the cause of great laughter by the crew until they realised he really was in pain, and freed him. 'I had to walk kind of funny for a few days afterwards,' Steve remembered.

Slowly he became aware of the responsibility of his job. On joining up he had only ever considered he needed to look after himself. He thought that if he made a mistake only he would pay the consequences, but now he had to be mindful of his crew too, and was responsible for their safety. This bothered him greatly. Quietly, and without fuss, Steve collected together the family details of his crew and kept them in a notebook, just in case he needed to write a letter explaining their demise. Luckily for him he never had reason to use the information in this way. He also made a decision that he would never drink heavily, especially before flying the following day.

One of the officers at Honeybourne was Squadron Leader Hamber, who had been a senior officer at SFTS Brantford. He was, in Steve's terminology: 'A regular guy who never tried to "high hat" you.' He made friends with Steve. At this time aircrew of his higher rank were rarely attached to a crew, as they were expected to become commanding officers of a squadron. He did eventually become CO of No. 426 (Thunderbird) Squadron in April 1944 at RAF Linton-on-Ouse. Hamber asked if he could borrow Steve's aircrew for a few exercises. After chatting it over with his men, they all agreed to help. On 24 October, in Whitley TY-E 'E-Easy' (serial number unknown), they had trouble getting the 'old bird' to climb. After about

2 hours they had climbed to about 5,000 feet. The port engine started to overheat, and then caught fire. Steve pressed the button for the fire extinguishers, but that did not seem to work, so he started looking for somewhere to land. Whitleys had a bad reputation and the airmen were wondering whether to bail out when Steve spotted the lights of an airfield and, resorting to using 'Darky' procedure (next important emergency after 'Mayday') called up that he was in trouble. He was worried this might be one of the 'Q-sites' – dummy airfields to confuse the Germans – but it turned out to be an American station, Dunkeswell. They called him in and he touched down safely. A small staff of RAF personnel took charge of the aircraft, and the crew were given over to the care of the USAAC and showered with American 'goodies'.

After a couple of days, the aircraft was patched up enough for the short flight to Honeybourne. As they were leaving, the RAF types gave Steve a list of seventeen items that needed attention, with a comment: 'Give this list to the flight sergeant.' On his return he passed it to the flight sergeant in charge of maintenance, and asked: 'Are the aircraft DI'd?' (given a daily inspection). The mechanic, a long-time NCO, said: 'Sarge, if I look out of the window and see the aircraft, it's DI'd!' That gave Steve no confidence at all.

For this incident, Steve received a 'commendation' in his log book for saving the aircraft, rather than having the crew bail out.

On 3 November 1943, in Whitley TY-B 'B-Bravo', they experienced their first operation over enemy territory in the form of a 'Nickel' leaflet run over the Paris area. Three aircraft were detailed, piloted by Warrant Officer Andy Gibb, Flight Lieutenant Kennedy, who had been an instructor on Steve's course at No. 5 SFTS, Brantford, and Sergeant Steve Puskas. This was a diversion raid while the main force of Bomber Command hit Düsseldorf. Only two aircraft returned, Kennedy's plane going down after an engine fire and only the rear gunner, Sergeant Al Spencer, surviving.

The following day was another eventful flight, in TY-J 'J-Johnnie', when, after a 'Bullseye' exercise with fighter affiliation, a red light appeared, showing that the undercarriage had not come down on approach for landing. They circled the airfield, narrowly missing another aircraft, when rear gunner Wilf Faulkner just gave them enough notice and tried to wind the gear down by hand. Eventually, with no visible luck, Steve ordered the wireless operator to cut the hydraulic line in a last-ditch attempt to remove any airlock. Lack of fuel meant they had one final chance to land, but – all warnings blaring away – they did so safely and without any damage. Steve was met by the engineering officer, who was livid at the hydraulic oil spilled everywhere, and gave him a telling off. There was, however, no comment on the faulty gear warning, except that 'safety equipment does not always work!' During these flights in November, Steve had a few hours as navigator to hone his extra skills.

At the commencement of their course all crews had tossed £5 into a 'pot', with the idea that the crew with the best bombing record would win the the amount pooled, and this would make for a more interesting competition. At this time the CFI called Steve into his office to say that his crew had won the 'pot' and completed the prescribed course ahead of the others, and that rather than sitting around waiting for some action, he was sending them on leave early. So they went off to London, and demolished their savings. Before they joined their next unit they were sent on an 'escape course' at RAF Dalton in Yorkshire, just to the south-west of the bleakest part of the Yorkshire Moors. The course was run by instructors from the local Yorkshire regiment, the Green Howards, with just a flight lieutenant and two PT instructors from the RCAF. Actually, the Canadian instructors were the two Sharp brothers, from Steve's home town of Hamilton; he knew them well, and they socialised together. Often the exercise would be to have the group dropped off on the moors, and told to find their way to a certain point using only maps and a compass. If you were caught on the road, you would be taken back 3 miles. It was a course not enjoyed by the airmen, but as can be seen from another story in this book, could be very useful after baling out over enemy territory.

On one evening the course was divided into two groups, and split on opposite sides of the airfield. The idea was for one group to light a lamp and advance with it across the field, and for the second group to 'defend' and capture the lamp. Steve and Wilf thought this a rather silly exercise. Steve recalled: 'We hid in a swampy ditch behind the lit lamp, and as everybody moved out, we moved to the lamp, we blew it out then carried it in the dark across the airfield and lit it again! The exercise was over, and a lot of time saved.' Here they were staying in primitive accommodation, and the winter's cold and damp weather was getting to the young Canadians. Keeping warm was a problem, and they never seemed to have enough wood, so they scrounged it from wherever they could. A lot came from a local farmer's fence, until he took to defending it with a shotgun; then they even resorted to chopping up the wooden toilet doors and seats! The Green Howards put up with their nonsense for so long, then they took the 'steam' out of the Canadians by making them go through the obstacle course.

On 24 January 1944 the crew headed just a few miles to the west to RAF Dishforth, alongside the A1 Great North Road, where they joined 1664 Heavy Conversion Unit, which had moved down from RAF Croft on Teesside. Here they were to familiarise themselves with their first four-engined aircraft, the Handley Page Halifax. It was now very likely that eventually they would be joining the Canadian No. 6 (RCAF) Group, also based in Yorkshire. Steve and his crew stayed for almost a month. This aircraft needed more help in lifting off the ground: someone to look after engine temperatures, fuel consumption and the like. Initially their bomb aimer, Ted Bowles, assisted, but they were soon joined by a new man, Jack Phillips. As previously, they were just put into a room and asked to 'sort yourselves out'. Like many RAF flight engineers, Jack was formerly an airframe fitter and ground crew mechanic before volunteering for flying duties, and had been in the air force a lot longer than any of the Canadian aircrew. Steve thought he looked trustworthy – about all he had to go on – so asked him to come and meet the rest of his men. They all stared at him and said nothing, and it was as though Jack could read their minds. 'I know you chaps would rather have a Canadian engineer, but there are none,' he said. They all felt rather sheepish. Jack became a reliable, trustworthy and popular crew member.

The aircraft were Mk II and Mk V Halifaxes, both with Merlin engines – just like the old Whitleys they had been flying – and were mostly tired old aircraft from operational squadrons. Steve's first flight in the Halifax was on 24 January in DH-E 'E-Easy', with Flight Lieutenant Smith on a familiarisation flight of 45 minutes. He took the controls for the first time and gingerly made some gentle turns. Smith said: 'You can throw this aircraft around without damaging it, you know!' So Steve proceeded to do so; it was a much sturdier aircraft than he had initially thought. After a few flights doing 'circuits and bumps' and a cross-country, on 31 January, while airborne without his instructor, the port outer engine overheated and he had to do a three-engined landing. The following day, Smith suggested they should practise a three-engined landing, and Steve retorted: 'Too late, we did that for real yesterday!'

Although Steve had a principle of never drinking more than two beers when on station, on leave it was a different matter. The relationship between NCOs and officers was always difficult for the young Canadian aircrew, and on one occasion led to an alarming incident. The crew had scrounged a meal in the mess by pretending they were on operations, and while they were eating, it was brought to Steve's attention that Jack Phillips had broken one of the rules of the mess by going behind the counter, and was chatting up a rather chubby female. Warrant Officer Yardley was giving him hell and, 'goaded on' by his crew, Steve felt it was worth a word to the warrant officer. One thing led to another, and some strong words were said. Yardley warned he would put Steve on a charge and sure enough two service policemen (SP) came over and took Steve's name and number. A few days later as they went to sign off for their posting to Leeming, the flight commander said that Steve could not leave as he had a charge pending; when one NCO charged another it was a court-martial offence, and the hearing was penned in for the following day. This was beginning to sound ominous.

The following morning two SPs took Steve to the station commander's office, removed his belt and cap, and marched him in. There were two wing commanders on either side of the group captain. The CO read out his name and Steve took one pace forward. The CO then read out the charge: 'Sergeant Puskas did say to Warrant Officer Yardley on the evening of 9 February 1944, "Go piss up your back and watch the steam rise."' There was little doubt he had said that and more besides. The wing commanders tried to suppress sniggers, but the CO was serious: 'Did you say that?' 'Yes Sir.' He proceeded to tell Steve the seriousness of the proceedings, and that it might hinder his chances of promotion, 'Do you not know this will be on your record?' After giving him a dressing down, the CO said: 'I know how keen you are to get at the "Hun", so I'm dismissing you with this warning.' Steve breathed a sigh of relief.

With this over, he and his crew signed off the station and proceeded to RAF Leeming, another few miles up the A1, to No. 429 (Bison) Squadron. This was now 'it', all their training and lessons were finally to be put to the test. Their war was about to begin.

Part I: Goldfish

3. Bison Squadron

No. 429 (Bison) Squadron was the tenth Canadian bomber squadron formed within Bomber Command in No. 4 Group, and commenced business on 7 November 1942 with Vickers Wellington Mks III and X. The unit was sited at RAF East Moor, a few miles north of York. With the formation of No. 6 (RCAF) Group early in 1943, the squadron transferred to the Canadian group on 1 April 1943.

In August they relocated to RAF Leeming, and changed to the four-engined Halifax, which was to become the 'workhorse' of the group, initially with the Merlin-engined Mk II and later the Mk V. In March 1944 they switched to the superior Mk III with Hercules radial engines.

Over its history in Bomber Command the Halifax was subjected to many modifications, as opposed to its rival, the Avro Lancaster, which changed little. The early Halifaxes were fitted with a nose turret and the triangular-shaped vertical fin. The weight of the nose turret, and poor handling, especially at height, meant that many of the Mk II and Mk V Halifaxes had the turret dismantled and replaced by a new fairing known as the 'Tollerton', named after the company who made them. Barrage-balloon cutters, bulky exhaust shrouds and fuel jettison pipes were also removed to improve performance, and even the thickness of paintwork was altered. It was found in tests on Halifax Mk V DG237 at Rootes factory at Speke, Liverpool, that a careful application of a single coat of rough night finish over the black paint increased the climb to 20,000 feet by 4 minutes. Some Mk Vs, though not all as will be seen, had the top turret taken away completely. The bulky Boulton Paul 'C'-style turret with twin .505 machine guns caused very significant drag. Later, with the appearance of the more powerful radial Hercules-engined Mk III and VII aircraft the mid-upper returned in a lower-profile form of the Boulton Paul 'A' series, this time with four guns.

Another problem overcome was rudder overbalance, initially tested on Halifax HR727 by extending the rudder downwards by a few inches, but then having the whole fin changed to its now familiar 'D'-slab shape. With the advent of these modifications and the Hercules XVI radial, the 'Hally', as it was lovingly called, could now hold its own in the bomber stream with the Lancasters. In fact the Mk B.VII with Hercules 100 engine could even climb higher than a Lancaster.

The Canadians loved the Halifax. With its lower than mid-fuselage wing and spar, the crew were able to move relatively freely about the aircraft in flight; not so simple in the Lancaster. It is a matter of record that it was easier to depart from a Halifax in an emergency. The air-cooled engine could take more damage before it seized up. One flight engineer told the author that it was not unknown for a Halifax to return from operations with one or more cylinders out of action. The only disadvantage in the later Halifax marks was the aircraft's inability to carry the huge loads of the Avro Lancaster, even though it had bomb bays in the inner wing sections. Conversely, although not really a part of this story, the Halifax took on a much greater variety of roles during the war, including meteorological, glider towing and transport duties.

When Steve arrived at Leeming, No. 429 Squadron was equipped with Mk Vs, and the commanding officer was Wing Commander J.D. Pattison, an autocratic commander but known to be fair to his crews. Along with his friend 'Doc' Murray, Steve was assigned to A Flight under Flight Lieutenant Bowen. On 18 February he was on his first operation, as 'second dickey' to the Australian Pilot Officer E.A. Giles. In Halifax V LL153 AL-A they were off to the 'Big City' – Berlin. It was a lengthy, and probably scary, trip for the first one, comprising some 7½ hours with a mixed bomb load of high explosives (HE) and incendiaries. A total of 891 aircraft took off in all, of which 314 were Halifaxes, and for the Giles crew fortunately uneventful. It was the penultimate major attack of Arthur Harris's campaign on the German capital and 43 aircraft were lost. It was not a good night for the bomber force; the Pathfinders were late as there was inaccurate wind information. The crew had to divert to Little Snoring on their return to England, due to bad weather at base, flying back to Yorkshire the following day. (On the last attack on the city on 24 March, Pilot Officer

Giles was lost in Halifax LW688 AL-J, two of the crew surviving to be prisoners of war.)

The day after, Steve was off on another operation as 'second dickey', this time with an RAF pilot, Pilot Officer A.E. Willey, in LK684 AL-E. This trip was a little more lively as their starboard inner engine packed up just after crossing the enemy coast. Since it was this engine that gave power to many systems on the aircraft, it was decided to return to base. For the next few days the CO gave the new crews as much local flying time as possible to increase their experience on the Halifax, Steve receiving his acceptance checks on 7 March. This was at a time when the squadron, like many others in No. 6 Group, were changing to the Halifax Mk III, with which they would see out their war. Detailed briefings were given to the crews, as there were different handling procedures to prevent engine misfires, especially on take-off.

Prior to departure on each operation, the crew would be issued with a 'Very' flare pistol with cartridges for the 'colours of the day' to be fired off in an emergency. These colours were changed every day. Also they were given a box of cartridges of the German equivalent to the Very pistol, to fire off if they were under attack from an enemy aircraft; the idea being to confuse the fighter pilot, and possibly give them an extra chance. Quite how the RAF knew what the German colours were, Steve never knew, but it was probably one of the many things decoded from enemy transmissions by Allied radio intelligence organisations.

Many of these Halifax Mk IIIs also had a modification, popular with the Canadian crews. Instead of having H2S radar, and its corresponding radome on the belly of the plane, the aircraft was fitted with non-rotatable 'Preston Green' cupolas with a 0.5-inch-calibre Browning machine gun firing downwards through a hole at the back. The Canadians had been badly 'mauled' by German night fighters equipped with the 'Schräge Musik' upward-firing cannon, and this was an attempt to counter this. Sergeant Ted Lewis, a gunner with No. 420 Squadron, told the author that the gunner, a new eighth man on the crew, sat on a basic heavy canvas seat, the gun being mounted on a simple gimbal, giving it a wide field of fire. However, the amount of ammunition was limited to one belt of shells. On daylight raids, crews often flew low on the return trip, to allow this gunner to expend his ammunition on ground targets.

About this time Steve heard his friend Albert Young had been killed. Steve was now waiting for his next 'second dickey' operation, so he could soon get going with his own crew. In the meantime, there was more training. On 10 March in the CO's new Halifax III LW685 AL-C they took off on a 'bullseye' exercise with twelve other crews. The CO was in hospital after an accident on the runway when an aircraft had dropped some incendiaries. While helping to remove them he had been badly injured in his legs. The exercise was a night operation, and Steve was told to '… take care of the Boss's plane'. But after an hour or so, over the North Sea, the port outer engine started to vibrate and run hot. Their flight engineer, Jack, kept an eye on the temperatures as they steadily increased, and the cowling started to shake heavily. Flying at 19,000 feet, suddenly the port outer gave a roar and threw the aircraft over on its right side. Revs were showing at 4,300rpm; cruising revs for the Mk III were 2,650rpm. The crew were yelling to Steve: 'What's going on?' The engine and wing vibration was so bad the throttles would not stay open without Steve and Ted holding them open. There were signs of fire, and the cowlings started to come apart. Ted had struggled back from the front of the aircraft to help his pilot. Steve put the nose down to roll the aircraft level, and soon they were down to 11,000 feet. As Steve pressed the fire extinguisher button the nacelle started to burn, and the cowlings dropped off. The extinguisher didn't do much good and the propeller was feathered.

The situation was getting serious. Steve considered asking the crew to bail out, but sea temperatures were very low at this time of year. They had to stick with the aircraft. He decided to try and keep the Halifax in the air, and make towards the coast. As they approached the shore, their speed was down to 150mph and ditching seemed the only option. He told the crew to take up their ditching positions, as by now the whole wing was on fire. As pieces of the wing came away the plane hit the crest of a wave at about 125mph. They slid along before the starboard wing dropped and then cartwheeled into another wave with a resounding crash. The force of the water shattered the Perspex nose and the sea rushed in. Steve was the only one left in the nose section, strapped in and under water. The pilot's escape hatch above his head was still in position. He struggled to undo his 'Sutton' harness and tear off his mask and radio connections. Then rotating he tried to kick the hatch free, but with no luck. He could hear the others walking about on the wing and in the darkness that engulfed him he started to panic, but then his training took over and he swam towards the back of the aircraft, eventually coming to the surface. Thank goodness for the wide-open space of the Halifax fuselage, something the Canadian crews were grateful for.

The crew were standing on the wing waiting for the dinghy to appear from its housing. It would not emerge, although it was supposed to automatically pop out and inflate as the immersion switch came into contact with the water. So Wilf kicked in the wing, pulled the dinghy out, threw it in the water, and topped up the inflation with the bellows. They all piled in, cut the cord that attached the dinghy to the aircraft and floated free. They were all safe, free and unharmed. Often the crew had teased him when Steve had carried out a heavy landing, but this time they laughed and said how smooth it was. Steve admitted later, 'I probably could not land as well again if I tried again in the same circumstances.'

As they gathered their wits around them, Steve asked, 'Have we brought the survival container?' 'No.' 'What else have we got?' 'Nothing but four tins of water', was the reply. Even though they had plenty of briefing on this subject, they were not well organised. Not a good show! He asked Jack to fire off the Very pistol, but Jack was fumbling with it. 'It's a new model and I can't find the safely catch,' he remarked. 'Give to me,' said Steve, but he could not find the projection in the pitch dark. Then Ted took control of it and eventually a bright red flare roared across the sky. He fired a second shot. Shortly after, they saw a light and realised someone was searching for them. A Scottish fishing boat gradually came into view; they had seen the burning Halifax and altered course to help. They pulled the exhausted crew to safety and offered them hot tea. Steve was the only one soaked through to the skin. As they were chatting to the fishermen an RAF officer came aboard. 'Are you ready to go?' he asked. The air-sea rescue boat had been sent to find them. Wilf, the radio operator, had done his job well, and had sent out an 'SOS' before abandoning the aircraft and had locked his transmit key down to give a fix on their position. As they climbed out of the fishing boat the fishermen gave them a twenty pack of 'Woodbine' cigarettes, known colloquially as 'coffin nails', a generous gesture indeed, and the aircrew were grateful for their hospitality.

The RAF launch took them to Aberdeen, where they were given spare cast-off clothing to change into; Steve refused to surrender his battledress jacket. Then they were conveyed to RAF Dyce, the nearest RAF station, nowadays the busy local airport. Here they were interviewed three times: first by an intelligence officer; then by the maintenance officer; and finally by a wing commander. It was the same information over and over again, after which Steve requested he phone RAF Leeming to inform them what had happened. He spoke to Squadron Leader Kenney, who was in charge in the CO's absence, and said he had ditched the aircraft. All Kenney uttered was, 'Everyone OK?' Steve answered, 'Yes, everyone but the aircraft.' 'We'll talk about it when you get back', was the succinct reply.

That morning they were lounging around in the mess awaiting transport when another officer came up to the group, and started quizzing Steve with another load of questions. Steve was tired and more than a little terse, but smartened to attention when he saw it was the station commander, a group captain. Steve enquired, 'What about the "Halley"?' 'Well, it's still floating, and the Navy is going to sink it, before it becomes a menace to shipping. You were very lucky. You ditched less than a mile from a minefield!' The group captain asked if they would like a lift back to Leeming with the air officer commanding the group who would be visiting the following day. The airmen jumped at the chance of a quick flight home.

The following morning Steve was told to get the crew out to the Watch Office. Air Commodore Boothman asked Steve if he had flown a Hudson before. He told him, 'No.' 'Don't worry, we'll manage.' On arriving at Leeming, the air commodore taxied to Flying Control, and before the aircrew jumped out he asked Steve to tell Air Traffic Control he was on his way to London, via Grantham. Steve ran to the Watch Office, 'Quick give A/C Boothman a green light. We don't want to keep him waiting.' After a short delay the air commodore was en route again. After a further debrief at their base, the crew were given a few days' 'survivors' leave', so after rekitting their missing uniforms they were off to London again. Steve's much-loved Gruen wristwatch was full of water and would not dry out, even though he took the case off and put it in a warm oven in the billet; but no luck, the watch was wrecked. This was his great loss of the experience.

The P.B. Cow Company in Farnborough, Hampshire, was one of the foremost British manufacturers of sea rescue equipment, including dinghies, and they decided to give an award to downed airmen who were saved by their product. It was in the form of an embroidered badge of a goldfish with wings, over a couple of wavy lines representing the sea. This was accepted by the RAF as special recognition for those who survived a ditching experience. Steve and his crew were about to join this select group, much to their surprise and delight.

Several years later, after the war, Steve visited Ted Bowles at his home in Victoria, British Columbia. During a walk along the beach Ted said that something had long been bothering him, and he had a confession to make. He said, 'Do you remember when we ditched?' 'Yes.' 'Well I forgot to release the escape hatch for you to get out.' 'Don't worry about it. It all turned out all right, didn't it?' Steve responded. Ted continued, 'Another thing. Every time we took off you cracked your knuckles with the "mike" turned on. It used to drive me nuts!' Steve recalled that particular habit. He had not realised how it could have been irritating for others. For him it was a way of easing tension.

On 15 March Steve was off on another 'second dickey' trip, this time with Pilot Officer Rawlinson in Halifax III LW723 AL-B. On the way to the target, the flight engineer, Sergeant A. Batad, informed the 'skipper' that the port inner engine was consuming as much fuel as two of the other engines. Nevertheless, the pilot decided to continue and, after bombing the target at 23.59 hours, when they turned back to base, he asked Steve to feather the faulty motor. The feathering knobs were in front of the pilot, and Steve groped across in the dark and accidentally hit the knob for the port outer. Normally this could be easily rectified, but the hydraulic line was broken and the oil was very thick at the freezing temperatures outside, and the motor became unserviceable. It was a terrible 'goof'. The flight engineer figured they would just get back to the English coast if they were lucky, but not enough power to return to base. The wireless operator/air gunner sent out an SOS, and they started a long glide with the engines just ticking over. RAF Thorney Island on the south coast heard their SOS and radioed them to come straight in without doing a circuit, which they did and safely taxied to a dispersal point, much to their relief. It was another lesson Steve learned well, and there and then he vowed that if he had a 'second dickey' pilot he would never ask him to handle any vital equipment. Two days later, after the leaks had been fixed, they returned to Leeming.

Steve's first operation as captain was on 25 March 1944 on a trip to Aulnoye in France. Apart from a heavy head cold, the trip was an uneventful one of 5½ hours. Steve had dodged sick parade; there was no way he was going to miss his first operation in charge. However, three of the squadron's aircraft were lost, including Pilot Officer Giles, the Australian who had been so kind to Steve on his first 'second dickey' trip.

They bombed the target from a relatively low altitude of 8,000 feet. This was part of the plan to be more accurate, and save the local civilian population from death and destruction of their houses. Steve remembered seeing the railway cars tumbling about under the power of the bombs. It was the first time they had seen such devastation up close, and they were satisfied with their effort. After the trip, as they were locking up the aircraft and talking to the ground crew, they were approached by a photographer for an official photograph. 'No way – go get someone else,' said Steve. 'I need to take some crew photos,' the photographer insisted. Wilf repeated Steve's comment and swung his crew bag at him. 'There are others coming in who you can photograph.' The man grumbled and drove off. The following morning Steve was called to the CO's office for an explanation. He told him they were not keen on a photograph after the operation. The CO replied, 'The people of Canada have paid for your training, pay your salary, and provide your equipment, and therefore have a right to see what they are getting for their money. Now get out there and "gear up" for some pictures.' So they washed up for their 'glamour pictures' and this time cooperated with the photographer.

Their next raid was on 26 March, and turned out to be a very eventful one. The crew were in LW415 AL-K for a second time and the Halifax lumbered off the runway at 20.08 hours. They were headed for the Ruhr, or 'Happy Valley' as it was known, and the industrial town of Essen. The visibility was poor throughout the trip. They were in the first wave of bombers and Jasper, the navigator, wanted them there early before the enemy gunners had really woken up, and sure enough there was little activity at the target. However, the target indicators (TIs) were several miles to port, and they were determined to drop right on target, which was the Krupps steel works. Steve banked the aircraft to port to bring it back on track to the aiming point, but by this time they were headed directly into the bomber stream. They flew into cloud and as they came out there were four glowing lights dead ahead. It was another bomber. 'Look out!' shouted Ted Bowles from the bomb aimer's position in the nose, and Steve tilted the aircraft to the right, just as the other did too, and they missed one another by just a few yards. Steve banked for the turn on to the target, and the aircraft's load of incendiaries went down on the target at 22.11 hours. Now it was flat-out for their home base.

However, the defences were now awake, and to add to that problem the aircraft was handling sluggishly. Steve tried to close the bomb doors but they would not shift. Ted took a torch to investigate, and he was gone longer than he should have been. He had disconnected his oxygen supply and had become groggy. Jack Phillips, the flight engineer, went to check on him, brought him back, and reported 'A1 clear, the bomb doors will close', which they did after another shove of the lever. They were now west of the River Rhine headed for the Dutch coast, and below Steve could see an airfield with its perimeter lights going on for a few minutes, then off, then back on again. It turned out to be fighters taking off to catch the bombers before they reached the coast. Steve called for the gunners to be on alert. Suddenly the rear gunner, Wilf, shouted there were flares astern, then 'Fighters, fighters!' It was a bad procedure and Steve was angry; he needed to know which direction they were coming from. 'Which side?' he yelled, anxious to start to corkscrew the opposite way. 'It doesn't matter – there are three of them,' returned Wilf. The Halifax was thrown into a violent corkscrew, and tracer was all around them. The enemy aircraft overshot them. It was relief for a few moments, but not for long.

The plane levelled out, and then the enemy aircraft attacked again, one at a time. Steve first corkscrewed left, then right, noting later in his diary that for about 31 minutes they fought off attacks from first one side then the other. 'It seemed like it would never end,' he wrote. After the initial pass by the fighter, Steve moved the crew around, putting Alvin, the mid-upper gunner, with his good gunnery perception, down behind the H2S radome to watch underneath, and moving Wilbur, the wireless operator/air gunner into the mid-upper. They were better covered that way. After several minutes there was a long burst from the rear turret; one enemy fighter was hit, then it exploded. A parachute was seen to open, and the aircraft hit the ground. Steve could see everything clearly; it was as though his night vision was improving – perhaps it was his concentration. As they levelled off again, Jack, the flight engineer, spotted another fighter to port at the same height. The enemy turned in towards them, and Steve veered to starboard and dived underneath it to give Wilbur a good angle, and he managed some telling shots into the belly of the aircraft, which then caught fire. Both the mid-upper and rear turrets got more solid hits, as the enemy peeled away, the gunners having no trouble finding him in the darkness. There was still a fighter on their tail, and Steve hauled the Halifax around, trying to shake it off. Wilf kept calling the distance, and their adversary pressed home his attack even though he was on fire. Eventually he ran out of ammunition and as the crew watched, the enemy aircraft blew up and fell to the ground not far from the other plane they had hit. No parachute was seen this time. The third fighter disappeared during the action. By the comments from Steve, and the notes in the squadron ORB, it is clear these were single-engined enemy fighters of the 'Wild Boar' defence system.

Jasper gave them a new course for home and, apart from some bullet holes, nothing important was hit and all the crew were fine. Within a few minutes an aircraft appeared off their port wing, which they identified as a Halifax, but it had all its running lights on, lit up like a Christmas tree! It did not make any sense and seemed to be getting closer. Rear gunner, Wilf, was sure it was a captured Halifax the Germans were using as a decoy, and was going to give it a burst, but Steve dived away and they lost it in the darkness. (The author can find no record of a captured Halifax being flown by the Luftwaffe.) A short while later, a Spitfire came into view, and made a visual check on their Halifax. Steve had the identification, friend or foe (IFF) switch on as they approached the English coast. Wilf again surmised it was an enemy aircraft, and was going to give it a burst, but Steve managed to manoeuvre the plane out of range, losing it in the darkness. He said to his colleague: 'How would it look if we shot down two "Jerries" and a Spit?' Wilf was not convinced. The rear gunner was becoming a problem, and who was not easy to deal with due to their locations in the aircraft. As they crossed the coast the British ack-ack opened up, and searchlights scoured the sky. Possibly they were off track. Wilf started cursing again, and let loose with his guns at the anti-aircraft batteries. Steve could hear their chatter as he dived and zigzagged away, to get as far from the flak as possible. The guns ceased firing and they were all silent on the return to base. After they parked the aircraft, the airmen and ground crew talked animatedly about the trip and the excitement. All the while Wilf stood off to one side, very quiet. Steve tried to involve him in the conversation, but he would have none of it. 'That's it,' Wilf stated, 'I've had enough. This was my last trip.' But Steve was sure he would change his mind after a good night's sleep. So ended a most eventful operational flight.

During all the action, Wilf, a husky chap, had perspired profusely inside his electrically heated suit, which eventually caused the suit to short-circuit, giving him some painful burns in the armpits and behind his knees. He was sure he had been shot, but it was not blood but perspiration trickling down his side. That morning after a few hours' sleep, the aircrew were summoned to the station commander, Group Captain J.G. Bryans's office as he wanted to hear about the operation. After they finished their story, the CO hinted that some aircraft recognition practice might be forthcoming, but to his dismay, the rear gunner told Bryans what he could do with that. Wilf informed him: 'That was my last mission, and that is all there is to it; nothing is going to change my mind.' This unexpected response to a senior officer clearly upset the station commander, a pre-war officer fresh from Canada who enjoyed the privileges of rank, although with no operational experience. Steve felt Wilf had displayed a lot of nerve to maintain his decision. He thought the beginning had been the ditching in the North Sea a few weeks before.

Lack of moral fibre (LMF) was something the RAF and RCAF found it difficult to deal with. The Americans sent their men to a hospital, known as the 'Flak House' for psychological tests and professional help; in the RAF/RCAF you were either fit to fly, or were out. They sent their men on a posting to the 'Aircrew Refresher Course' in Sheffield, basically an open-arrest barracks where a rigorous course of physical training was the regime. The RCAF did not totally agree with this and sometimes the punishment for NCOs was removal of all badges of rank, reduction down to AC2, and a posting to another station. Canadian officers were dispatched back to Canada, after a reduction in rank; an officer had to face a court martial first. Wilf Faulkner was posted off the station without delay. Alvin Williams took over the rear position; shortly after, Harry Venn, like Steve also from Hamilton, transferred in from another crew, and took over in the mid-upper turret.

Several years after the war, Steve was holidaying in the Vancouver area and called in to see Ted Bowles, and Alvin Williams, who advised him he should make an effort to find Wilf. This he did and Wilf came to his hotel, still in his working clothes, and certainly he had a lot to tell Steve. They sat drinking until 2am. Wilf said the thing that bothered him most was that second fighter. Out of ammunition and on fire, he still kept coming straight at him. Boring in and getting closer he was convinced the pilot was trying to ram him. Him personally. No wonder he was shook up.

The RCAF was now gradually increasing the percentage of aircrew who were officers, and the plan was ultimately to have all aircrew as officers. The Canadian egalitarian society never really got on with the more 'classed' structure of the RAF. It was often problematic, as in Steve's case where the pilot was an NCO (the captain of the aircraft) and there was an officer in the crew, in their case, Pilot Officer James Still, the navigator. Although this 'caste' system carried on into the RCAF, it was not easy for many crew members to deal with. NCOs were going through the same rigours and difficulties as the officers, for less pay and privileges. It certainly did not 'hang easily' for Steve. On 4 April the group tactics officer came to the station to give the crews some tips. It was Squadron Leader Barney Rawson, DFC, and he had been a schoolfriend of Steve's at Westdale High in Hamilton. Steve was about to say 'Hi!' but Barney just ignored him, as if he did not exist. Steve asked Harry Venn, another from the same school, 'Does Barney talk to anyone?' 'He doesn't talk to NCOs', was the reply. The lecture left little impression on Steve.

Several days after the Essen trip there was a fighter affiliation exercise with a fighter based at RAF Dalton. Steve and his crew flew towards the station a few miles to the south, contacted them, and a Hurricane arrived to commence attack practice. All the action was photographed by cine cameras, to give an assessment of the skills. On return to base, they were eventually summoned to the gunnery leader, Flight Lieutenant L.V. Pollard, RAF, to talk about the exercise. He said: 'The fighter pilot, a "so-called-ace", doesn't think much of your ability.' But the film showed they had shot him down three times, and he did not hit them once. Pollard thought it was 'sour grapes'. He then told them: 'Your "kills" on the Essen raid are confirmed.'

April was a very busy month for the 'Bisons', and the Puskas crew. The next raid was to the marshalling yards at Villeneuve St George on 9 April. Sixteen aircraft took off, fifteen making it to the target, which was truly 'plastered' with well-placed TI markers and lots of debris was seen to fly up in two vivid explosions.

They were now joined by another officer in the crew as a new rear gunner, Pilot Officer J. Morgan. Twenty-four hours later they were on their way again, and according to Steve's log book, this time in an aircraft that would become their regular 'mount': Halifax III MZ282 AL-A 'A-Able'. The plane eventually had artwork applied to the nose with the name 'Sweet Adelaide'. This aircraft had the Preston Green ventral cupola fitted, so they would include a regular eighth member of the crew, often a 'spare' gunner from the squadron manning pool. This was the time that Bomber Command was concentrating on the enemy's transport infrastructure in the build-up to D-Day.

The following day they returned to Belgium, and the marshalling yards at Ghent. Their standard bomb load on these operations was 6 x 1,000 lb and 9 x 500 lb of high explosive general purpose (GP) bombs. There was almost no flak at this target. The next couple of operations were to Le Bourget aerodrome, Paris, and the rail centre at Lens on 18 and 20 April respectively. (The Le Bourget/Noisy-le-Sec operation is covered elsewhere in this book as three of the aircrew featured were also on this operation. There is an anomaly, as some log books record it as Le Bourget, others Noisy-le-Sec. The major rail yard was very close to the French airstrip.) It was on one of these operations they returned to Leeming to find their airfield fogged in. They, and the other aircraft, circled while they waited for diversion details and, as they did so, one pilot who had been an instructor at HCU, called Control and said: 'Why don't you let someone land who can?' There was a short pause, then Control gave him permission to try, and the Halifax disappeared into the fog. A few moments later the station fire engine also disappeared into the fog, and instructions to divert to another airfield came through immediately afterwards. On their eventual return the crews found that that 'mouthy' pilot had landed long and run off the end of the runway into a stream – fortunately no casualties, but certainly a case of dented pride.

On 22 April it was a return trip to Germany and Düsseldorf in LW689 AL-J, followed by Karlsruhe two days later; their load this time was a mixture of HE and incendiaries. They were back in 'Happy Valley' so the flak was intense. As they approached the target, the mid-upper gunner reported enemy aircraft, and sure enough there was a Messerschmitt Me 410 flying off their starboard wing on a parallel course, just out of the range of their guns. Harry Venn in the top turret said: 'Slide under him and we'll nail him.' Steve replied, 'We're here to drop bombs, not chase night fighters. Let's stick to our job.' The Me 410 continued to fly alongside, and after they had released their bombs, the aircraft slid away into the night. Steve was convinced the pilot had seen them; it was a strange sort of exercise.

The squadron commander, Wing Commander Pattison, returned from his injuries on 7 May, only to be posted back to Canada and to be replaced by Wing Commander Al Avant. He was transferred from No. 426 (Thunderbird) Squadron at Linton-on-Ouse, and at twenty-two he was the youngest squadron commander in 6 Group. He called Steve into his office a couple of days later, and informed him he would like to send the crew to No. 405 (Vancouver) Squadron in No. 8 (Pathfinder) Group. It was an honour to be selected for this, and Steve was stunned, completely taken by surprise. The only drawback was that a crew in the Pathfinders had to complete two full tours. Steve was concerned that would be stretching their luck, but he would talk it over with his crew. 'That's OK. I understand,' said the new CO. After chatting to his men it became obvious it was a 50/50 split. The additional trips were discouraging for some of them, so it was likely they would get some new crew members, breaking up the team just when they had got used to working with each other. Steve was in a dilemma.

The following day it was back to Ghent in 'Adelaide', bombing the target just before midnight. It was an uneventful trip. Not so the next operation to Boulogne on the French channel coast the day after, when they had to turn back due to navigational problems. Steve had had an uneasy feeling about this raid, and his intuition was right. As they were on their way he asked Still, the navigator, if he was sure of their track. 'Absolutely on course,' replied Still. Another ten minutes on he asked again, and got the reply: 'Sorry we are 100 degrees off course.' The navigator informed him that if they were to correct their course they would arrive at the target 5 minutes after the raid was over. This was an impossible position, and the only option was to abort and return early. This was the only mistake Flying Officer Still made, but it was a bad day to do it. Before they had set out the CO had asked Steve for his reply to their earlier conversation about a Pathfinder posting, and Steve promised to let him know later. As they approached Leeming, Control asked: 'Are you light or heavy?' It was not one of Steve's good decisions landing with a full bomb load and most of their fuel. The CO told him that it was his fault; as captain of the aircraft he had to take responsibility for his crew, even though he was only an NCO and the navigator was an officer. It effectively squashed their chance of the transfer to the elite 'Vancouver' squadron. Warrant Officer Cadogan and his crew went instead, were badly shot up by a night fighter, and seriously injured. Steve thought: 'There but for the grace of God go I.' For him that mistake was a sign they were not meant to go.

These raids were also difficult as bombing infrastructure targets in France were generally at low level, and they had to maximise accuracy and minimise the losses to the French civilians. It was about this time the crew encountered an incident that had fatal consequences. As they approached the French coast on their way home from a raid, they saw two Halifaxes way off to starboard. One called: 'Hello Harry.' 'Is that you George?' 'What do you say we go lower and shoot up Dieppe?' 'OK', replied the other. This was against procedure, as radio operators were listening for aircraft in distress. They watched as the two fools in their prank lost altitude. The 'flak' from Dieppe was accurate, and the second Halifax was hit; smoke came from the aircraft as it caught fire and fell into the Channel; no parachutes were seen. Not a very good result and a total waste of aircrew lives.

It was becoming apparent that all pilots new to the squadron had commissions, with a lot of them being ex-instructors with plenty of flying hours. A notice appeared in the 'Daily Routine Orders' to the effect that an NCO could apply for a commission if he felt he deserved it. This was the RCAF's way of compensating NCOs on operations caught up in this new system. It was one thing Steve felt very strongly about, and he had had a terse conversation with the CO about it. He had always felt the system was unfair, and the captain of a Halifax should be an officer if he was shouldering the responsibility of the crew. He got the forms from the adjutant, Flight Lieutenant Higgins, and told him what he was about to do. 'The CO might not like it,' Higgins said. The following day the CO called Steve in and said he would sign the papers, and shortly thereafter others members of the crew were also offered the choice, though some preferred not to put themselves forward.

The next operation was on 12 May, to Louvain, and they were in LW137 AL-K. It was a very hazy target so they bombed at low level of 9,500 feet on markers, and a huge explosion at 00.30 hours was seen high into the sky, obviously a hit on an ammunition dump. It was on this raid that a No. 426 (Thunderbird) Squadron aircraft was lost: LW682 OW-M was shot down by a night fighter and crashed into a bog. The crew of Flight Sergeant Benz were all killed, but three bodies were never recovered. Over fifty years later the remains of the aircraft were found and the missing three crew members retrieved and interred in an appropriate final resting place with due ceremony. A large amount of aluminium from the aircraft was salvaged, melted into ingots, and shipped to the Bomber Command Museum in Nanton, Alberta, by the team leader, Air Canada airline pilot Karl Kjarsgaard. Eventually this aluminium was donated to the Bomber

Command Memorial in London to become the main component of the roof structure, a fitting memorial to the Canadians of Bomber Command.

A subsequent rail target for Steve and his crew was Le Clipon on 19 May, another straightforward trip, though problems with their radio and bad weather meant a diversion to Tuddenham, with a return to Leeming the following morning. The build-up to D-Day continued with the next operation on the 22nd to Le Mans in central France, again at low level, this time 8,400 feet and with 16 x 500-lb GP bombs from the USA. In spite of heavy 'flak' only one aircraft, a Halifax, was lost out of the 133 Lancasters and Halifaxes sent over. Steve remembered it as a frightening experience seeing five aircraft on fire around MZ282, all at one time, but obviously four of those made it home. On 24 May it was back to Germany, to Aachen on 'Battle Order 90'; one of the three crews lost was from No. 429 Squadron, that of Flight Lieutenant Rawlinson, with whom Steve had completed a 'second dickey' trip, and with whom Harry Venn had been their mid-upper gunner. The sad irony was they were on their last operation before screening.

On 27 May came an operation to Bourg Leopold, a target they had attacked before, and involved a low-level assault on the large military camp. The weather was poor, but markers were clear, and during the course of the raid a large explosion was heard, so Steve reckoned they had hit something important. Their return to England was also marred by the weather, and they had to land at Ouston, in Northumberland. Flying back to Leeming the following morning, they had arrived to find the base covered with fog, but Steve thought he could see enough to land. The wireless operator called to say he had received instructions to divert. To give a pilot that news so late on was very bad timing. When they landed Steve asked him: 'Why didn't you give me that information earlier?' Sergeant Wilson told him that the radio became unserviceable after they had taken off, so he had dismantled it and got it working again just as they arrived back over Leeming. Steve said: 'Never take the radio apart on a raid again.' They could have ended up going on alone if an abort had been transmitted, though it was unlikely.

Now it was back to pre-invasion targets, with a raid on a German radar/radio station near Cherbourg at Au Fèvre. In their MZ282 AL-A, and in good visibility, the Puskas crew hit the location hard. A single Me 110 was seen as they left, and that was attacked by one of the other squadron aircraft, but not seen to go down. The bombing was scattered and 'A-Able' had one bomb hung up, so it was a dicey return to base. The night before the D-Day Normandy invasion on 6 June, the squadron was ordered to bomb a gun battery at Merville, just inland of the coast to the north of the Orne river and the main beaches. The squadron bombed just after 23.00 hours, and they could see a red glow on the target. This was in advance of a parachute drop over the area that took place a few hours later. The drop was not that successful; it took a long time for the parachutists to gather together, and it was found, when the battery was captured, that far from heavy guns, the big concrete emplacements contained only small anti-tank weapons.

The crew could see the wakes of masses of boats heading for France in the moonlight, and they were told to avoid returning back over the centre of England, so were instead sent south of Cherbourg, over the Bristol Channel and Wales, and thus well away from beachhead traffic. When they got back to Leeming the ground crew were all over them, asking what they had seen, as rumours abounded on the invasion. About this time airmen were asked if they wanted to be issued with a .38 revolver. Many thought it was pointless, including Steve. 'If we came down, what were we expected to do – shoot it out like John Wayne?' Some took up the offer; one of his gunners used it to shoot rabbits to supplement their diet, but skinning them and hanging them in the kitchen of their billets did not look too appetising.

Shortly after D-Day, Hitler instituted his 'Vertgeltungswaffe' programme, the first salvoes of V1 flying bombs (in truth, the first 'cruise missiles') being fired on 12 June. Most of the sites for these weapons initially were in the northern Normandy and Pas de Calais area, north of Paris. The V1s were largely aimed at London in a random fashion; not any specific target, but generally to hazard the population. There was talk of restricting crew visits to London, but nothing came of it. Steve experienced one V1 attack. The author was told by his Aunt that if one heard the missile's engine 'pop-pop popping' overhead you knew you were safe, as it would glide and land somewhere else, but if the motor stopped before it reached you, then that was another matter! Steve was in the bathroom of his 'digs' when he heard the buzz, but where was it coming down? There was no option but to grit his teeth; there was a loud bang not too far away. In the morning he went to look, and found several houses had been damaged a short distance along the road. It had been a close thing. He pitied the poor Londoners.

Now it was Bomber Command's turn to hit back and, over the next month, many trips to France were part of 'Operation Crossbow's' attacks on the flying bomb bases and storage depots. Most of the storage sites were more inland from the coast, and the launch sites were known as 'ski sites' due to the shape of the buildings. The V1 needed a ramp for take-off and these were orientated toward the coast. At a V2 site, in the Éperlecques woods, near Watten, a huge concrete bunker was constructed that was over six storeys high with a roof 18 feet thick. Reconnaissance by the RAF in May showed this structure was definitely out of the ordinary for 'Atlantic Wall' defences, and as such received special attention. Even today the bunker is so huge it is impossible to demolish, so it has been turned into a museum. In the event, the Germans never got to use it. Although the site was targeted repeatedly, the strikes had little effect on the main building until Barnes Wallis's 'Tallboy' bombs wrecked the main entrances and exit. The launch sites and storage depots, often scattered in woodland, were a different matter, and for 6 Group and Bomber Command demanded more regular attention.

During a sea search on a dull and very windy day, looking for the crew of an American bomber over the North Sea, Puskas's aircrew encountered some heavy turbulence; the conditions at their allocated height of 1,000 feet were causing some difficulties for the airmen. They were doing timed runs from the coast out to sea and, as they continued, it became obvious they were off course. Steve called to Flying Officer Still, the navigator, but there was no reply. The wireless operator reported he was out 'cold' on the floor of the aircraft, and had lost all control of his bodily functions. It was obvious they could not continue so they turned for base, aiming to blame the weather for their early return. By the time they arrived back the navigator was up and around, and he bribed the ground crew to clean up the aircraft. It was difficult for Steve; he was sympathetic, but it was risky to fly with a navigator who got air sick. Still asked Steve not to report him, as he would surely be taken off flying duties, but after that Steve made sure he got back to Leeming as fast as he could from a raid, often landing before the rest of the squadron. It was normal for one squadron to land, then the other, the routine reversed for the next operation. The commanding officer noticed and asked him why he did not wait. Steve offered: 'I had a heavy tailwind.' But the CO said: 'Don't give me that "crap". Land with the others.' Years later, at an Allied air forces reunion, Steve confessed to him as to why he did this, and Al Avant admitted: 'Yes, I probably would have taken him off flying, or at least looked into his medical records.'

After a relatively routine raid on Cambrai on 14 June, the crew participated in their first daylight mission, on an E-boat base at Boulogne. (The Cambrai operation was eventful, however, for an aircrew from No. 419 (Moose) Squadron, flying a Canadian-built Lancaster KB726 'A-Able'. Over the target their aircraft was hit and the rear fuselage caught fire, trapping the rear gunner, Flying Officer John Brophy, in his turret and cutting his intercom. The mid-upper gunner, Pilot Officer Andrew Mynarski, went back to help his comrade but was unable to get through because of the flames. After a few unsuccessful minutes, and with his clothes on fire, he returned to the exit door, pivoted to salute his comrade, and jumped. Sadly he did not survive, but remarkably Brophy did and was taken prisoner of war. Only after the war was the full story told, and Andrew Mynarski was awarded the first Canadian Bomber Command Victoria Cross.) For Steve and his crew in AL-A, it was significant as they had a fighter escort from the RAF for the first time. It was fascinating to observe the target clearly in the late evening sun, and they could see the gunners on the light flak guns firing directly at them. It was unnerving, though, to view the other aircraft so closely, which was not so apparent at night. The E-boats had been causing problems for the invasion forces, and this was a quick and effective way of hitting back. Some large explosions were seen and one looked to be a petrol dump.

The following day it was a V1 storage depot at Sautrecourt, an arrangement of scattered buildings consisting of concrete blocks in woodland on the road to the coast from Arras. The Pathfinder markers were crucial for a target such as this – particularly hard to knock out – and the crews bombed on the red TIs, with several fires being started. There was heavy cloud cover over the area, which made taking 'photo-flash' pictures pointless. This raid was part of a concentrated attack on V1 sites, with strikes on the same night against storage sites at Domléger, Renescure and Beauvoir, the latter being the primary focus. For Steve the matter was complicated by the need to return for a second run over the target, always a 'dodgy' time.

On the 20th, the crews were all called for a briefing. From the fuel load and urgency it looked like it was planned to be a deep-penetration raid. Steve rounded up his men but the navigator could not be found. His attendance was mandatory. Outside the officers' quarters Steve found someone who told him that Flying Officer Jasper Still was at the Willow Tree pub in the village, booking a room for his girlfriend who was up from London. Steve was livid, and with a couple of his crew borrowed bicycles and went to the inn. When they knocked on the door of the room, asking for Jasper, they could hear the girl, Betty, telling him to get rid of the NCOs. Steve shouted, 'There's a briefing in half an hour. You'd better get your "ass" back to Leeming!' Still was back in time – just – but in the event the operation, planned for Berlin, was cancelled. It was to have been a reprisal raid for the V1 attacks on London, but could have caused heavy casualties in the bomber force, so calmer voices in the hierarchy prevailed.

Instead, their next operation, this time in HX339 AL-O, was on 21 June to Oisemont, another supply site near Abbeville, but the master bomber could not be heard and the site was obscured. There was heavy flak, and one piece caused a hole near the flight engineer's position. It was pointless to bomb in these conditions so the load was brought back, with the exception of two 500-lb bombs that were dumped in the 'safety area' in the Channel. Jack Phillips reported to the medical officer, on Steve's advice, because it had given him a fright, and he was taken off operations for a few days. But he was back in their regular aircraft, MZ282 'A-Able', for the next raid on Gorenflos on 26 June, a morning daylight attack – his second daytime operation – on a 'ski site'. The campaign against the V1s continued unabated.

The following day the target was of a different nature, at Wizernes, just to the south of St Omer. Here was a huge construction site with a massive concrete dome that was planned to accept the V2 rocket, built over many months by slave labour. The Germans' aim was to deliver the weapons horizontally on rail trucks, assemble them vertically and then roll them on to a truck taking them outside for launch. This site received much attention from the RAF, including by No. 617 Squadron and their 'Tallboys', and in the end was never brought anywhere near to operational capability, in spite of much effort by the Nazis. The crew of MZ282 were among eighteen aircraft dispatched from the 'Bison' squadron, and although hits were seen, no results could be assessed. Actually, the small bombs (up to 500 lb) of the Halifaxes had little effect on the site, and it took the huge Barnes Wallis penetration bombs to eventually bring work to a halt.

On the way back, Steve – by this time a warrant officer second class – took the opportunity to obtain some flying practice for the crew; a good idea if it ever happened that he was injured. On the Sautrecourt raid a few days before, a No. 425 (Alouette) Squadron aircraft, NA518 KW-I, had lost its pilot due to inadvertent 'friendly fire' from another Halifax. The captain, 21-year-old Pilot Officer Harold Romuld from Dunblane, Saskatchewan, died in the aircraft, and the bomb aimer had managed to fly the aircraft back to the UK and land safely at Woodbridge. So Steve's precaution was a wise one.

For the next operation to Metz marshalling yards on 28 June, they climbed into their regular MZ282 'Sweet Adelaide' to find the fuselage full of packs of 'Window', the anti-radar aluminium strips, and Steve queried the quantity. They were to drop twice as much on this trip for some reason he never determined. However, the aircraft began to leak petrol, and they had to change to the spare. This plane also leaked as they started it up, so it was back to 'A-Able', which had now been repaired. Frustrated at the messing around, Steve and his crew eventually took off late, so he had to make up time on the journey. It was very unsettling for the mid-upper gunner, Harry Venn, who had just been told he would be screened after this operation, having completed his tour. The target was clear, and the master bomber worked well; they dropped their load of 16 x 500-lb bombs centrally. Messerschmitt Me 210 fighters over Paris accounted for several bombers; the squadron lost one, that of Pilot Officer P.S. Agur, MZ302 AL-E; three of the crew became POWs, the others, including the pilot, evaded. A total of 20 aircraft were lost out of 230 on the raid, a relatively high loss of 8.7%. Harry was relieved to be home safely, and was screened, so now Steve had to find another gunner.

He found him in the form of John Mangione, DFM. Shortly before, on 8 June, Mangione's aircraft, LW128 piloted by recently appointed flight commander Squadron Leader Bill Anderson, had been hit by flak on its way to Achères. Anderson was badly wounded, the aircraft going into a steep dive, and three of the crew bailed out. Flight engineer Gilbert Steere dragged Anderson off the controls and regained command of the plane. As they struggled back to England, having dumped the bomb load off Dieppe, it became obvious that Anderson's wounds were serious. Over the English coast the three remaining crew, including Mangione, decided it was risky to try and land the aircraft with their wounded skipper aboard, so he was parachuted out of the aircraft through the escape hatch. Then they exited themselves, all coming down near the wreck of their Halifax half a mile north of RAF Benson in Oxfordshire. Sadly, Anderson died of his wounds, although Gilbert Steere was awarded a Conspicuous Gallantry Medal, and gunners Gordon Richie and John Mangione both a Distinguished Flying Medal each. He was a good man to have as part of Steve's crew.

Two more operations to France followed, the first to the Villeneuve St Georges rail junctions on 4 July, and then a daylight to Siracourt, a specially built V1 launch site building north of Paris. This edifice, known as 'Wasswerwerk No. 1 St Pol', was another of the massive structures the Nazis had constructed and was a low concrete building 700 feet (215 metres) long and 120 feet (36 metres) wide, with a railway entering at one end and a launch exit halfway along, pointing towards the UK. Fortunately it never got anywhere near completion, with No. 617 Squadron's 'Tallboys' causing severe damage on 25 June. On a visit to the site in 2008, it was apparent to the author that the smaller Allied bombs had made little penetration of the main concrete structure, although there was shrapnel damage to the ventilator outlets. The wrecking of the infrastructure around the site by the bombing meant it was impossible for the Germans to bring in materials to finish it. It was part of a plan of ten such buildings, only three of which were started and all of which were never completed. Good visibility meant the 'Bison' squadron aircraft were able to bomb accurately.

It was at this time that Steve eventually received his commission. The adjutant, Flight Lieutenant Higgins, told him the commission had been backdated to May, so the back pay was welcome. Steve took off his WO2 rank and put on his skinny pilot officer braids. However, he liked living with the crew and so stayed at the house they had billeted in, until he was told in no uncertain terms by Higgins to move into the officers' mess. He was given clothing coupons for his new uniform. It felt funny to have the flat officer's cap, but he soon got used to the advantages, particularly having a batman to help with his routines in daily life. Two of his crew, Ted Bowles and Jack Phillips, were commissioned shortly after.

As the Allies pushed through Normandy, the bomber crews were tasked with supporting the advance, and there were several raids on France. No. 429 Squadron were tasked with a German strongpoint at Mondeville, in the area where the 21st Panzer Division were active. The operation was close to Allied lines and the plan was for the bombers to attack in waves, moving forward. As Steve's crew approached the aiming point they could view the markers clearly and bombed on the flares. As they turned away they could see the 'rolling' markers on the far side of the smoke, but although the master bomber was directing the main force to 'bomb to the right of the markers', the second wave bombed on the first lot. There were many ground casualties. One No. 429 Squadron aircraft was lost, that of Flight

Lieutenant Gardiner in LW127 AL-F, three of the crew surviving. At a post-raid analysis by the squadron, one of the deputy flight commanders, Flight Lieutenant George Arbuckle, was found to have bombed short and was disciplined; he was posted to No. 424 (Tiger) Squadron at Skipton-on-Swale. Even though the bomb aimer had dropped the explosives, as captain of the aircraft it was deemed his responsibility.

As part of their continual 'on the job' training, the crews had to complete 'bullseye' flying exercises, especially with the ongoing advancements in radar. On 13 July after one such exercise, and the airmen were piling into the crew bus, Steve and Jack, the flight engineer, were fixing the control locks to the control surfaces when they became aware of a loud engine noise. Looking up Steve saw a Halifax banking around the aircraft at the opposite dispersal. He instinctively shouted to Jack, 'Duck', and the Halifax crashed about 10 yards off their starboard wing. One of the propellers broke off and rolled just past the nose of MZ282, smashing into the rear steps of the crew bus, where the airmen were sitting waiting for them – a lucky escape. Jack and Steve ran over to the now burning aircraft and managed to pull the pilot, the squadron commander, Wing Commander Avant, from the plane. His face was a ghastly sight with blood all over it. They then jumped on the wing and tried to open the escape hatch. The ammunition started to explode, and there was a 'whoomf' as one of the fuel tanks went up. They thought they could hear voices inside. The fire crews had arrived by this time but there was little pressure as the water was hosed on to the burning aircraft. Steve asked a fireman what to do next. 'Use that pump handle', came the reply, pointing to the vehicle. Steve grabbed it and it broke. 'What now?' 'I don't know,' the fireman shouted, 'it's my first day on the job!'

Luckily there was no one else in the aircraft. As the explosions became worse they retreated. Someone had already started to move MZ282 away from the area, as the detonating ammunition was a threat. The aircraft was left to burn out. The CO was fortunately not too badly injured; the blood on his face looked worse than it was. The irony was that only a week or so earlier the CO had announced that there were to be no flights with just a pilot on board, after one skipper had taken a Halifax for a test flight, got lost and had to land away. A minimum of four crew were to be on an aircraft. Years later, Steve found out that the CO had allowed his flight engineer to go off to town with the rest of the crew, thus breaking his own rule!

The next operation, to Hamburg on 29 July, started badly. The crews were told to approach the target at low level, below radar coverage, and then climb to bombing height, returning to base at low level to see if that made a big difference from interceptions. As they climbed into their aircraft, MZ282, Steve noticed oil dripping from one of the engines. Flight Sergeant Olliver, in charge of the ground crew said, 'Don't worry, it's just from the overflow, probably after over filling. Not to worry.' As they took off and turned to the east of the Vale of York, to their allotted height, there were two big crashes. With aircraft fully loaded the bangs were spectacular. Two aircraft had crashed into the Yorkshire Moors. One of those was MZ686 6U-U of No. 415 (Swordfish) Squadron on the unit's first operation as part of Bomber Command. It was not a good beginning.

As they approached the German coast, Jack informed Steve the port inner engine was starting to overheat. By the time they reached the target the temperature was at the critical stage. Steve decided to keep the motor running until they had dropped their load of 9 x 500-lb GP bombs, then he shut it down and feathered the propeller. Due to the problem he stayed at 5,000 feet for the return trip. The following day Steve went back to Flight Sergeant John Olliver and found there were pieces of metal in the engine, and the motor had to be replaced.

Two days later, as their MZ282 AL-A was out of action, the Puskas crew were in DV965 AL-J as part of a squadron operation of thirteen aircraft for a raid on Coqueraux, another attack against a flying bomb site, this time in the Seine area. Steve had a 'second dickey' pilot with him, Flying Officer Kingsland. There was little flak so the crew were relaxed. As DV965 approached the target an aircraft blew up right in front of 'J-Jig'; there was no way they could avoid the explosion, and pieces of metal and other material bounced off their Halifax. It gave Steve a shudder to think there might be bodies in the debris. They could not identify the aircraft, but when they got back to base they found out that the squadron had lost Warrant Officer (Second Class) Irish and his crew in LV970 AL-C, all the crew being killed in the resulting crash.

August commenced with a raid on the 3rd on a V1 storage depot in the Forêt de Nieppe, a large forest with the target being difficult to identify. The following day No. 429 Squadron was back in the same area, this time attacking the Bois de Cassan, another storage area near Paris where flying-bomb components were brought together and shipped to storage and launch sites. That day other squadrons bombed a number of V1 sites. Altogether over 1,000 Lancaster and Halifax aircraft pounded this region around the Oise Valley, north of Paris. (This locality also features later in this book.)

After this raid, the second of only two Canadian Bomber Command Victoria Crosses was awarded to Squadron Leader Ian Bazalgette of Calgary, Alberta, flying a Lancaster of No. 635 Squadron. After being hit and losing both starboard engines over the V1 railhead at Trossy St Maximin, Bazalgette continued to bomb the target; then as the aircraft started to lose height he ordered his crew to bail out. However, the bomb aimer was badly wounded and the mid-upper gunner was overcome by fumes, so he bravely kept the aircraft in the air, and made for a crash-landing in an open field near Senantes. Unfortunately, the aircraft blew up after landing and the three crewmen were killed. Bazalgette is buried in the nearby churchyard, a grave – visited by the author – which is immaculately tended by the villagers to this day.

For Steve and his crew their daylight operation proved routine. Fighter cover helped, and it was a lot easier to spot the target. Passing the Abbeville area they saw a formation of Messerschmitt Bf 109s, but they made no attempt to attack the bomber stream. As they flew over Paris it was like a 'tourist' trip and even Wilbur, the wireless operator, came out of his 'cubbyhole' to see the view of the Arc de Triomphe from the cockpit. As they started the bomb run, suddenly there was a bang to port and a hole appeared right in the centre of the wing roundel. As the aircraft jumped on the release of the bombs, more 'gravel-like' sounds were heard and flak hit the aircraft, damaging the radio and the window in front of Steve. They went into a dive to escape the ack-ack, and luckily the flak gunners turned their attention to another aircraft, and they were able to head for the coast. When they touched down at Leeming, Wilbur showed Steve the hole in the fuselage by his seat. His visit to the cockpit had been fortunate.

The next raid in 'A-Apple' the following day, 5 August, was to another V1 depot, this time at St Leu d'Esserent, which features in more detail elsewhere in this book. Some 742 aircraft were assigned to bomb in clear conditions, with only one No. 425 (Alouette) Squadron aircraft lost over the target, and three of the 'Bison' squadron aircraft landing away from base. Two days later it was back to supporting the invasion forces with an evening attack with full squadron strength of twenty-one aircraft to La Hogue. Bombing at 23.00 hours, the target was well covered by smoke, and results were seen to be good. As a continuation of Operation Crossbow and raids on the V1 sites, La Neuville – a launch and storage site – was next on the list to be attacked.

On 11 August RAF Leeming had been paid a visit by the King and Queen, in company with Princess Elizabeth. The day before, the flight commanders had been called to a meeting where they were told to assemble all aircrew. They were to be detailed to tidy up all loose debris and trash they could find on the runways and airfield. That did not go down too well with the crews, who felt that the task should have been given to the ground crew. They figured it might be a visit by the Canadian prime minister. The King had come primarily to award medals, but he also met some of the crews, and the aircraft, including Flying Officer Murphy's LW130 U-Uncle of No. 427 (Lion) Squadron, which had been hit by bombs from above, damaging the fuselage and losing one of its fin and rudder assemblies in the process.

The evening of 14 August saw a major effort in support of ground forces when strikes were made on five aiming points near Aisy. Bombing was from 9,000 feet, and although conditions were hazy, the Halifax crews could hear the master bomber clearly. The raid started well, with MZ282 AL-A in the first wave. About halfway through the operation, some aircraft started to bomb short, and Steve believed the master bomber's choice of yellow target indicators was a poor one. There were casualties, sadly in the Canadian 3rd Division advancing on Falaise. A few aircraft were so unsure they did not bomb, and brought their loads away from the target.

On 15 August the target was La Rochelle on the east coast of Brittany, France, and what was to be a 'gardening' mission, the code name given to the mining of estuaries and naval operations areas. It was to be Steve's first mining experience, and his last sortie. The commanding officer drove out to their dispersal to confirm this would be their final outing as a crew. Steve's thoughts at the time were: 'I wish he hadn't done that, not just before a trip. The crew is nervous enough as it is, without making it worse.' Mining operations were often regarded as risky as naval targets were well defended and flying was often below 10,000 feet. In this case, six 'Bison' aircraft were briefed, each with a specific area to cover, including Steve and his crew in MZ377 AL-D. The Halifax was loaded up with 2 x G716 Mk IV and one each of B406 Mk IV and F362/14B Mk IV mines, which were so bulky the bomb doors had to be left partly open, causing the aircraft to 'waddle' around on the runway, and affecting its flying performance.

Every aircraft was given a camera to record exactly where the mines, each fitted with a small parachute, had gone down.

The harbour at La Rochelle was protected by two islands – Île de Ré and Île de Oléron – both well equipped with flak positions. However, the ack-ack did not bother the Puskas crew too much, but there may have been some panic on the Germans' side, as they saw some naval ships firing at one another. After dropping their mines in light cloud from 8,500 feet using H2S and Gee references, Ted Bowles, the bomb aimer, photographed the radar screen for the intelligence team. Then it was over the town itself where they experienced some heavier flak. Yet they were soon through safely and on their way back to base for the last time together. En route for home, Jack asked if he could fire the 'Very' pistol. It was something he had wanted to do for some time. Steve said, 'OK, but fire the colours of the day only. It's our last op – what can they do to us!' Jack fired off three cartridges, satisfying his long urge to do it.

Four years later there was an adjunct to this, Steve's last operation. Back home in Canada there was a talk given by the West German military attaché to Canada, a former U-boat commander. In conversation with Steve he confirmed he had been at La Rochelle that night. Steve asked, 'What was the outcome?' 'Not much damage,' he replied. 'One of our submarines picked up one of the mines and was out of commission for only three months.'

At the end August 1944, their eventual paperwork came through, with details on future postings. Steve had promised his loyal ground crew that if he and his men finished their tour safely, they would give the ground crew a 'bash' they wouldn't forget. That was a promise, as they wanted to show their appreciation and to say thanks for their efforts in helping to keep them alive. They invited Flight Sergeant John Olliver and his team to a party at their favourite pub, the Wagon & Horses in nearby Bedale. However, some 'killjoy' remembered the pub was not opening that night due to a beer shortage, so the trip to Bedale was scrubbed. Then one of the ground crew recalled another pub nearby that would be open, but they would need bicycles to get there. So bikes were borrowed and scrounged and away they went. It was a great evening, the group even joined by a few strangers who heard of the free beer! All too soon the landlord cried: 'Time gentlemen please!'

Now there was a problem. How were they to get all the paid-for but unconsumed beer home? They decided to stuff the bottles into their uniforms and coat pockets. It was amazing how minds were sharpened after a few beers. As the men trickled out of the pub, 'cohorts' inside passed the beers through the window, to be hidden in their clothing. All was going to plan until the local policeman turned up on his bike to check on closing time. He realised what was going on and started to blow his whistle. The Canadians took the unanimous decision to retreat, and pedalled furiously out of the village, with the 'bobby' in hot pursuit. Even though they were hindered by the bottles in their tunics, it was remarkable the speed they made, especially as there were few torches and the road was unlit due to the blackout. A short distance away someone shouted: 'Short cut – turn left now!' Too late for some, but Steve went with the 'flow' until they got to a stream with only stepping stones – no bridge! How nobody was hurt crossing the river Steve never knew, but they got through at the expense of some bent bicycles and wet clothing. However, those who missed the turn were not so lucky; as they rounded a bend there was another 'bobby' with his bike blocking the road, chatting to a young lady. Alvin Williams, Steve's rear gunner, could not stop and crashed into him, toppling the policeman on to his back and Alvin into a ditch. The others stayed long enough to assess the situation and then charged off to the airfield, remembering the base curfew. After a conference with the 'bobby', Alvin and one of the crew's mechanics, Rod Williams – during which Rod pointed out the policeman's bicycle had no lights – a fee of £10.00 was agreed to repair his machine, and it was understood that no further action would be taken. The airmen trudged onwards to base and it was a sorry crew who arrived back at Leeming to find some of the quicker crew already in their house, toasting bread on the fire and consuming the remains of the beer.

The following day news of their postings was circulated, and the crew – who had spent so much time together – were now to be scattered about England. Steve was transferring to No. 82 OTU at Ossington; Jack Phillips (flight engineer) and Ted Bowles (bomb aimer) were being posted to No. 1659 and 1666 HCUs respectively; Jasper Still was remaining at Leeming on an instruction basis; and Bill Wilson (wireless operator/air gunner) was leaving for No. 83 OTU.

Just before they all separated, Ted Bowles got married in London to his fiancée, Joan. Of the crew, Steve, Harry Venn, Jack Phillips and Jasper Still attended the wedding; it was one of the last times they were all together. (Ted passed away as this was written in November 2014 – the last surviving member of the crew.) After ten days' leave, Steve arrived at his new base, RAF Ossington in Nottinghamshire. Here Vickers Wellingtons were flown at a unit designed to prepare new crews to learn from those who, like Steve, had completed their operational tour. However, on these aircraft there was only one control column and the student had use of that. On one of the cross-country exercises Steve's student froze at the controls and they crashed on landing. Steve was out of the aircraft in seconds, tearing his trousers in the process. He told the subsequent inquiry committee, and flight commander Flight Lieutenant Middlemiss: 'I didn't survive a tour to be killed by a bad student!' (Middlemiss had been with Steve during his time at an OTU on Whitleys.) The CFI was not too happy and expressed his concern, and Steve decided if an opportunity came up he would move on. A chance soon presented itself, and in November moved to RAF Gamston nearby and No. 91 General Service Unit and Ferry Flight.

The members of No. 91 were supposed to get roomed at the station headquarters, but the CO, a permanent-force type, hated the 'colonials' and they were billeted at a distant abandoned site. They did not complain as they were happily 'out of sight', but nevertheless did their best to irritate him. There was no fuel for their stove, so they chopped up any wood they could find, even acquiring (was it stealing?) tables and chairs from the officers' mess. They even rigged a radio up with a wire to the nearest electricity pole to power it. They kept curtains closed, and door locked, so the CO could not carry out any inspection. When he moaned, they said they needed to keep the door locked for security in their remote location. They could not let an inspection ruin their 'acquired' possessions. After a couple of refresher flights in dual mode, Steve was off on his duties. His room-mate, George, had completed a tour in the Middle East and had a lot of 'catching up' to do. Their 'batwoman' was a local country girl; in Steve's parlance: 'You could say she was a "homely" girl.' One morning he had walked on ahead on his own to the mess for breakfast, when he remembered he had forgotten his raincoat as it was starting to rain. Returning to the room he opened the door to find George in bed with the girl. He recalled: 'I didn't say a word, or look at them, just picked up my coat off the door and left.' When he next saw them, no embarrassment was shown by either. Shortly after, George announced he was getting married to a local girl he had met at a station dance, and as far as Steve knew they were blissfully happy.

On 4 November Steve was 'gazetted' for the award of Distinguished

Flying Cross on fulfilment of his operational tour (a total flying time of 191 hours 30 minutes) from 15 February to 15 August 1944. It had been put forward by the No. 429 Squadron CO on 19 August. The citation said: 'This officer has completed a notable tour of thirty-eight attacks on enemy targets, including attacks on such heavily defended targets as Berlin, Leipzig, Stuttgart, Karlsruhe and Düsseldorf. Throughout his tour he has shown a keen offensive spirit and a great desire to come to grips with the enemy. He has been an outstanding captain of aircraft and has encouraged and trained his crew so that they have invariably carried out their duties satisfactorily and in the course of which [he has] invariably displayed the utmost fortitude, courage and devotion to duty.' Steve wore his ribbon with pride immediately, though the award itself was presented to him on 27 July 1949 when he was at RCAF Mount Hope, Hamilton in Canada.

At No. 91 General Service Unit and Ferry Flight, Steve put together his own crew, both English – Atherton as navigator and McCarthy as wireless operator/air gunner (author's note: no ranks are known). Atherton was 'prim and proper' and a stickler for procedure, whereas McCarthy, who was from London, delighted in getting away with anything he could. He used to listen to the US armed forces radio station American Forces Network (AFN), and they could hear his feet tapping away through the airframe.

They had a relaxed job, sometimes picking up aircraft from factory or repair depots and then delivering to operational units, or for storage at satellite landing grounds (SLGs) or even to 'graveyards' of aircraft parts. Slade Farm was one such place in the Midlands. It was tight flying in, and the plane had barely enough fuel for the trip. There were just two officers there (Steve only ever saw one) and a few ground crew who directed them into the woods to a clearing, where the aircraft would be stripped of anything useful and then scrapped. They had a great time visiting these sites. There was always a good lunch offered, often with home-grown chickens and vegetables, and locally sourced food. For example of a typical trip, on 4 November they delivered Wellington LN407 to Slade Farm, returning in HE587, then two days later they conveyed HE587 to its final destination, arriving back in BK392. The following day it was X3461 to go to the graveyard – and so it went on every day or two. Steve's last flights over in the UK were on 5 January 1945, taking Wellington HF758 to No. 8 Maintenance Unit (MU) at RAF Little Rissington and coming home in BJ456.

Steve had asked for a posting to the RAF's Light Night Striking Force,

PART I: GOLDFISH

A snowy RCAF Brantford airfield
in southern Ontario.
Mrs. M. Puskas

Billets at Brantford - typical of BCATP airfields.
Cold and damp in winter.
Mrs. M. Puskas

Early aerial photograph of RAF Leeming showing camouflage taken in 1942.
A couple of Wellington bombers can be seen dispersed.
After the Battle magazine archive

Steve Puskas during pilot training.
Mrs. M. Puskas

Airborne mine leaving bomb bay
of a No.427 Sqn Halifax
Douglas Petty 429 Sq.

PART I: GOLDFISH

RAF Leeming taken 28 May 1943. Halifaxes are clearly shown on dispersals.
RCAF Archives via R. Koval

Steve with Jasper Still, left and Jack Findlay right.
Mrs. M. Puskas

PART I: GOLDFISH

Handley Page Halifax Mk.III MZ282 AL-A 'Sweet Adeline' with ground crew and 'Cookie' 4000lb bomb.
RCAF Archives via R. Koval

Puskas air and ground crew next to their Halifax. Standing left to right N. Osborne, Rod Williams, Jas Still, John Oliver (Crew Chief), Steve, and Alvin Williams; front row Jack Phillips, Harry Venn and Wilbur Wilson.
Mrs. M. Puskas

Puskas crew at OTU next to Whitley. Left to right: Wilf Faulkner, Steve, 'Gopher' Wilson, Ted Bowles, Alvin Williams, Jasper Still.
Mrs. M. Puskas

PART I: GOLDFISH

Preston Green mid under cupola, here fitted to a No.420 'Snowy Owl' Sqn Halifax.
The weapon is a 0.5in. machine gun, with gunner Ted Lewis.
Author's collection

Alvin Williams cleaning the 0.303
machine guns in his turret.
Mrs. M. Puskas

King George inspects damage to No.427 Sqn
Halifax 'U-Uncle' during visit to RAF Leeming
on 11 August 1944.
RCAF Archives via Author's collection

PART I: GOLDFISH

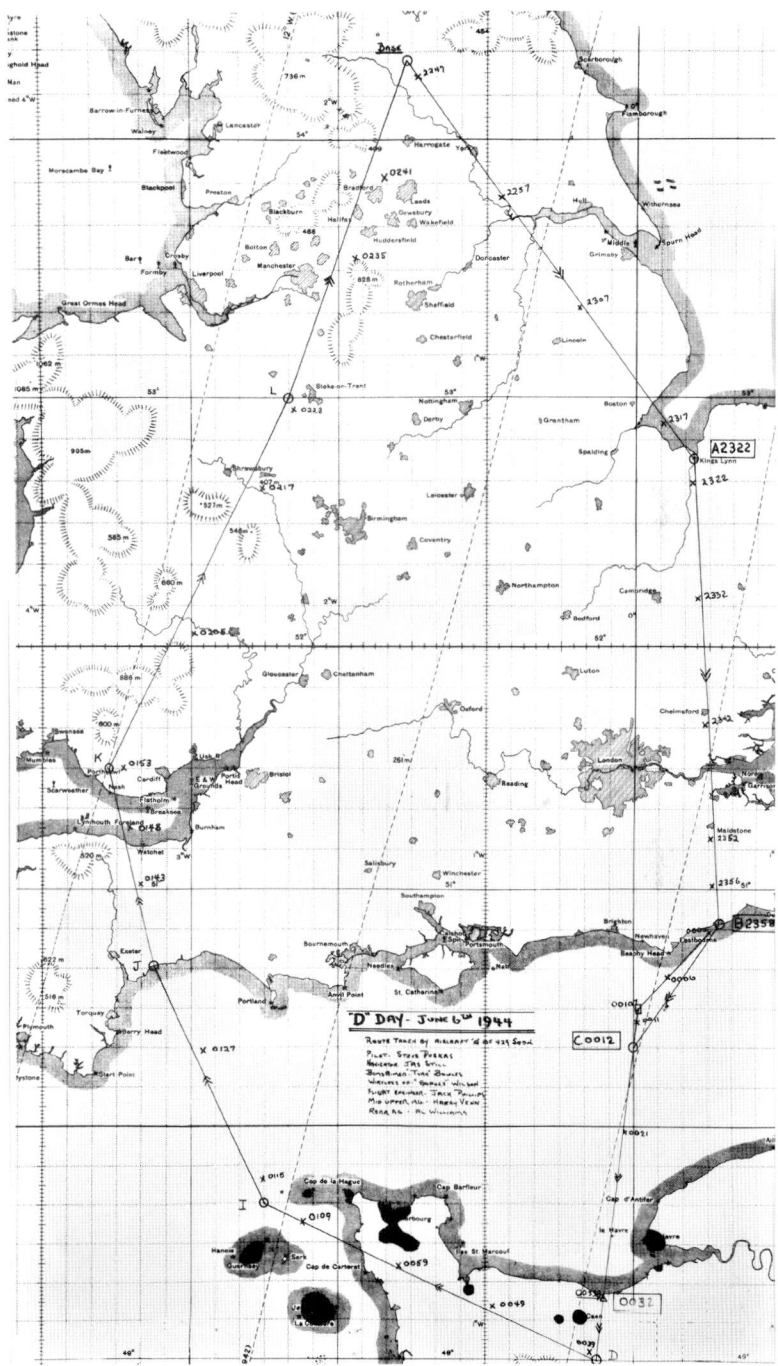

Route of 'Sweet Adeline' to target at Franceville over D-Day invasion 5/6 June 1944.
Mrs. M. Puskas via RAF Leeming Museum

PART I: GOLDFISH

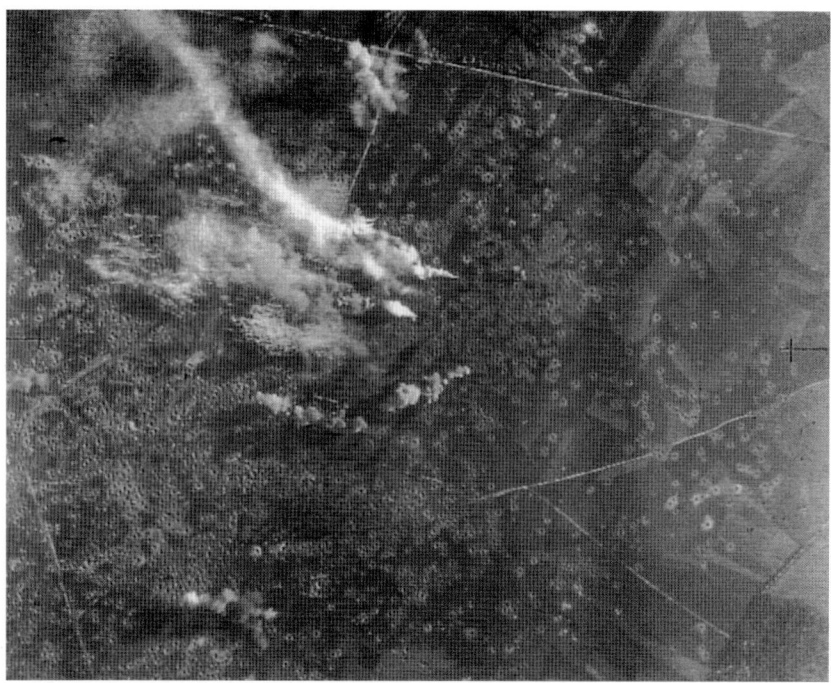

Target photograph of Siracourt, taken by AL-A crew 6 July 1944. Note heavily pockmarked area around target, that is partially obscured by defensive smoke.
RCAF Archives via R. Koval

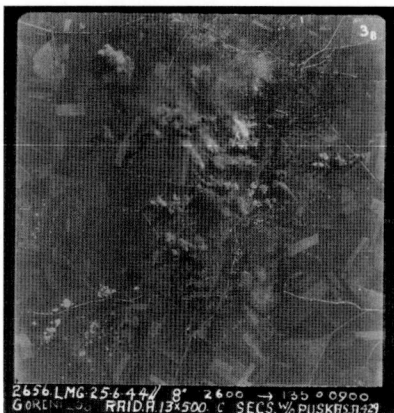

Target photograph of Gorenflos, taken by AL-A crew 25 June 1944.
RCAF Archives via R. Koval

Target photograph of Metz, taken by AL-K crew of W/O Irish 429 Sqn 29 June 1944. AL-A crew were on this operation.
Author's collection

PART I: GOLDFISH

Top of huge V1 bunker at Siracourt taken in 2008. Note top shows little evidence of damage in spite of large number of bombs that hit it.
Author's collection

'Operation Crossbow' target at Siracourt taken in 2008. This was bombed by AL-A crew on 6 July 1944. Damage on right is the result of a Tallboy bomb.
Author's collection

PART I: GOLDFISH

THE GOLDFISH
GOLD FOR THE VALUE OF LIFE · FISH

CHARLES A. ROBERTSON, HON. SECRETARY
BEEHIVE WORKS, HONEYPOT LANE
STANMORE · MIDDLESEX

TELEPHONE : WORDSWORTH 4521 - 4530
TELEGRAMS : "BECOW" PHONE, LONDON

CAR/EF

May 27th, 1944.

F/Sgt. S. Puskas,
R.C.A.F.,
Leeming, Yorks.

Dear F/Sgt. Puskas,

    I have your letter of the 15th inst. for which I thank you. As a result, you have all been enrolled as life members of the above Club, and I am having your official membership cards prepared. I hope to receive these from the processors during the next two or three weeks, when I will send them along, together with the Club badges.

    I should like to congratulate you on your escape, and hope that you sustained no injuries.

    Would you be good enough to let me have the full addresses of the crew members? I should like these in connection with post-war activities of the Club.

    Best wishes to you all,
    Yours sincerely,

C.A. Robertson.
Hon. Secretary.

This Club has been made possible by the courtesy of P. B. Cow (Queensbury) Ltd. in appreciation of many gallant airmen.

This is to Certify that
F/Sgt. S. Puskas
has qualified as a member of the Goldfish Club by escaping death by the use of his Emergency Dinghy on
March 10th, 1944.

Letter and Certificate issued by P.B. Cow (Queensbury) Ltd. of Steve Puskas' membership of the 'Goldfish' Club after his successful ditching of Halifax AL-C 10 March 1944.
Mrs. M. Puskas

PART II: EVADER

Pilot Officer James Moffat during leave visits Edinburgh Castle.
J.Moffat/M.Thomas

PART II: EVADER

Roger Fournier, Jim's friend from Timmins, Ont. Roger saved Jim's life in the mine.
J.Moffat/M.Thomas

PART II: EVADER

No. 427 'Lion' Squadron Commanding Officer
W/Cdr. Bill Newson in cockpit of Handley Page Halifax Mk.V.
RCAF Archives via R. Koval

Handley Page Halifax LV687 ZL-W 'Whisky' with ground crew.
RCAF Archives via R. Koval

PART II: EVADER

Unidentified Halifax crew checking the rear turret of No.427 Squadron Halifax Mk.V. Note doors through which Jim bailed out of the damaged aircraft.
RCAF Archives via R. Koval

PART II: EVADER

W-'Whisky' crew checking guns in armoury after third operation.
Jim Moffat 2nd from right.
J.Moffat/M.Thomas

Crew at Leeming 1943. Back row left to right: Sgt Pat Clapham, Sq Ldr George Laird, WO1 Joe Corbally, F/O Jim Moffat, F/O Paddy McClune. Seated left to right: Sgt Lloyd Smith, Sgt George Lorimer.
J.Moffat/M.Thomas

PART II: EVADER

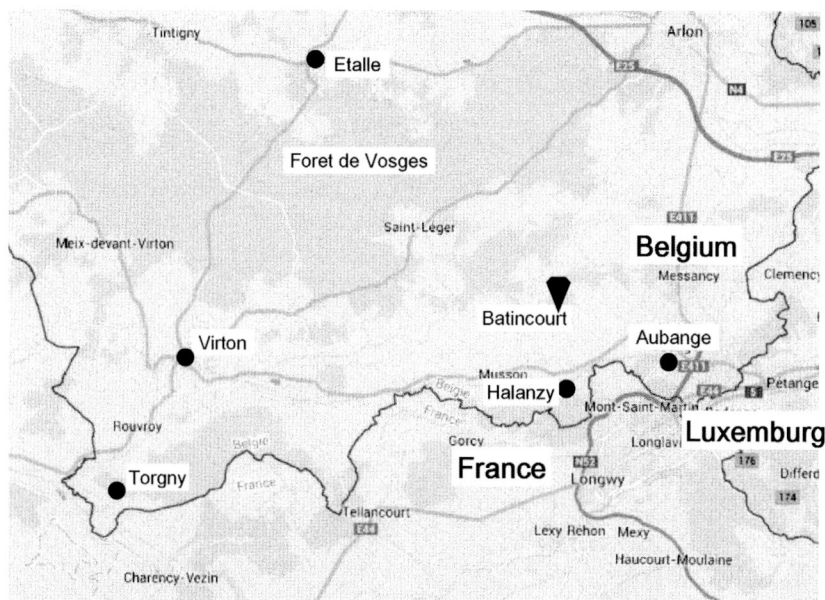

This map shows the area around the French, Belgian/Luxembourg border
where Jim Moffat was active with the resistance.
Google Maps

Laird Crew at RAF Leeming. Left to right:
pilot George Laird, navigator 'Red' Soeder, bomb aimer Joe Corbally, wireless op. Pat Clapham,
flight engineer 'Paddy'. McLune, mid-upper gunner Lloyd Smith, and rear gunner, Jim Moffat.
RCAF Archives via R. Koval

PART II: EVADER

Jim with fellow RAF evader Bill Jones at Etalle.
J.Moffat/M.Thomas

The Hermitage at Torgny.
It was here Jim hid in the loft area.
J.Moffat/M.Thomas

The Authphene family with Jim (2nd from left).
J.Moffat/M.Thomas

PART II: EVADER

The house in Etalle. Jim's hiding place was above the archway. Messien family house to the right.
J.Moffat/M.Thomas

James Moffat with Arsène Martin, who initiated the monument at D'Aubange in memory of the two crews who died. Unveiled at Rachecourt 31 March 1990.
J.Moffat/M.Thomas

flying the much-vaunted Mosquito, an aircraft he dearly wanted to fly. Just one day later the adjutant called him into his office. Steve thought: 'Here it is, the transfer I want.' But it was to tell him he was being posted back to Canada. During his embarkation leave he returned to London to see his old girlfriend, Peggy, now working in RAF offices in Aldwych. They went to a couple of shows together and over a drink she told him she was getting married to an RAF pilot who was coming to the end of his tour. Steve still had some clothing coupons left (two years' worth by civilian standards) and he gave them to Peggy so she could buy new clothes for herself, and bid her a fond farewell.

A few days later he was at Padgate, near Warrington, waiting for a ship to Canada. Just days afterwards he boarded the SS *Louis Pasteur* at Liverpool. Built as a liner in France just before the war, it had taken the French gold reserves to Canada before it was captured as France fell. Converted to carry prisoners of war, and also acting as a troopship, by the time Steve alighted, the vessel was showing signs of its hard life; he described it as a 'rust bucket'. Steve was entitled to a cabin on this trip across the Atlantic, but at the last minute in Liverpool the officers were asked to give up their cabins for wounded being repatriated to Canada. 'How could I refuse?' he recounted, 'I had come over in 1943 sleeping on a table, so I could do it again.' Unfortunately the crossing was a bad one, stormy all the way with the ship pitching around as it changed course regularly. Navy officers travelling with Steve suggested a hammock may be better, but not so. The ceiling swaying back and forth only make his queasiness worse, and he swore he would never get in a boat again – not even a rowing boat! Eventually the *Louis Pasteur* berthed in New York and Steve was greeted with genuine coffee and doughnuts, a real treat. After a train journey back to Canada, he ended up at Lachine in Montreal, where he was documented, paid up to date and received travel warrants home to Hamilton for a month's leave.

During the last week of his leave, he received a telegram telling him to report to RCAF headquarters at RCAF Trenton, east of Toronto. He was informed he had been selected to remain in the post-war air force, and was to be sent to British Columbia for retraining. He asked for overseas or Mount Hope, and the wing commander asked: 'Why Mount Hope?' 'I live in Hamilton', was the reply. 'OK,' he said, 'Mount Hope it is.' There was not much flying to do and Steve soon became bored. After being inveigled into doing some speaking to various organisations, he decided he wanted to leave the air force and had his discharge papers prepared. When these came through, he had to report to the RCAF Manning Depot in Toronto for a quick medical check before becoming a civilian again. 'I was back where my flying career had started!' he told this author. He planned to return to his pre-war employers, Westinghouse, as his former manager confirmed there was a place as an electrical draughtsman for him. His final parade was on 5 June 1945, when Flying Officer Stephen Puskas, DFC, fronted the parade, the only one he was ever to lead, and his last. 'I think it was because I was the only one with a DFC!'

After he left the air force he returned to Westinghouse, where he remained for the rest of his working life, ending up a senior manager. Steve married a local sweetheart, Mary, and they were together until she passed away in 1987. For a while he joined an RCAF Reserve unit at the local Mount Hope airport, where he flew Chipmunks. In the 1990s he became a regular attendee at the annual Allied air forces reunions held at the Royal York Hotel in Toronto, becoming an organising committee member. He wed his second wife, English girl Marie, in September 1989. In June 1990 he returned to the UK for the 6 (RCAF) Group reunion held in London and York, and had the opportunity to visit his old base, RAF Leeming, again. His last trip over the pond was in June 1999, to a gathering of the 6 (RCAF) Group Association founded by this author, of which he was also a founding member. It was his last journey, as he passed away, aged seventy-eight, on 17 July 2000.

UNDER THE
MAPLE LEAF

PART II

EVADER

Jim Moffat (2nd from right).

Part II: Evader

4. From Mining to Flying

The thorns were very sharp and Flying Officer Jim Moffat from Timmins, Ontario, had not realised just how pointed they were. In fact, he had not known it was even a thorn bush when he had dived in. And now, here he was, half naked and in the middle of one, somewhere in the Belgium/France border area and just inches away from the boots of a German soldier searching for him, determined to kill or capture him. He had lost his trousers in the chase, and was wondering just how on earth he had got himself into this dicey situation.

Jim was born on 4 August 1921 and grew up in northern Ontario. The family were homesteaders; his mother, Elizabeth, was from Pontefract, Yorkshire, in England, and his father, David Moffat, was scraping a living from the earth. Life was tough, and his education limited, although his parents were well read and ensured he could cope with the world outside. Timmins was a gold mining town, and leaving school early, Jim was used to 'roughing it' in the bush.

Then the war came and changed everything. Jim decided he wanted to join the Canadian Navy and so he walked overnight 25 miles to Timmins, then took the train to Toronto and made his way to the Navy recruiting office. Jim recalled: 'I told the recruiting officer I wanted to be a gunner. "Sorry, no vacancies for gunners. We are looking for stokers," he said.' Jim had read a paper on the train, and a feature about a destroyer that had been sunk had told that all on board had been saved except the stokers, who got trapped in the engine room of the ship. 'No thanks,' he stated, and decided to return to Timmins.

Back home he signed on at the mines' recruiting office, and in no time he was shovelling rock in the Naybob Mine, about 10 miles outside Timmins. It was hard work – very hard work – and after a while he managed to change his job to 'cage tender'. The 'cage' was the lift that took the miners up to the surface; one day one of the miners had broken a safety rule and looked up the shaft to see if the cage was coming down and it had severed his head. Even this work was not much easier. Accidents were common.

At this time Jim became friends with another local young man, Roger Fournier. A few months later, one morning, Jim went down the mine to switch on the air blower to clear the dust and gas after the nightly dynamite blast, but this time the explosion had damaged the equipment. He could not make it work and called up to Roger to ring the emergency 'nine bells' and get him out of there. Roger acted quickly and the next thing Jim knew he was being brought around by the shift boss with smelling salts. Roger had saved his life that day, something Jim remembered a couple of years later in his turret over Germany.

Working the mine was tough, and Jim built up a close friendship with Roger, and his girlfriend Elda, and together Roger and Jim worked on the cage for almost two years, Jim often working extra shifts in the dark and just by the light of his helmet lamp. They were not supposed to work alone, but they got 'risk money', so often it was long dark hours on his own at the bottom of the cage shaft.

After a couple of years, in September 1941, he and Roger decided to have another attempt at volunteering for the military; this time for the air force. Roger was accepted and went out west for training, but Jim was turned down as, lacking a high school graduation certificate, he had insufficient qualifications. Six months later there was an advertisement in the Timmins newspaper saying that the air force was accepting recruits if they had 'the equivalent' of a high school education. Armed with this advert Jim quit his job and hurried down to North Bay, about 226 miles south from Timmins, to sign up. The recruiting team in North Bay said: 'Your education is not exactly what we want, but you could be ground crew.' At this time Jim's thoughts were based on the grim stories of a hard life told by his father after his experience in the First World War. 'I don't want to be mucking around in the mud', he told the recruiting sergeant, and the man replied, 'Well you could be a gunner, I suppose.' Jim was advised to return in September, so it was back to Nabob. As he had given up his job operating the cage, he was employed elsewhere in the mine, working with a miner called a 'driller'.

But by September 1942 Jim was at last in the air force, and with all the other recruits at the Manning Depot. This was based in the old exhibition centre down by the waterfront in Toronto, a place known as the 'Cow Palace'. It was a rude awakening for a naive 'north country boy', and after eating they were 'herded' together into the barracks, which had about 500 bunk beds; Jim managed to get a top bed. Within a couple of days he had the unfortunate experience of having his camera stolen. For the next two months life consisted of early morning runs and 'square bashing' to the shrill calls of the NCOs. After the grim time down the mine, Jim thought he was in heaven, and life was just beginning.

Shortly after, they all moved to Dunville, in south-west Ontario, to learn ground duties and to mix with aircraft for the first time. This was No. 6 Service Flying Training School (SFTS), mostly using North American Harvard and Yale aircraft. The Yale was a Harvard with fixed undercarriage, widely used by the RCAF. There were also a few Avro Ansons on which some New Zealanders were taking navigational courses. One of these chaps offered Jim his first experience of flight. They flew out over Lake Erie, covered in ice. Jim wondered: 'How thick is the ice?' Without further ado the pilot lowered the wheels and they touched the lake's surface, and after that Jim thought flying was the best experience ever. It was not without its dangers, though, and a few days later the same pilot tried another trick of knocking over a haystack, but this one was solid ice, and he was killed.

On New Year's Day 1943, at the traditional mess dinner where officers served the enlisted men, Jim was told it was good luck to get the tip of an officer's tie, so he clipped off one tip from an officer serving him, and this became his lucky mascot throughout the war. A few weeks later he transferred to Canadian Forces Base (CFB) Trenton, east of Toronto, which was now the main Canadian Air Force transport base. Jim found the training in navigation, gunnery and wireless operation easy to learn compared to some of the recruits, and even took time to go down to the gunnery section and help others to dismantle and assemble some of the weapons. By the spring he was selected to man a precision marching squad at the station, and on the campus of the University of Toronto; this entertained at various banquets and official functions.

Jim's next move was out west to No. 3 Bombing and Gunnery School at Macdonald, Manitoba, beginning his course in April 1943. At the airfield they used Fairey Battle aircraft, an early light bomber of the RAF that had proven unsuccessful and had taken a terrible mauling from the Luftwaffe during the Battle of France in the spring of 1940. However, for training in Canada, 750 Battles, built in the UK and shipped over for the British Commonwealth Air Training Plan (BCATP), had powered turrets fitted halfway along their fuselages, and served the Canadians well in gunnery training. They used to fly out over Lake Manitoba, and practise shooting at drones. On one occasion the gun jammed, so Jim reported it to the pilot and they turned toward base. Jim realised he had made the cardinal sin of allowing the empty shells to collect and this had stopped the gun. A little bit of quick thinking and he recognised a 'number two stoppage' was a broken cable, so in the 15 minutes it took to fly back he had snapped the cable. On return he responded to the training sergeant's question – 'Did you find the problem?' – with, 'Oh yeah, a broken cable', and so Jim got full marks!

Much of the training was in a turret simulator mounted in a building that was used for night-firing practice, and one could watch the tracer bullets arc over the lake. Occasionally students could be clumsy, and one lazy chap actually ended up spraying the building interior with bullets, the sergeant having to grab the gun from him after yelling for everyone to 'Hit the deck!' The Battles did suffer from leakage of fumes from the engine coming up from below the turret. Once, this made Jim so ill and caused him to vomit out by the gun sited toward the tail. When on the ground preparing for a flight one day, one of the trainees in a turret fainted and collapsed on Jim down below in the fuselage. At the same time there was a 'thump' at the front of the aircraft. Jim grabbed the intercom to relay the information of the sick trainee to the pilot who said: 'I think we've hit somebody.' It turned out two airmen had been walking across the tarmac with some ammunition and had walked into the propeller. They had their helmets on and could not hear the engine; one was killed and the other lost his arm. It was a hard price to pay for lack of attention.

Jim completed over 23 hours in the Battles, and by 25 June graduated second in a class of 122 and he was promoted to sergeant. Next day he was earmarked for service overseas in the UK, and was sent back to Ontario for pre-embarkation leave. Two days after arriving at his mother's house, now in southern Ontario, he received a telegram to say he had been commissioned as an RCAF pilot officer. After spending a few days with a fellow No. 3 B&GS student, Kenneth 'King' Cole, who had also been promoted, they went to Toronto for their new uniforms. However, at this time such items were not often available, so they were given white armbands to signify their status, and four of them – along with all the NCOs – left on the train for Halifax, Nova Scotia.

Halifax was heaving with humanity from all services and Jim was excited, probably 'walking on air' and not paying attention. On his way from the clothing stores, he was strolling down the corridor and suddenly realised there were women in underwear all around him – he had strayed into the women's division barracks! He left as quickly as possible. After 'blagging' his way into receiving two 12oz bottles of liquor, instead of the single-bottle ration, he headed for entertainment downtown. They were only there a couple of days before they embarked for Greenock, Scotland, aboard the *Ile de France*, a French transatlantic liner built in Saint-Nazaire and launched in 1926, now requisitioned as a troopship, and wearing 'battleship grey' paint.

Equipped with their new uniforms and wearing the regulation pistol, tin helmets and carrying their kitbags, the servicemen found the situation rather strange, with people and kids waving along the streets. On board who should be there but the New Zealanders from Dunville. Being officers, Jim and his friends were accommodated four to a cabin, with white bed sheets, and ate in the main dining room with silver service. All the hard work studying and not 'fooling around' had paid off. Occasionally Jim was 'duty officer' and had to inspect the lower ranks' accommodation, and that was somewhat of a shock, with sleeping quarters in hammocks and picnic tables for dining on the basic fare. 'Oh my God,' he said to the NCO showing him around, 'you sleep in hammocks?' 'You should see our bathroom,' remarked the NCO and led him to the rear of the ship where there was a simple board across an open space, and you could see thrashing propellers below. The sergeant wryly commented: 'In stormy weather the sea splashes right up here and washes us off!'

Due to the high speed it could make, the *Ile de France* made its own way across the ocean, via the Denmark Strait, past Iceland, and the only company they had on the trip was from a Coastal Command B-24 Liberator, which exchanged messages by Aldis lamp with the ship. Disembarking at Greenock, they immediately boarded a train for Bournemouth, on the south coast, and the overseas aircrew reception centre. Jim could have been here for weeks, enjoying the rigours of cross-country escape training (which might have proven useful in the light of later events), but instead quickly volunteered for operational training, and having good marks was an important criteria.

In just a few days he was on his way to No. 1659 Heavy Conversion Unit (HCU) at RAF Topcliffe in the north of England at the Vale of York, arriving at the beginning of August 1943. Here he roomed with two of his friends, Cole and Stewart, and a Pilot Officer Jack Findlay, who had been at No. 82 OTU on Wellingtons. He had already mustered with an aircrew and said to Jim: 'You can join our crew if you want.' In the mess several flight lieutenants were talking together; 'King' Cole joined Don Arnott's team and they eventually went to No. 405 (Vancouver) Squadron, and Jim joined Flight Lieutenant George Laird's crew. It was a very informal way for crewing up but it was essential to form a good relationship with your fellow airmen as your life may later depend on it. Sadly the navigator, Flight Sergeant George Lorimer, was not an officer, which Jim would have preferred, and George Laird would often give him a hard time. He was unforgiving of any mistakes.

At Topcliffe the crews were half British and half Canadian, though Topcliffe was within the area administered by No. 6 (RCAF) Group. This group had been formed in October 1942, becoming operational in January 1943, in response to the Canadian prime minister, William McKenzie King's, insistence for an all-Canadian bomber group in return for allowing the wide open spaces of Canada to be used for aircrew training. The commanding officer of Bomber Command at the time, Air Vice Marshal Arthur T. 'Bomber' Harris, was not in favour of this, as he did not want international politics, and a 'foreign outfit' as he called it, within his command, but he was pushed into accepting the deal by Winston Churchill. Harris wrote to the RAF Chief of Staff, Air Chief Marshal Sir Charles Portal: 'I fail to see why we should give these people, who are determined to huddle into a corner by themselves on purely political grounds, the best of our equipment at the expense of British and other Dominion crews.' In the end he came to love his Canadian crews and praised their courage.

Jim started his flying training in the unit in a Handley Page Halifax Mk V, equipped with four Merlin engines, his first flight on 10 August 1943 being as mid-upper gunner in FD-X 'X-Xray' (serial number unknown) doing 'circuits and bumps' with George Laird and being tutored by Squadron Leader Bob Turnbull, who had already completed one tour of operations. On 13 August in FD-T 'T-Tommy' they completed their first 'bullseye' operation, flying around the UK, with British towns simulating targets: bombing a range at Strensall, north of York, then returning to base via Gainsborough (Lincolnshire), Fishguard (West Wales), Market

Drayton (Shropshire) and Waterbeach (Cambridgeshire). The following day there was another 'bullseye' of over 5 hours' flying again. The Mk V Halifax had a mid-upper turret that had originally been designed for the British turret fighter, the Bolton Paul Defiant, and could catch out the unwary; they were warned never to stick their arms out to feel the breeze. One day Jim did and the slipstream nearly pulled him out of the turret. This was a grim time for Bomber Command and the news media told of the fatalities. There were also heavy losses from the conversion units due to the crews' unfamiliarity of UK weather and landscape, and No. 1659 HCU's experience was no different.

At last on 27 August 1943 their operational posting came through and the crew were transferred to No. 427 (Lion) Squadron at RAF Leeming, just a few miles to the west of Topcliffe, alongside the A1 Great North Road. All the 6 Group squadrons were 'adopted' by various organisations across the Atlantic. In the case of No. 427 it was the Metro Goldwyn Mayer studios in Hollywood, USA. Some of the aircraft carried the names of movie stars, such as Lana Turner (on Halifax V ZL-L DK186). No. 427 Squadron was the only Canadian unit 'adopted' by a US organisation, and squadron members were given free passes to see any MGM film.

The first training operation in the new squadron, on 27 August, was another 'bullseye' operation, flying at about 10,000 feet – a pleasant height as one could see the ground and the roads of England clearly. Jim had made friends with the pilot on this operation, Flying Officer George Pierre Vanderkerckhove, a 21-year-old with twenty-nine operations and a DFC to his credit, and they used his motorcycle to charge up the main road to Darlington for a few drinks on a bright moonlight night, with the headlights off. It was great fun. Just a few days later on the 31st, on his final operation to Berlin, George was dead. His Halifax EB251 ZL-T was brought down by flak 10 miles north-west of Osnabrück and all but two of the crew were killed. It was a hard lesson to learn for Jim, so soon after joining the squadron; making friends in wartime was difficult.

On 5 September the Laird crew, with Jim as mid-upper gunner, Jack Findlay as tail gunner and Canadian Sergeant Bill Cardy joining the crew as flight engineer, were tasked for their first operation to Mannheim. It was just under three weeks short of a year since Jim had signed up at North Bay, and he was thrilled to be off over Germany; this was what he had joined for. Being an inexperienced crew, they were in the fifth wave of the operation, flying Halifax Mk V LK687 ZL-W 'W-Willie'. However, problems were about to manifest themselves on the raid. On the way to the target the starboard inner engine started to 'run away', from 2,400 to 6,000 revolutions, and Laird called out: 'Where's that damned engineer?' Cool as ever, a calm voice came back: 'That damned engineer is right behind you, skipper.' Jim could see the wings flapping. The constant speed unit on the propeller had failed so Bill Cardy 'feathered' the propeller to reduce drag, and cut the engine.

They were now flying on three engines and losing height fast. The Mk V Halifax was a poor performer, even though it had the reliable Rolls-Royce Merlin 22 engines. Things would change later when the squadron would receive the Mk III Halifax with the more powerful Bristol Hercules radial engines. George Laird asked the crew for their opinions as to whether they should keep going, and the response was unanimous to continue on to Germany. Jim said later: 'We had come all this way and we were anxious to get our first "op" out of the way.' They reached the aiming point at 10,000 feet – instead of the assigned 21,000 – 'so we had to watch to see we did not get bombed by another aircraft'. They found themselves in among the Stirling bombers – quite a surprise for the Stirling crews – and away from flak that was targeting the higher aircraft. Jim could see everything from the mid-upper turret. They limped back to England, carrying out an emergency landing at Boscombe Down in Wiltshire due to fuel shortage, and returning to Leeming in another aircraft, due to the serviceability of W-Whisky (the crew called her 'W-Willie').

On that operation Bomber Command lost thirty-seven aircraft in all, with No. 6 (RCAF) Group losing three: JD210 VR-oS and JD410 VR-V from No. 419 (Moose) Squadron and Sergeant Fletcher's crew in LK63 ZL-H from No. 427 Squadron. As far as the crew of 'W-Willie', was concerned, the 'Lion' squadron's Operations Record Book (ORB) notes that ' ... the bombing was concentrated, and well worth the effort'.

Jim was delighted to have finally gone on their first bombing raid and wrote home to his mother two days later. The letter is quoted verbatim:

Well it happened, Mom at last I got what I was waiting for. We bombed Mannheim the other night and let me tell you this. It is not like what I thought it would be. It doesn't matter how much I try to explain it, I couldn't recount an idea of how I saw, or how it was. Lots of lads have told me what to expect, but you can't picture it at all ...

then when you see the target there is at first a small red glow in front, and you never seem to get to it, and then at about 20,000 feet you see down below a hell of a lot of fires; in fact it looks like molten metal with smoke coming from it, and two or three cones of searchlights about twenty or thirty lights in the area. But we had some bad luck going into the target our motor went and we lost 4,000 feet before we could drop our bombs. I saw three fighters, they didn't see us, though I saw two kites [aircraft] go down they are held in a cone of searchlights for a while and then you see tracer machine gun fire and he goes down in flames but the whole thing doesn't seem real just like toys. ... Well, Mom say Hello to Charlie [Charlie Carron a First World War veteran and friend of the family] for me and tell him I am giving the 'Jerries' hell, it is different this time, one night we are over Germany fighting and next we are dancing at some dance hall or in a nice billet or to a show or to a pub. Sort of hard to get used to it. Best of luck be seeing you in a year or two. Don't worry about me I am over 21. Adios, Jim.

One can almost feel the excitement in his mind when he is writing the letter. The crew's second operation on 22 September was in 'W-Willie' again and was a 'milk run' to Hanover, taking off at 18.55 hours. This time they bombed with their mixed load of 2,000 lb of HE and incendiaries in what was recorded in the ORB as: 'Many bombs bursting within the vicinity of the markers, and large concentration of fires east of the markers – a well "pranged" target.' For Jim it was somewhat uncomfortable in the turret as his battledress was at the cleaners and he had to wear his dress uniform, with the escape kit in the hip pocket, sitting on it throughout the flight. The squadron lost no aircraft that night but No. 6 (RCAF) Group lost five.

Shortly after, Bill Cardy invited Jim to a family wedding near Epsom. Bill's relatives were all in the Army and he did not want to be the only airman. Most of the men at the event were Scottish Army types with ceremonial dress and kilts. It was a good spread for wartime and there was plenty of alcohol. Eventually, when it came time to return home, Jim and Bill staggered to the station with a major from the Essex Scottish, via another local pub, only to find their train had gone. There was nothing to do but wait until the following day, so Bill Cardy suggested they sleep in the local park, but Jim said: 'Officers don't sleep in the park. Let's try the local police.' The constables were happy to put them up in cells, but the sergeant vetoed that, until a small bald-headed constable came in and offered them a room in his house. His wife had been killed in the Blitz, and there was room to spare. After a good night's sleep, they awoke to the smell of bacon frying – a luxury in wartime Britain. Jim thanked their host profusely and gave him all his clothing coupons to help with his young son before they left for Yorkshire.

On 2 October operations were scrubbed, and the following date there was intensive training, Jim doing some air-to-air firing over one of the ranges. Sometimes during night flights, Jim used the navigator's instruments to 'shoot' the stars. Then on the Laird crew's next operation on 3 October, things went horribly wrong. They took off from Skipton-on-Swale, just south of Leeming, as their runways were being repaired. The target was Kassel, and just as they got to the coast near Texel, at about 20.10 hours on the outward trip, the 'Monica' aircraft proximity warning system bleeped into action, telling them of an enemy fighter in the vicinity. George Laird dived and weaved the Halifax, their regular LK637 'W-Willie', through the moonlight sky but Jim, in the top turret, and the rear gunner Jack Findlay could not see anything because of the haze. Then the night fighter, likely coming from below, gave the Halifax a full burst of the cannon. Their aircraft shook as the shells raked the underside, 'Like peas on a tin roof' Jim described, and fire erupted from the bomb bay. He could see the fighter and from his position in the mid-upper turret called out advice to his skipper, and helped direct evasive action.

The German fighter pilot must have thought he had done enough to bring the bomber down. Laird then put the aircraft on a reciprocal heading, turning back toward the UK, and asked for an appraisal of the damage. The aircraft was ablaze, and much of it was due to the 500-lb incendiaries in the bomb bay. He dived the aircraft to put out the fires and they dropped about 5,000 feet, and then called to the rear gunner, Jack Findlay, 'Are you OK? Are you OK?', but there was no response. Jim said: 'I think he might be dead as I can see bits of his turret sticking up in the air.' Laird asked the bomb aimer, 24-year-old Sergeant Joe Corbally, to go back and check on the crew. Corbally reported back a little later. 'The tail gunner is dead, so is the wireless operator, Rogerson, and the engineer is badly hurt.' He bandaged up the engineer's arm as he lay unconscious on the fuselage floor: 'Cardy is hurt, but should be OK.' Laird asked him to return to his position and drop the bombs as they were over the English Channel, but the bomb doors were stuck and they would not open. The hydraulic lines were badly damaged. By this time the fires were out. 'There's an emergency lever for the doors, but we'd better not try it as we might need to use it to lower the undercarriage,' called George Laird.

Jim thought he saw a fighter, possibly a British one, as they were approaching the English coast, so Laird asked Corbally to fire the 'colours of the day' from the Very flare pistol, since the wireless operator was dead and the IFF system was not working. They looked up the right colours; good to check as after midnight colours had changed, and Corbally struggled to fire the pistol. Jim said: 'Maybe I should try being a gunner.' 'Are you not hurt at all?' called Laird. 'No,' replied Jim and he climbed down from his turret. Only then did he see the two rows of bullet holes either side of his position; one had left the turret between the guns and later he found nine rounds in his ammunition cans – a close shave indeed. He flicked the safety catch off the Very pistol and fired the colours as they crossed the coast into English airspace. To him it seemed unreal that two of his colleagues were dead, including his friend, Findlay, who had brought him into the crew at the HCU; only Joe Corbally had seen the enemy fighter.

Rather than land at a nearby aerodrome, Laird decided to try to make their base. When they arrived in their home airspace the CO, Wing Commander Bob Turnbull, immediately said: 'For God's sake, aim the thing out to sea, put it on "George" [the automatic pilot] and bail out!' Laird answered: 'I can't do that because our engineer, Cardy, is badly wounded and I won't toss him out. If you don't find him right away he could die. We're coming in.' The wing commander wanted half an hour to get everyone in shelters in case the rest of the bombs went up. It seemed to the crew to be a very long half-hour.

'Where are we?' Cardy said as he came round. 'We are circling the airfield and can't get the wheels down. The hydraulics are shot up and the lever won't work.' He just managed to offer, 'I can cut the hydraulic pipes and the undercarriage will come down on its own', before he promptly passed out again. Jim called to the pilot, 'Keep flying round, Cardy is coming to again and we might get the wheels down.' Jim and Corbally dragged the flight engineer to the pipes running along the side of the fuselage. There were both fuel lines and hydraulics. With the phosphorous still simmering in the bomb bay it would be fatal to cut the wrong one and allow petrol to flow down. They had to be right first try. Eventually, Cardy identified the correct line and Jim swung the escape axe with all his might, and oil flowed. With a loud clunk the wheels came down and Laird called: 'I have the green lights, wheels are locked; we're going in!' Jim remembered: 'We laid down on the fuselage floor, and Laird gave us a smooth landing.'

Then the whole aircraft burst into flames, and they left the badly damaged Halifax as quickly as they could. The fire crews were on the scene and soon extinguished the flames, but they could not find the 2,000-lb bomb. Perhaps it had dropped out down the runway, so the fire crews checked that out, but no sign of it. They inspected the release cable, and discovered it had been cut by a cannon shell entering the front of the Halifax. One shell had hit the wireless operator, Flying Officer Jack Rogerson, and one shell the rear gunner, Flying Officer Jack Findlay. As soon as he could get back to the aircraft after it had been dampened down, Jim rushed around the tail to see Jack Findlay, his friend and room-mate. He was thirty-eight and a kindly father-figure type who had taken Jim under his wing. But that was Jim's big mistake; he wished he had not gone there! They rolled the aircraft into a hangar and locked it up.

For that operation, George Laird received the DFC, and 23-year-old Sergeant Bill Cardy was awarded the Conspicuous Gallantry Medal, the highest award – apart from a Victoria Cross – for an NCO. Jim got three days' survival leave, and went up to RAF Middleton St George to see some friends, McGurty and Lamontaigne, from their bombing course at Macdonald, who were both still sergeants. As Jim could not go into the NCOs' mess, being an officer, they had coffee and chatted on the roadway for a couple of hours – just ' ... shooting the breeze'. Three days after, both his friends were dead, when their pilot spun into the ground on an air test. Such was life on a bomber base in the Second World War.

Part II: Evader

5. Operations with the 'Lions'

The fragility of life was brought home again just a few days later. Jim was on duty at the gunnery section with 'Rocky' Durocher, just in case a spare was needed, and Jim heard a familiar voice. Coming up the corridor towards him was his old friend from Timmins, Roger Fournier. He had been posted to No. 429 (Bison) Squadron, who shared the base with the 'Lions'. 'Roger, when did you arrive on the base?' was the immediate question from Jim. Roger replied, 'This morning.' Although he had joined up six months before Jim, after the reception centre at Bournemouth he had transferred to an operational training unit in the Midlands, before going to an operational squadron. 'My God,' said Jim, 'you're on "ops" already tonight?' 'Yes.' 'Well, I'll still be on duty at four o'clock, so I'll see you later.' Jim never saw Roger again. It was his first and last operation on a trip to Kassel, on 22 October. The No. 429 Squadron aircraft, JD363, was brought down by flak over the target.

For their next operation Jim was in the tail again. Laird said: 'You're experienced now so I want you in the tail so you can spot any trouble.' It was a much tighter fit for Jim's 6-foot frame and, as he was still thinking about the last operation, he wore his parachute throughout the trip. It was very uncomfortable and he never did it again. He was not at all happy, but orders were orders. It was 3 November and this time the raid was to Düsseldorf, and they were in a new 'Whisky' LK965 ZL-W, with a 'second dickey' pilot, Flying Officer J. Matherley, an American Seminole Indian who had volunteered for the RCAF (he was to last until early January 1944) and Sergeant L.K. Smith replacing Jim in the mid-upper position. They were joined by two English RAF crew: Flying Officer J.A. McClune as flight engineer and Yorkshireman Sergeant W.T. Clapham as wireless operator. They took off at 16.45 hours and the trip was relatively uneventful, although there was activity over the target and flak was heavy. Over the target, Jim heard Matherley say, in his Southern accent: 'Ah say Skipper, what are them 'purty' lights?' The skipper swore and put the aircraft into a weaving motion over the sky; the 'lights' had been a fighter heading for them with guns blazing, but Jim never managed to get a shot off. In fact he never fired his guns at the enemy in all his trips. They were back at Leeming by 22.50 hours.

The news of George Laird's DFC came through on 2 November and there was a terrific party in the officers' mess. In fact so much so it warranted the following comment in the squadron's Operations Record Book: 'In one of the rowdiest mess whirls that there has ever been experienced by an officer, either living or dead, members of the mess met last night to celebrate F/L Laird's award … during the course of the drenching, our Wingco was instituted in the Royal Order of Leos as the 'Grand Lion', and was duly initiated under the revised policy in said order, whereby all potential Lions are required to (in official terms) osculate the rectum of Leo, the M.G.M. Presentation …'

It really must have been a party to remember. Events like this helped relieve some of the stress of being bomber crew. The continual change of one minute over Germany in flak and the next waiting at the airfield for details of the next assignment, took its toll of human emotions.

Jim found himself carried on by the rush of events and the busy life on the squadron. He tried to retain the thought he would survive, even though the odds were against him. He did not want his family to worry, but in truth he was devastated by the loss of so many friends in such a short time. His letter home seems to belie the feelings he was going through:

> Dear Mom, Just a line to let you know how I'm getting on. Health perfect and outlook on life marvellous. You might have seen my picture in the paper by now and wondered what the score was. Well, my skipper was awarded the DFC, and our flight engineer the CGM for a 'shaky do' on the Kassel raid. You see, we were shot up badly and the skipper did a marvellous job of bringing the 'kite' back. His picture was in the Toronto Star along with three other chaps next to a Halifax – just cut it out and send it to me because it's is a good line

to shoot a picture. Boy, Mom do you remember Roger Fournier? Well, he is missing he went for a bust on his first trip over Germany. Sort of tough luck. You see Roger and I used to work together at Naybob. There is a chance he might be a prisoner of war. Well I say those who play with guns are liable to get hurt, but I don't play ... not much else to tell you except there is quite a bit of fog around at times. Do you remember Ripon, Harrogate, Darlington, Northallerton or Thirsk? We can get good eats at Ripon, and then go by bus to Harrogate to the pubs and to a dance. There is quite a dance floor there, and a very nice band also so[me] Canadian WAAFs. ... It sure is good to chat to a Canadian girl for a change. Sort of makes you think you are back in Canada. Adios, Jim. PS. I go on leave on the 6th November. I am going down to Somerset to a Mr. James Steel – a great Uncle. Hope there is a pub down there, Ha Ha, Night.

By now it was late November, and it was the crew's first trip to the 'Big City' – Berlin. This was the beginning of 'Bomber' Harris's major campaign against the German capital. A previous raid a few days before, for which the 'Lions' had been stood down, had been unsuccessful. Now it was Jims turn to see Berlin for himself. In LK 965 ZL-W again, at 17.30 hours the crew lifted off the runway knowing they were probably in for a tough trip. They knew Berlin was well defended, with both flak over the city and particularly night fighters on the approach routes. The Luftwaffe was using the 'Wilde Sau' (Wild Boar) system promoted by Oberst (Major) Hajo Herrmann. His idea was to have single-seat fighters, not normally used at night, in the main searchlight areas. The searchlights were guided by radar and often locked on to a bomber for some time. It would then be easier for a manoeuvrable or a small aircraft to bring the bomber down. As soon as the defenders had predicted the target, the fighters would be moved into position. On most raids Jim saw few other aircraft, but over Berlin he found it as bright as 'driving down Broadway', like a fully lit street with Halifaxes all around him, and with aircraft also dropping flares into the bomber 'stream.

The crew gave George Laird, newly promoted to squadron leader, a new nickname, 'Turkey', as he kept exploding: 'The turkeys, look at those bloody turkeys! Look at those turkeys dropping their bombs early. We come all this way and they don't go over the target.' They went through the maelstrom, and at 21.15 hours dropped their bombs – again a mixed load of 2,000 lb of HE and including 840 x 4-lb mixed incendiaries – on the Pathfinder's 'Wanganui' coloured flares, from 21,000 feet, and then flew home. Jim saw no enemy aircraft, but their log notes that five large explosions were seen.

Just three days later they were over Frankfurt. The target was completely covered in 10/10ths cloud, as was the trip out to Germany, and there were no identifiable flares to bomb over the city. Laird 'stooged' the Halifax around for a few minutes before a flare was seen going down over a flak position and so they bombed on this, before a harrowing trip home, harried by fighters all the way. At one stage a Messerschmitt Me 210 was recognised, but they lost it in the cloud after Laird put the Halifax into a 'corkscrew' evasive manoeuvre. Joe Corbally, in the nose, complained: 'I wish to hell he'd shoot us down and get it over with! I'm sick as hell down here.' They lost an engine over France and eventually landed at Wing airfield in Buckinghamshire, returning to Leeming the following day. Laird logged the trip as an unsatisfactory sortie in the squadron ORB, and it had to have been a sobering experience for the 'second dickey' pilot, Flying Officer Shannon.

Most of December was taken up with training and cross-country flights. Jim was asked to teach aircraft recognition and train the gunners, so took them clay pigeon or 'skeet' shooting to improve marksmanship. They would go out over the North Sea for air/sea shooting practice and it was on one of these trips that Laird called out to the wireless operator: 'OK Pat, you say you live on the Yorkshire Moors. Give us directions and we'll buzz your house.' Pat's family had been moved out of Hull because of the bombing. They circled the house a couple of times and Pat's mother came out waving a tea towel in greeting.

December also saw Jim's promotion to flying officer, and Sergeant Cardy – their wounded wireless operator from the October raid on Kassel – recommended for suspension of flying duties and repatriation home to Canada. Fog pervaded the Vale of York for much of the month and on the 20th the crew's only December operational sortie was to Frankfurt again in their faithful 'W-Willie'. They had Flight Sergeant Clibbery as 'second dickey' and, although it was a straightforward operation for them, Jim notes in his log book that it was the first time they had seen ground-to-air rockets fired at them.

They did get a chance of some formation flying with their CO, Wing

Commander Bob Turnbull; his brother, John, was also flying with the group at the same time, with No. 419 (Moose) Squadron at RAF Middleton St George. George Laird also had the idea that after their ordeal over Kassel, when they had been shot up, each member of the crew should be able to step into another's job. So on some of the training flights, Jim got the opportunity to take control of the Halifax, guiding it through some slow turns. It should be remembered that the Halifax did not have dual controls, so George remained close at hand! To quote Jim, 'I was in heaven', and he found the episode great fun. Two Canadian Army officers, including Cardy's brother-in-law, Captain Cross, joined them in some practice flights. The military were starting the build up for the invasion, and it was thought that such participation would provide good training for the airmen. On 29 December the Laird crew lost its navigator when Warrant Officer George Lorimer was posted to Sergeant Arthur Darlow's crew. Lorimer had been a successful navigator in the Laird aircraft, especially during some long 'bullseye' exercises during their instruction, and it was felt that his knowledge would help the less experienced crew on its forthcoming first long trip to Berlin, a trip that Jim and the Laird crew would miss.

On quieter times, outings to the public houses of Yorkshire kept them sane and let the crews relax. In one pub in Harrogate Jim had become well known as a chap who would get up and sing. After starting with a few Scotch and rye whiskies, which usually ran out after two drinks, he would go to the piano and sing. One night there were two soldiers with wonderful voices singing at the other end, and Jim tried to catch their attention – but without luck – so he threw his hat at them. In an instant he was on his back on the ground with the soldiers at his throat. 'I only wanted to buy you a drink and ask you to join us,' he croaked; they were not best amused.

Laird's predecessor as OC of B Flight had been Squadron leader V. 'Gandy' Ganderton, later to become CO of the 'Lion' squadron at the end of its tenure at Leeming. Soon to be promoted to wing commander, he had been promoted to 6 Group headquarters at Allerton Park, a stately home about 15 miles south of the airfield, next to the A1 Great North Road. On one occasion 'Red' Soeder, a good friend of Jim's, and Ganderton's navigator, decided to go with Jim for a night out in his little Hillman car. They stopped at a pub at Wormald Green near Harrogate, and during a drink Red asked the barmaid: 'How are my finances today?' He was a gambler, often going to race meetings when he could at Ripon or Pontefract, and he had a deal with the girl that she would keep a stash of money in a little cigar box behind the bar; he topped it up when he was flush, and he could scrounge cash when he was short of funds.

One evening they went to Allerton Park to see 'Gandy', only to find their friend on the floor of the officers' mess shooting dice, with the commanding officer of the group, Air Vice Marshal C.M. 'Black Mike' McEwen, a figure much admired by the Canadian bomber crews, looking on at the game. A wing commander walked in and informed them: 'Boys, you're not supposed to gamble in the officers' mess. Please cease and desist', and then walked out. Quietly, 'Black Mike' spoke up: 'Gentlemen, I think you'd better pay attention to him.' So they decided to take 'Gandy', who could barely walk, to Harrogate to keep him out of trouble. 'Red' called up the Transport Section and in an official voice said: 'Squadron Leader Ganderton would like transportation to Harrogate.' Within a few minutes they were on their way. In 20 minutes they were in their favourite bar, whereupon 'Gandy' suddenly sobered up and walked to the bar unaided – a remarkable recovery!

On 5 January 1944 the Laird crew went on a 'messing run' to Middleton St George. George Laird had been made responsible for buying for the officers' mess, and to get the low-down on this he wanted to discuss it with a friend at another base. They loaded up Halifax V LL194 ZL-C with sufficient fuel, and supplies to trade with their colleagues at Middleton St. George, and made the 20-minute flight with the CO, Wing Commander Turnbull, in the pilot's seat. He was an amazing example to his men, having risen through the ranks from sergeant to wing commander in a remarkably short period, collecting on the way a DFC, AFC and DFM. After a few hours, problems were sorted, and they flew back to Leeming. The following day, Turnbull went on leave and George Laird took over as No. 427 Squadron commander until 20 January.

Their first operation of the New Year was to Berlin on the night of 20 January, in another Halifax V, DK268, ZL-V 'Victor'. This turned out to be a bit of a 'rogue' aircraft. By this time the old Halifax Mk Vs were getting 'long in the tooth', and were soon to be withdrawn from operational squadrons, to be replaced by Halifax Mk IIIs, with Hercules radial engines and 'slab fin' rudder assemblies. These were altogether much better aircraft, with higher ceiling capability. After a couple of hours their starboard inner engine cut out, then their 'Gee' navigation aid and wireless went down. Laird thought it inadvisable to continue, so they turned back, dropped their bombs in the sea, and headed for Leeming. After four hours they touched down at base. Jim tried opening the turret to get out, but it was jammed. Assuming the pilot had turned off the intercom, he let go with a string of abuse, only to hear: 'Would the pilot of V-Victor please report to the control tower.' Laird had a strip torn off him for the use of foul language in his aircraft. But in many ways they had been lucky. The 'Lions' lost two aircraft of No. 6 Group's eleven aircraft casualities, including EB246 ZL-S and LL191 ZL-N. Among the crew of ZL-S was Sergeant J.S. Child, an RAF NCO, who at eighteen years old was one of the youngest to be killed in service with Bomber Command.

That was the Laird crew's last operation in a Mk V, and after an initial flight with the CO in LV821 and several training flights over the following couple of weeks, including a cross-country, Laird took over Halifax III LV836 ZL-W 'W-Willie' after an acceptance flight at the end of the month. Jim recorded: 'It was a beautiful plane, with radial engines and handled much better.'

On 19 February they were back in action on their eighth operation. Sixteen aircraft took off on a raid to Leipzig, but only thirteen made it to the important rail target through 10/10ths cloud. They had with them a 'second dickey' pilot, Flying Officer Weiker from Kitchener, Ontario, later to be decorated and to lose his life with No. 100 Squadron, RAF, at the end of March 1945. He had a high-pitched voice and as they neared the target he stared yelling, 'Fire, fire, fire!' The navigator quickly dashed to the cockpit with a fire extinguisher, only to see a fighter diving on them, and told the pilot to 'Corkscrew now!' The fighter dived past just missing them, as the Halifax went over on one wing. Weiker had been yelling 'Fighter', but nobody could understand what he was saying because of the pitch of his voice. Just one aircraft was forfeited from the squadron, LV829 ZL-D, the all-Canadian crew of Pilot Officer D. Olsvik, though the group tally was running at 9.5%, a higher rate than normal. This was a bad time for Bomber Command.

By the time of their next operation, to Augsburg on 25 February, the loss rate of aircraft was more than Bomber Command had expected. For the Laird crew in LV831 ZL-P, this was somewhat of a 'milk run'. The Canadians followed the US 8th Air Force, who had bombed the target during the daylight hours. There was only light flak that did not reach their altitude of 20,000 feet. The raid was outstandingly successful, although the majority of the old medieval centre of this historic city was destroyed, causing the Germans to publish it as an example of 'terror bombing'. No. 6 Group lost only six aircraft, the 'Lions' sacrificing only one, LK759 ZL-Z. The next trip was to Le Mans in France, considered by the flight crews to be 'easy going'. On this trip, in LV831 'P-Peter', they took with them base commander Group Captain Bryans as 'second dickey', and they bombed from a lower level of 10,000 feet; the plan was to be more accurate and cause less casualties with the local civilian population. However, still thirty bombs fell outside the target area, killing thirty-one French civilians, and injuring forty-five.

Jim's eleventh operation, in LV789 ZL-W, was to Frankfurt on the night of 18/19 March. The squadron put up a full effort and only two aircraft were lost on the raid, Flying Officer T.W. Cooper's LW551 ZL-G and Sergeant W.C. Miller's crew in HX279 ZL-Z. Aircrews reported haze over the target, but the Pathfinders had marked it well and bombing was accurate. Jim noted in his diary that they blew a cylinder in one engine and landed at Bury St Edmunds out of fuel, returning to Leeming the following day.

The next operation was to change everything for Jim and his crew members.

Part II: Evader

6. Nuremberg

On the night of 30/31 March 1944 the Laird crew were scheduled to bomb Nuremberg. This was considered to be a controversial raid, as it was during the full moon period when crews would normally be stood down. However, the 'met. man' promised there would be cloud cover at high level to protect the main force. A reconnaissance Mosquito was sent out and reported that cloud was unlikely, but there could be a smattering over the target. Some 795 aircraft left the UK and enemy fighters were waiting for them; the battle lasted for over an hour. Over 80 of the 572 Lancasters, 214 Halifaxes and 9 Mosquitoes were lost on the outbound route, and a further 13 on the return flights when most of the German fighters had to withdraw. The majority of the crews reported they had bombed the target, but reconnaissance showed that many aircraft had bombed Schweinfurt, 50 miles to the north. The casualty rate was 11.9% of the bomber force – Bomber Command's biggest loss on any raid in the war.

For Jim all seemed well on the route to and over the target, but on the return flight, as they reached the Belgium–Luxembourg border, there was a shattering crash and Jim was thrown back against the rear of his turret. Their 'W-Willie', ZL-W LV923, had collided with Lancaster ND767 GI-D of No. 622 Squadron, flown by Sergeant E. Picken and his crew. They had hit at a 45-degree angle with tremendous force, and Jim could see the Lancaster they had hit drifting downwards into the darkness. Everything went quiet, and he tried to contact the crew on the intercom, but everything was dead. His first thought was, 'I'll go up front and see how it is', but the door by the tailwheel was damaged so he crawled back to his turret and plugged his intercom in again. Still nothing, but the oxygen was working all right. A further notion crossed his mind: 'Well we've been damaged before. We'll get back OK.' The aircraft seemed steady enough, but when he looked out each side of the turret he could see the port-side tailplane was missing. 'Oh my God, even if Laird is alive, he'll never be able to control the aircraft.' In an instant he knew it was time to bail out.

But Jim had not realised the aircraft was already spinning down tail first, and he was on the inside of the spin. He heaved himself out of the turret again and reached for his parachute, clipped on the inside wall of the fuselage, and managed to stand up. It was then he saw a large part of the fuselage had gone too, as from the waist up he appeared to be on the outside, with one foot on the rim of the turret and the other on the tail-wheel housing. The aircraft was spinning like a leaf. He quickly fastened the first hook of his parachute to his harness, but could not get the second hook to grip hold, so he took off his gloves, straightened it and clipped it on. He put his left hand over the front of the 'chute and pulled the rip-cord. Then he realised: 'Oh shit. I should jump first!' Luckily he still had his hand over the spring on the front of the pack, preventing the main canopy from billowing out prematurely. Using his other hand to push himself from the fuselage, he leapt into space. For a moment he saw his four guns pointing at him, so he kicked at them and was propelled away from the falling aircraft.

It was his first jump. They had never been given any formal parachute training, but at gunnery school at Macdonald, Manitoba, they were shown how to clip on a parachute and pull the ripcord. Now in the skies of Europe, Jim was trying to think it out. He did not count the traditional 10 seconds, but just let his hand release the spring and the parachute spilled out. It opened with a snap, jerking his body as the aircraft disappeared into the darkness. His friend and navigator on the aircraft, 'Red' Soeder, had bailed out once and he had told Jim you could never tell distance at night, so be prepared to hit the ground as soon as you jumped. Remembering his advice, Jim pulled his feet together, bent his knees, grabbed the cords and looked earthwards. 'I can see plain as day,' he thought. 'There's a big forest, a clump of trees, and I'm going to drift over and land in that clearing.' Then – bang! He hit the ground. The 'clump' was not trees, it was bushes and he had indeed misjudged the distance. Luck was with him, though, and he was safely down.

He learned later that the flight engineer, Jock Morrison, had bailed out as well, but he was severely wounded when he landed in a tree and died twenty days later in Arlon hospital. The rest of his crew – George Laird, 'Red' Soeder, Joe Corbally, Will Clapham and Les Smith – died in the crash, along with Flight Sergeant Stainton, RCAF, the 'second dickey' pilot also along for the trip. Four aircrew exited the Lancaster they had collided with, all too late to deploy their parachutes, and died when they landed near their aircraft crash site.

Jim was therefore alone, and very tired, so he walked into the forest, rolled up his parachute, and went to sleep. He woke in the morning to snow and the sound of church bells, and appraised the situation. While he was covered in blood from a nose bleed incurred from the jump, he was otherwise unharmed – no injuries, or even aches and pains. He had no idea where he was, but guessed he was somewhere in Germany and that the war was over for him; probably the next stop would be a prison camp. Certainly he had been very lucky, as he was sure everyone else was dead.

He decided to hide his electrical suit and parachute and squashed them under a log in the forest. His survival kit was in the top pocket of his battledress. This pack, issued just before they boarded the aircraft and about the size of a packet of cigarettes, consisted of energy tablets, water purification tablets, a plastic tube with drawstring for water, a small hacksaw, a tiny compass and a silk map of Europe, along with some foreign money, presumably to be used for bribes.

Jim heard the sound of woodcutters in the forest and walked to where three old men were chopping wood. Although he could not speak French, he tried, 'France, France, aviateur!' They looked at him and continued with their task, obviously ignoring him, so he decided to head towards the bells. Across in a nearby valley he could see a village about half a mile away, surrounded by forest. A boy, aged about twelve, came out of a farm building to relieve himself and Jim called 'France? France?', and the boy shouted 'Nein. Nein' but he did not look German. That was the one German word Jim knew. He thought, 'I'm in Germany', and decided to head across country and determine where he was on the silk map. He saw a road sign that might help; it said 'Halanzy' so he decided to head in that direction. It started to snow again and Jim was feeling confused and exposed. He was in his blue RAF battledress uniform, with no hat and carrying his outer flying suit. The boy certainly had not looked German, or alarmed. The name 'Halanzy' did not appear to sound German. A man on a bicycle rode past him, making tracks in the deepening snow. Then the man on the bike rode past again and Jim could see he was in some sort of uniform, blue with a red stripe – a postman perhaps? Jim thought: 'What if he stops me? I'll have to brave it out. I'll go through the village and head for the woods on the other side.' As he was leaving the village four young men, all in their twenties, cycled past then turned in front of him and called 'Prisonniere, Prisonniere!' and crossed their arms in front of them as though in handcuffs. 'This is it,' considered Jim. 'They'll report me to the Germans and turn me over for the reward.' Aircrews had been told that the Germans were handing out big rewards for Allied airmen – and if locals helped and were caught, they would be shot. However, that did not stop many brave French and Belgian people helping downed crew members.

Suddenly another man ran up and urged: 'I'm from Birmingham, England. I'm here to get you back to England as soon as possible. The bloody "Boche" are just behind you. Jump behind the hedge and hide!' With that everybody disappeared, so Jim sprang over the nearby dense evergreen hedge and lay flat. He stayed there and made himself as comfortable as he could, thinking of the warm heated suit he had abandoned in the forest. As the day wore on, hunger started to take over; he was very cold and had not had anything to drink since he had left Leeming the night before. There were trucks and vehicles going up and down the road all day. Knowing that two aircraft had crashed nearby, the Germans were looking for survivors. Jim dared not look up, so he lay there shivering but knowing there was help nearby, which gave him hope and courage.

When he had been at Bournemouth, Jim had skipped escape training to volunteer to go straight to squadron flying. He had been told to approach a person only if they were on their own, so if they looked untrustworthy you could run away. He was very lonely, and desperate for a drink, but at least the snow had eased and had melted from the ground. As evening fell, things quietened down, and eventually one of the men he had seen earlier appeared and motioned for Jim to follow him; he took him to the back of a building on the outskirts of the village. It was a bakery and they entered the living quarters at the rear. Jim blinked at the light as one of the men gathered there told him to take off his uniform. 'You come in here,' he said in broken English, 'we'll give you clothes and burn your uniform.' He asked where the parachute was and Jim explained about hiding it. They would go later and pick it up; the silk material would be useful for turning into underwear as the war had made materials scarce. 'Can you ride a bike?' the leader asked. 'Yes.' He pointed to one of the men and said: 'He can't speak English, but he is going to take you somewhere you can hide. We'll come after dark and find you. OK?' Jim could only mumble 'Yes' again and quickly slipped into the civilian clothes they gave him. He could see a woman in the background talking on the telephone and that worried him, but from her look in return he was reassured. The English speaker told him he had parachuted into a corner of Belgium, at Batincourt; France was only 200 yards in one direction and Luxembourg 200 yards in another. Jim was feeling better by the minute; at least it was not Germany.

The woman busied herself around the kitchen preparing some food for him. There was also a little girl of about six or seven years old, and she shyly brought an egg across the kitchen for her mother to cook, but dropped it on the kitchen floor – no egg tonight! They gave Jim a bottle of beer and he took a swig, then put it in the pocket of the coverall he was wearing along with a sandwich – bread coated with bacon grease – in another pocket, and nodded his thanks. Outside they brought another bicycle and without a word they set off. After a short time, the guide pointed to a nearby forest of beech, oak and maple. Unfortunately Jim spilled some of the beer as he dismounted the bike, but managed to save half of it. He sat down by a large maple tree, ate the sandwich and drank the rest of the beer. He was contented as he knew there were friends nearby who would help him. After a while he saw a man walking through the forest and somehow felt sure that this was not 'his' someone, so pretending to be another farmer he got up and strolled as nonchalantly as he could toward another clump of trees of tall pines, and stood behind one. The man disappeared.

Jim stayed there for about two hours and the next time someone came they were softly calling, 'Albert, Albert.' The man had a big floppy beret and was short in stature – certainly not German. Jim stepped out of his position and returned with, 'Canada, Canada.' The man ran over and grabbed his hand warmly, like an old friend, and started speaking his 'code name' again, 'Albert'. Two 'gendarmes' in heavy black coats with high collars appeared, startling Jim, one of whom could speak a little English. He explained they would walk into France, then Luxembourg, and then back to Belgium. One of the gendarmes was the little man's brother, and Jim later learned they were Vital, with the beret, and Albert Paul. Following the policemen they wandered through the countryside around the hills, over three borders, and into the rear of Halanzy village, to the back yard of Vital's home at the edge of the settlement. It was a long way round, but it ensured they were not seen by anybody. The two gendarmes left and Vital introduced Jim to his wife, Marie-Claire. She led him into the kitchen, which was warm and cosy. She was a young, short woman with her hair drawn back from a round friendly face, and she made Jim welcome by sitting him down at the table and giving him a small amount of food. There were also two young children, Christian aged eight and Anne, seven, but they were kept in another part of the house and not allowed to see their 'visitor'. Vital took Jim upstairs to a small room where Jim took off his outer clothes and crawled into the lovely soft, warm bed and immediately fell into a deep sleep.

The following morning, after a decent wash and shave with a rather lethal-looking razor, feeling much better, and now dressed in fresh clothes of a white shirt and vest and dark trousers, Jim transferred his escape kit and checked out his currency, which consisted of the few thousand French and Belgian francs. The only Canadian identity he now had was his 'dog-tags' engraved with his service number; if he was unfortunate to be killed one was to stay with his body and the other to be returned to Canada.

The Paul family lived a reasonably comfortable life in the village in a typical two-storey house. Vital was an accountant with the railway, and Jim later learned they had joined the Resistance in 1941, along with Albert and his wife. They had been involved in several Resistance operations, including one where Marie-Claire had travelled on the train to Albert, about 40 miles away, with explosives in her bag for a demolition job. Very risky considering the German troops were already on the lookout after a French Resistance raid a few days earlier. Vital regularly supplied London with details of rail movements and loads, through an intermediary. After breakfast, the two gendarmes returned with a black saloon car, and it was then Jim learned his first lesson on French etiquette. As he left the little house he waved a goodbye to the family, Marie-Claire and Vital, who had cared for him. One of the policemen came over and told him: 'You've insulted Madame Paul, the lady of the house.' 'Why?' asked Jim, 'I've said my thanks.' He shook his head: 'No, no, you have to go and kiss her on both cheeks.' So Jim returned to Marie-Claire at the front door, did so, and said his goodbyes again.

The car was to take him to Albert Paul's house in Étalle, about 40 kilometres away. As he climbed into the back he noted with some surprise there was a woman with a baby and an English airman, also wearing civilian clothes. The woman was Albert's wife, Cecile, and the Englishman was

Sergeant Bill Jones, the wireless operator of a No. 158 Squadron Halifax, LW634 NP-P, that had been shot down over Metz, south of Halanzy, also on the Nuremberg raid. Later, Jim found that all of the No. 158 Squadron crew had survived and were taken as prisoners of war. It was good to be able to chat away in English, though they were relatively silent on this journey. They wondered: 'What happens now?'

But there was a plan in hand. After a stay at the Pauls' house they were to be put on a train to Brussels, and from there to join an escape route that should take them across the Pyrenees to Spain and freedom. Jim found out that Albert and Cecile had been staying with her parents in Halanzy when his Halifax came down in nearby Rachecourt. They had gone to view the wreck, and had seen the bodies of his crew. The Germans were warning everyone not to help any survivors. There had been a party of them in the village that day, removing the church bells to melt down for war material, and the villagers had been ringing them for the last time. It was that sound that had attracted Jim to the village, and a near encounter with the Maquis. It was 1 April, 'All Fools' Day', and Jim could feel his luck holding. It was snowing a little as the black car pulled into the garage of a house in the village of Étalle, and Bill and Jim were shown into an upstairs room, a solarium with frosted glass all round. They were told, 'Stay here. You will not look outside into the yard, and don't let anyone see you.'

The room was fair-sized, with clear panels at the top and frosted ones on the sides. It was obvious they would be staying here until the false papers they needed were prepared, and plans put in place for their journey. They became part of the family and got to know their hosts. Albert Paul was in the Étalle brigade of the gendarmerie, and had been so when the Germans invaded in 1940. It was a lightly armed police force, with rifles and hand guns, and had also been armed with motorcycle-sidecar combinations with machine guns at the time, and had fought the invaders. Albert was about twenty-nine, short in stature like his sibling, and had a bad scar on his face from the fighting. His brother, Vital, was younger and slightly taller, dark and handsome with a back as straight as a ramrod, and a prominent nose. The black uniform they wore was piped in red and had riding breeches and knee-high boots, and they were armed with a P-38 pistol in their holsters. The area in which they lived was hilly and heavily wooded, an extension of the Ardennes area, with small villages in the valleys and being close to the border; many of the locals spoke both French and German. These factors made it an ideal working area for a resistance movement.

Albert would do his daily regulation rounds, then in his other life as head of the Resistance in the area go out two or three nights a week organising his group, and performing acts of sabotage. He always left the pistol with Cecile while he was out, and there was a Sten gun in the house. The visitors were told: 'If two Germans come, shoot them and then run. If a bunch of them arrive, don't shoot, just run!' So Jim and Bill decided on a plan to make for the forest about 500 feet away. To flee along the hedgerows would be difficult as the little garden plots were still surrounded by barbed wire from the First World War.

Their accommodation was comfortable enough. They had the run of the house. It was a terraced house with front and rear access only. Downstairs was a large living/kitchen room with a toilet in the corner, and upstairs a single bedroom the full depth of the house, which was shared by all. The airmen were separated from the family with a divider, but they all slept there. The solarium was at the end of the bedroom and had a tub and toilet, as well as a couple of chairs and a table. As they settled in, they realised there was a need to communicate with the Pauls, so decided to try and learn the language. Bill had been taught French at school, but had forgotten most of it; Jim spoke none at all apart from basic numbers. It was difficult as there was no dictionary in the house. They would be given about five to ten words daily to learn; they would study these for hours and then be given more by Cecile. They could see Allied bombers flying overhead on their outward trips, then observe the main force and stragglers returning from their operations; often a fighter would scream across at low level. As they improved with their vocabulary they tried reading the local papers, getting an idea of what was going on, even though they were heavily censored by the Germans.

Occasionally Jim and Bill would slip out of the back door under cover of night, and go into the house of the Messien family next door. Marcel Messien was the town notary, a lawyer, and they shared the concealment of the airmen. Their first visit was memorable as Marcel's wife Rose had a real treat for them. Their language skills were coming on now as, although the Messiens could not speak English either, they were beginning to converse better. The 'treat' was real meat. Up to now they had been living on one strip of bacon and potatoes with bacon grease smeared over them. Marcel announced: 'We are going to cook this meat for you.' He put the frying pan on the stove, cut the meat up and put it in, then after a short time flipped it over – just searing the outside. It was like eating raw meat, and the airmen struggled to chew it, requesting if it could be cooked a little more. 'We hope you like it,' said Marcel. 'Do you know what it is? It's horse meat!' He smiled at their reaction.

Étalle village was not far from the town of Arlon, which was the German headquarters for the area, and the enemy raided the village three times while Jim and Bill were there. One raid was on the night they were at the Messiens, while Cecile was away. Rose had been with a neighbour and came running back into the house screaming: 'Les Boche, les Boche.' They knew they were all in danger, especially their hosts. Rose was terrified. They scuttled back to the Paul house, and Albert showed them to a crawl space over the garage. It was dark and smelly, but it was the only place they could hide. The Germans stayed for the next 24 hours or so, trying to find out who was running the resistance units. One of Cecile's best friends was taken away, never to return. When that happened it usually meant questioning and torture, then being sent to a labour or concentration camp in Germany. Cecile cried for some time. They stayed in their crawl space for a few days, only coming out to eat.

As time passed, Jim loved to hold the baby, Monique, and they bonded after a while with Jim singing softly as he held her and rocking her to sleep. As they became closer to the family, Cecile would tease Jim. Bill was quiet and had a girlfriend at home, but Jim did not. 'Why do you not have a girlfriend?' Jim just shrugged the question off. While they were in hiding, another problem presented itself. Cecile's brother, 24-year-old René Ravet, arrived. He was on the run, having escaped from a forced labour camp in Germany He had made his way back to Belgium, but could not stay at home, so was living at various safe houses and using various aliases. He would often deliver messages for the Maquis.

Time was passing and Jim was becoming worried they were not going anywhere. He chatted it over with Bill. They now had their papers. Jim was a Belgian labourer, 'Charles Lebrun', and Bill was 'Jacques Lenoir'. Jim had the idea to walk to Switzerland, but Bill was against it. It would be difficult to get across the border. Albert Paul was horrified: 'No, no – you won't get in. Spain, you might have a chance. We are making arrangements.' Only a month previously they had passed a British squadron leader down the line and back to England. Jim was reassured; they had been coached by the Allies on what to do.

After the German invasion of Belgium and France in 1940 there had been several organisations set up to help Allied airmen – and, in the early days also soldiers – to escape the Germans and return to the UK. The two major operations were the Comet and the Pat O'Leary lines. The Comet line was created by a young Belgian woman, Andrée de Jongh (nickname 'Dédée'), who was twenty-four in 1940, lived in Brussels and had joined the Belgian Resistance. She was the younger daughter of Frédéric de Jongh, a headmaster, and Alice Decarpentrie. A heroine of 'Dédée's' in her youth had been Edith Cavell, a British nurse who was shot in 1915 in the 'Tir National' in Schaerbeek for helping troops escape from occupied Belgium to neutral Netherlands. Dédée had taken a British soldier, and a couple of helpers, across France and over the Pyrenees on foot to Bilbao in Spain where they made their way to London and made contact with the British Secret Service, MI9.

The second, and larger, group, the Pat O'Leary organisation based in Marseilles, had three lines operating through from Paris to Toulouse, via Limoges, and then over the Pyrenees, via Esterri d'Àneu to Barcelona. Another O'Leary line ran from Paris to Dijon, Lyons, Avignon to Marseilles, then Nîmes, Perpignan and Barcelona, from where evaders were transported to Gibraltar. The third route from Paris (the Shelborne line) ran to Rennes and then Saint-Brieuc in Brittany, where men were shipped across to Dartmouth in Devon. These were run by Albert Guérisse, a Belgian Army officer, who operated under the name 'Pat O'Leary'. He was born in Brussels, and qualified in medicine at the Université Libre de Bruxelles before joining the Belgian Army. At the outbreak of war, Guérisse was serving as a 'Medecin-Capitaine', a captain in the Medical Branch, as the medical officer of the Guides, a Belgian cavalry regiment. After Belgium was forced to surrender, he escaped to Britain through Dunkirk. It was a very risky business, especially after the annexing of the 'Vichy' government area of France into the German administration in 1942 and there was no mercy from the Germans if caught.

Both lines were infiltrated by German agents, and both Andrée de Jongh and Albert Guérisse spent a terrible time with their captors before being incarcerated in concentration camps. These brave people fortunately survived the war and were both awarded the George Medal for their courageous work. The official history of MI9 cites that 2,373 British and Commonwealth servicemen and 2,700 Americans were returned to Britain by such escape lines during the Second World War. The RAF Escaping

Society, of which Jim is a member, estimated that there were 14,000 helpers by 1945. When Jim was in France, in 1944, there were large numbers of airmen 'holed up' in chateaus and farms around northern France and Belgium.

For some reason unknown to Jim, their 'courier' never showed up, and the Gestapo kept the pressure up on the Belgians. Apparently they were looking for a Jewish girl taking cover locally, but never found her. Jim and Bill kept hiding in their little space in the roof every time the Germans came near. After six weeks' stay in Étalle, in late May 1944, Albert announced: 'I'm taking you out of the village overnight to show you something exciting.' The two airmen, who had been incarcerated in the house for many weeks, except for visits to the Messiens next door, were intrigued. Albert ushered them out of the back door after midnight, away from villages and across the meadows to an isolated farm. In the middle of a field was a lone barn, which they entered. Albert flashed his torch around and they could see about twenty or so new metal containers like barrels, about 3 feet high and 2 feet around. Albert took the lid off one and they could see chocolate bars and explosives and, nestled in between, a bunch of .38 revolvers made in Montreal. Albert became excited. 'From Canada,' he said, 'all for my unit.' They replaced the top on the container, and headed back to Étalle. Certainly Albert had been proud to show Jim and Bill his stock, but it may have been a fateful move in the light of events shortly afterwards.

Part II: Evader

7. With the Maquis

It happened at daybreak, unexpectedly. Jim was asleep when there came a loud banging on the front door. Cecile ran upstairs with the baby, crying, 'Les Boche, les Boche!' Jim woke to see his comrades, including Bill, already exiting out the window. He had not stopped to wake Jim. He pulled on his trousers and, without time to put on his boots, leapt out of the window, 8 feet on to soft ground below. They all ran to the bottom of the garden and over the chicken-wire fence. Bill was short and had difficulty so Jim shoved him head first into the field behind, and they both started running for their lives. The soldiers were now at the window; one had a rifle and the other a machine pistol, and Jim could hear the 'whizz' of the bullets as they passed his ear. How they missed his legs he never knew, but his luck was holding.

They were in the open, so he yelled, 'Let's duck behind this hedge!' He lost track of René and Bill. René was long gone; he had got a head start on them, and was clear away. With bullets still around, Jim ran along the hedge line, under a fence into another garden, then dived under some barbed wire. His trousers got caught on the spikes so 'To hell with them' he thought and pulled them off, sprinting over another fence into the undergrowth beyond. But the grass had been cut and you could see 300 yards all round. 'Which way?' He was short of breath, and gasping for air. Jim looked back. The soldier with the machine pistol was on his tail; others were behind him. Jim was out of range and sight for a moment, and two or three clumps of bushes were nearby. He ran past the first two and dived into the third bush, the densest, about 10 feet high and 20 feet around. He crawled into the centre and lay down, puffing hard. Jim watched the soldier's feet run by, and thought, 'Why can't he hear me – panting as hard as I am?' But he ran by and nobody followed immediately. Then through the thicket Jim could see German boots and a dog's paws. It was a German Shepherd dog. 'Oh my God, they're going to get me this time!', but somehow the dog led them past, probably following the earlier soldier's tracks.

It was five or six o'clock in the morning, about daybreak. And with the rush of adrenalin Jim had not realised his feet had been cut on the stubble in the fields and he was now in the middle of a thorn bush. He decided to stay right where he was, for the rest of the day. He was frightened and alone, and half naked. He did not even know which direction he had gone. After dark, he decided to get out of the bush – much more difficult than getting in, which had been easy. The thorns were about 2 inches long and cut his skin. Yet those thorns had probably saved his life. Jim wandered back into the woods, and found somewhere to hide that was not so prickly. He made a bed on the soft leaves, sat down and covered the bottom half of his body with leaves to afford some protection from the cold. It was still only May after all, and it was cold at night. He fretted about what to do next; all sorts of thoughts ran through his mind. His 'dog tags' had been in his boots, so he now had no identity apart from 'Charles Lebrun', on his false papers in his shirt pocket, and this preyed on him. 'How will my mother know what has happened to me? Nobody will know who I truly am. Did Cecile escape?' She had bravely run upstairs to warn them as she knew what the knock on the door had meant. 'What about the baby? Where are they now? Did they manage to get away?'

More thoughts struck him: 'What about Albert? Did the Nazis capture him? Here I am alone again.' After a while he fell into a fitful sleep, awaking as dawn was breaking again. He could hear the sound of someone calling, 'Yoo hoo, yoo hoo!', but it was only a Cuckoo bird. At that moment he was close to losing hope, and he was at his lowest ebb. 'I can't even head across country without trousers or boots,' he remonstrated with himself. Jim headed to the road to see if he could get help, and after a while two gendarmes on bicycles rode by. 'Canadien aviateur!' he called and they responded, 'Tonight, later tonight.' He had no trouble understanding their French now. But they never came back, and he spent another cold damp night in the forest with the leaves for a bed. The Germans were probably still searching for him, and the gendarmes would not be taking any risks.

Eventually he decided to make his own move. Growing up in the bush land of Ontario, he was no stranger to the forest, and it helped his independent attitude. Late that afternoon he heard sounds in the woods again and cautiously made his way toward the noise. There was a woodcutter chopping down a tree, so from a distance of about 25 feet, in case he had to make a run for it, he offered a 'Bonjour.' The man's face said everything as he looked at this stranger in the forest, naked from the waist down, with scruffy hair standing on end and several day's growth of beard. He walked over. 'Oh the dirty Boche,' he uttered. 'You wait here and I'll go and get you some trousers and food.' As he ran out of the glade, across the road to his home, Jim moved to a safer place of hiding where he could still see out. The man came back a few minutes later with a sack containing a dirty old pair of trousers, a pair of pantouffes (slippers) and some black bread coated with bacon grease. Jim ate that first – he had not eaten in three days – then he put on the clothes and shoes. 'Come with me,' the man indicated. He was in his early thirties. 'I'll check the highway, and if there is nobody there we'll cross over and go to my farm where I live with my mother.' Jim guessed he might be hiding from the Germans too, and thought they might be about two or three miles from Étalle. They stepped into the tiny house, immediately into the kitchen where the mother had some cabbage soup in a pot on the stove. She dipped a bowl into the liquid and handed it to Jim, who tucked into the meal right away. She offered him some money but he refused. 'What will you do?' she said, and Jim replied, 'Make some sport for the Germans', at which she burst into tears. A bad joke in the light of what the enemy would do if they caught them hiding Allied airmen. 'I'm going to make my way south', he continued, 'and see if I can get into Switzerland or Spain, or something like that.' The woman gave him another grease sandwich, which Jim put in his pocket for later, and offered his sincere thanks to the good people before he left. They had no contacts who could help, and it was obvious they did not want him to stay there.

Jim walked all night along the deserted highway. It was quiet except for animal sounds, and reminded him of his childhood in Timmins. He was ready to jump in the ditch alongside but did not have to. As daylight filtered over the horizon, Jim could see a few houses, then a village in the distance, with the highway dropping down the hill into it. He decided to climb over the roadside fence into a terraced field. The terraces were lined with barbed wire, so in the half-light he had to scramble over the wire on each one as he made his way down the hillside. About halfway down he came to a higher terrace, which was more difficult, and as he hopped over the fence he realised too late there was a drop of about 15 feet the other side and he fell awkwardly, spraining his ankle. Resorting to crawling on all fours under the last three ditches, he made his way to a river and crossed it with the aid of a fallen log, then struggled up a path into more forest. His only interest was to hide among the trees and get some rest.

He awoke to the sound of voices; two men were talking. He stayed hidden until after they left, then made his way down a sandy path towards the village where he thought he might be able to scrounge some food and a drink. The pain in his ankle had eased a bit. He came across a man working in his garden next to a tiny cottage, and called in French: 'Bonjour, I'm headed for Switzerland. Which way do I take?' The man was surprised, but helpful, and said: 'I know how it can be. I was in the Great War. I can help. Take this road here', pointing to a small lane, 'that will get you where you want to be.' It was only a minor lane into the forest, but Jim started down it anyway. Somehow he lost his way and found himself on an even narrower pathway, heading into a field of sheep shared with a little house and a haystack. He saw a shepherd and his wife, and asked for food and a drink; they gave him some water, but were obviously very scared. 'Is there anywhere I can spend the night?' They pointed to the haystack, so he crawled into the centre, and quickly fell asleep, in spite of the ache from his ankle after walking on it all day.

In the morning he awoke to a shout from the shepherd: 'You've got a friend; a compatriot.' 'Oh a fellow airman,' thought Jim and a voice from a small man shuffling towards him said, 'I am Desiré Paul, Albert's cousin, I've come to take you back to Belgium.'

Desiré was older than Albert Paul, who had hidden Jim in his house earlier, and was about 5 foot 5 inches, with a slender face and light sandy, wavy hair. He was in the green uniform of the Belgian Forestry Service. They set a slow pace out of the field, because of Jim's ankle. He was still only wearing slippers, with no socks, and it was painful going. He had apparently walked about 15 miles into France. Now they had to walk back to Belgium. Jim found out that Albert had been taken by the Germans, and his brother, Vital, had warned Desiré to keep an eye out for him. Whether or not the young shepherd had tipped the Resistance off, Jim never knew, but it was a sign of their persistence that they eventually found him. Maybe it was their worries over Albert that they were determined to help him, or perhaps because of Albert's situation they were going to make sure Jim was all right. He felt he was 'one of their own'. Jim acknowledged their bravery, knowing the Germans were on the look-out for him.

They were headed for the Paul family's home town of Torgny, a village of about 300 people to the south of the town of Virton, situated on the French–Belgian border. They kept to the road most of the day, not talking that much, and entered the village down a hill. Desiré's house, a small one-storey, two-bedroomed cottage on the edge of the settlement was accessed from the hillside. Once again this brave family took him to their hearts. There were two young girls in the kitchen; one was blonde, about three years old, wide-eyed and staring at him and, another, older and more sickly in demeanour. Madame Paul cooked a meal for him and, after eating, over a cup of coffee they were able to review the situation. 'You can't stay here,' Desiré said, 'but I know a place you can go.'

When darkness fell, Desiré took him along the village road to what looked like an old church building – Jim guessed about 200 years old – with a bell tower and a large doorway in the facade. This was 'L'Hermitage', first an old church then a closed-down museum, with boarded-up windows. Desiré removed one of the boardings from a lower window and they climbed inside the church and up into the rafters, towards the bell tower. Through an opening in a wall into the uppermost part of the tower, they found themselves in a small room about 10 feet by 10 feet. The windows were also boarded up, but could be removed. There was a small fireplace in one corner and a bed of straw to rest on. Desiré said: 'You will sleep here at night, and go into the forest in daytime. I will bring you food in the forest every day.' Jim relaxed for the first time in a long while. His belly was full, and he was with friends again. Although he was not on his way to Switzerland, he was safe for the time being. He curled up and went to sleep, content with his fate at this time.

Next morning Jim climbed down from his hiding place and went into the woods, where he waited for Desiré in the cover near the edge of the forest. It was now late May and the days and nights were getting warmer. It was not long before his friend approached, bringing the now inevitable bacon-grease sandwich, and some water. It became a regular routine, and with him there was news. 'The Germans have taken Albert, and an English airman to prison,' he said. 'We don't know where they are, or what has happened to them.' According to what little Desiré knew, after Jim had leapt out of the upstairs window, the Gestapo had held Albert at the front door, and they had shot Bill Jones in the leg as he raced across the field.

WITH THE MAQUIS   91

Many years later, Jim learned that the Germans thought they had shot and killed him. The two were taken to the German prison at Arles. That was about as much as Desiré had gathered from his cousin Vital. He was not as worldly-wise as his cousins, and was not directly involved with the regular Maquis. Vital, on the other hand, was in personal contact with London, and Albert had been part of the attacking forces, having already been in Army service before and during the 1940 invasion, and both had played a key role in the organisation. To Desiré, having a simpler life, it was a great blow.

Desiré's job, being a forester, was to maintain and patrol the local woods, and this gave him considerable freedom to move around. The village was about 15 miles south of both Étalle and Virton, the other side of the main forest in the area and literally on the border with France, which was only a few yards south of the village. Desiré would plod to the forest and spend much of his time on his hobby of collecting beetles for the museum in Virton. To help pass the time he asked Jim if he would like to help, and Jim agreed; it would assist in relieving the boredom of his days, and improve his French. Regularly Edmond-Pierre Fouss, the creator and curator of the Musée Gaumais in Virton would join them. He was the local historian, had a special interest in Jim's new home, 'L'Hermitage de Notre Dame de Luxembourg', and knew its history in detail. It had been damaged by shells and abandoned; an ideal hideaway for Jim. Once Edmond brought a 1918 edition of the *Illustrated London News*, which Jim enjoyed greatly. By now the Germans were moving around by night, mainly due to Allied fighters and low-level bombers roaming the skies unchallenged.

After about three weeks, Jim saw Desiré running towards him, obviously excited, and he was nervous what the news might be. The Germans could easily be raiding the village. 'Le débarquement! Le débarquement!' It was 6 June 1944 and what turned out to be the D-Day landings. It was what they had all been waiting for, and he was ecstatic. Jim thought: 'In about a week I'll be liberated and on my way home.' It was not to be that quick, though. About a week later Desiré had more news. 'Pilotless aeroplanes bombing London', Jim was told. They were the German FZG-76 'V1', Hitler's 'Revenge weapon No. 1', fired from sites near the coast. Perhaps the war was not won yet?

During the daytime he watched the formations of American B-24 Liberators and B-17 Flying Fortresses on the way to and from their targets in the Reich, often with holes in the formations on the return trip where aircraft had been lost. He so wished he could be up there with them. One day the valley was 'buzzed' by a low-flying Focke-Wulf Fw 190 flying close to the treetops – magnificent sight, even if it was the enemy. In addition, Desiré had given Jim a book on bird watching to help pass the time, and he used it to improve his French further.

About this time, Jim began to itch. He thought it was the straw from the bed, but as he got warm it became intolerable, and he was losing sleep. He paced the room, before investigating further. It took a long time to take off his trousers, as they were stuck to his rear. He had boils from his poor diet, and scabies. They were caused by little 'mite' insects that burrowed under the skin to lay eggs. He had probably got them from the trousers that he had been given weeks earlier, and the raised red spots they caused were now bleeding. He was in bad shape and told Desiré one morning: 'I need a doctor; I need a doctor, badly.' Knowing it was dangerous, and contagious, he took Jim down into the village to his home, where he met Desiré's wife, Henrietta, once more. She was taller than Desiré, and more authoritative. She obviously 'ruled the roost' and really was not too happy to deal with this, unless she had to. It was her decision whether Jim would see the doctor. 'Down with the pantaloon,' she commanded. 'No way,' said Jim, but she convinced him she would have to look. 'Oh, mon dieu!' she exclaimed, 'tonight you stay here.' The following morning there was a knock on the door and an ensuing whispered conversation; then Henrietta returned into the house and said: 'Tomorrow a truck will come. It will take you to a nice lady's home where you will stay, and they will take you to a doctor.'

The next day an ancient flat-bed truck 'wheezed' up to the house, with a big black bag attached to a charcoal burner, which somehow powered it. Jim climbed in and they made their way to the next village, Dampicourt, about ten minutes away. He stayed with the local mayor, Monsieur Adam, and his wife, an Englishwoman. She welcomed him in his native tongue, and Jim guessed by her accent she was from Yorkshire. 'Where are you from,' he asked. 'A little town you've probably never heard of – Pontefract', was the reply. 'Oh my God, my mother is from Pontefract,' said Jim excitedly. They chatted for ages about their experiences. She had been a nurse in the First World War and had married a Belgian soldier and stayed in the country. Monsieur Adam, in addition to being the mayor, was owner of the local sawmill, but he was sympathetic to the German cause. That did not stop his wife working for the Resistance. She added, 'If he doesn't like it, I have threatened to burn his sawmill down.' Jim reckoned she meant it! She might have been joking but he did not think so. They had two children in their teens, and she was upset at how the war had disrupted their lives.

After a meal, Jim was offered a bath; his first in two months. He was now clean again and in a nice warm bed, but still scratching. The following morning, there was blood all over the bed, and Madam Adam said: 'You poor thing. You definitely must see the doctor. A truck will come this morning.' The transport arrived and they rumbled down the road on their way into the forest. After a while it slowed down, as there were young men with guns waiting for him. 'Where's the doctor?' They were urged on further down the road. After about a mile, two of them started whistling and they received a similar whistle in return. The truck had obviously passed through a checkpoint. As they neared the camp, Jim spotted a Slavic-looking chap with short blond hair. He was walking a German soldier in front of him at gunpoint. Jim's companion said: 'He's going for his final walk.' They arrived at the camp, a large underground dugout under the forest trees with the door made of blankets and heavily camouflaged with shrubbery. Jim was now in the care of the local Maquis group.

In this region of the Luxembourg border the Resistance had been very active. The Ardennes countryside, with mountains and forests, was ideal for their operations, and they had taken over many old iron mines in the Halanzy and Musson areas, which had been shut down during the war. Many of the Maquis used the mines, which the Germans disliked due to the dangers posed by unsafe roofing. These resistance units were mostly made up of former Belgian, French and Flemish soldiers, with many young men under their care. There were also many Russians, mostly escaped forced labourers, who formed Communist-based pockets, known as 'Patriotic Guards'. They were living on the breadline and doing what damage they could, such as putting iron dust in railway oil boxes on rolling stock, cutting telephone wires, and destroying electric power cables and transformers.

Records show that these men worked hard under the most dangerous conditions, even derailing a train on one occasion and blocking the line for over thirty-six hours. The Germans often took reprisals, but sometimes limited their searches to hunting out secreted radios and confiscating bicycles. By late 1944, the Resistance were also tracking down members of the Gestapo and local 'collaborators', and handing them to Allied troops when they could. They also made identity cards that could be used by evading airmen – like Jim, and Belgians who had escaped the German clutches – and produced a regular journal, *Le Maquis de Musson*, which was circulated throughout the units. Jim had heard about the organisation, but had no real idea of the scale of operations.

On arrival in the camp, Jim was led into a cave. It was about 30 feet deep and 15 feet wide and contained about twenty men, all with various rifles and handguns and ammunition. There were introductions all round, first names only, and Jim introduced himself as 'Charles Lebrun' – the false identity given to him in Étalle – as he had no proof of his RCAF identity, his 'dog-tags' having been lost in his earlier escape. They were a motley lot, with a couple of Russians, two Algerians who had escaped from the French Army, and a chap from Luxembourg, all the rest being Belgian, led by a tall blond chap who could speak Flemish. Nobody could converse in English, so Jim was glad he had spent so much time learning French during the time he was hidden.

He was assigned a bunk, but it was cold in the cave as there was no fire and all cooking was done outside. Later Jim heard two of the Algerians and Russians talking and thought he detected broken English, but it was actually a fractured mixture of German and French. Yet at least it was a way to communicate. One of the Belgians told Jim he would have to wait another day for the doctor, and in the meantime he had to take his share of guard duty. The leader explained they were remaining in hiding, often moving their camp, until they had instructions, probably from their leadership or MI9. Jim was allocated guard duty with one of the Russians, Nikolai Sapranov, and they initially 'spoke' by drawings or hand gestures, until Nikolai taught Jim a few words of Russian, and German, which he had learned in various prison camps from which he had escaped. His background was similar to Jim's, being a Russian Air Force bomber pilot who had been shot down.

After about a week, the doctor arrived, rattling away on an old motorcycle that he left in the wood before making his way into camp. After checking Jim over he got out a big old-fashioned needle and gave Jim a shot in the arm, which caused him to pass out. When he came round he could hear the doctor saying to the leader: 'You'd better get him somewhere where he can get good food. He's suffering from malnutrition. He also has "scabies" and there are other things wrong with him.' So once again Jim had to wait for treatment. A few days later one of the men motioned him forward. 'Come with me. We're going to take you to a home where you can stay.

They will give you good food, white bread, lots of greens and lettuce.' 'Thank goodness no more medical treatment,' thought Jim. They walked about 3 or 4 miles to the little town of Couvreux, a couple of miles west of Virton. It took a while as Jim was unable to walk quickly. They came to the home of Madame Germaine Autphenne, whose husband, a major in the Belgian army, had been a hero during the 1940 invasion, his anti-tank unit of some thirty men holding up an entire German division for two days. He was now in a German prison camp in the Hamburg area.

Germaine Autphenne had the bearing of an old-fashioned schoolteacher, which she was, and had two little girls. She welcomed Jim into the house and gave him biscuits with butter and honey. Her job with the Resistance was to look after those who were ill, or just needed good food to build them up. She had a well-stocked vegetable garden and six beehives. Jim was told: 'Do not leave the house.' Her brother, Guy Giot, known to Jim as 'Emile', another Maquis fighter, was also staying with her while recovering from an accident, having blown a hole in his hand from a German 'Teller mine' he was handling. The house was a large one, right in the centre of the village, and although there was plenty of space to move around, Emile was restless. He had spent months fighting in the Resistance and was eager to get back into action. Jim's appearance seemed to act as a catalyst to him. A few nights after his arrival, Emile acquired the key to the liquor cabinet and they had a few drinks, becoming very relaxed and enjoying listening to the BBC on the radio. However, when Madame Autphenne arrived home, trouble was in store. She was furious – after all, she was risking a lot during the German occupation, not least the lives of her young daughters, and she gave Emile a real dressing down and switched the radio off. If anyone else had heard it broadcasting – or indeed the Germans themselves – there could have been severe retaliation.

Jim was now beginning to recover from his health problems, and started to sleep well, but he was still rather weak. After a few days, Emile decided they should go swimming. 'I've got no swimming trunks,' Jim said. 'No problem,' dismissed Emile, and he went to his sister's drawer, and pulled out a pair of her 'bloomers'. 'Try these,' he urged with a cheeky grin, and off they went. The local river was the Semois, which made a natural border between France and Belgium. It was July and the weather had improved considerably, being fine and warm that day. They followed the riverbank to a secluded area and swam for an hour or so. The exercise was good in helping Jim's recovery, though no doubt Germaine would not have approved. Spurred on by this success, a few days later Emile decided they should try fishing. He had some bamboo poles and hooks. Jim thought: 'Well, at least this won't involve bloomers!' There was a problem, however. Belgium required a fishing licence and Emile did not have one. 'We'll cross the border to France,' he said, 'we don't need one there.' It seem ironic to Jim to worry about a fishing licence in the middle of a war, but it made sense to avoid trouble.

After a short walk, they made their way to the village of Écouviez, on the French side of the river. There they found a bakery and bought some bread and a beer each, then headed a mile or so out of town to the river. Jim relaxed. The walk had given him the exercise and fresh air he needed, and he was enjoying the sunshine when he spotted someone in uniform. It was a dark navy outfit with a peaked 'pill-box' cap. He whispered to Emile: 'A French policeman?' It was actually a French border guard, and he chatted away to Emile about fishing. Then he turned to the airman, but Jim, cautious of his very poor accent, just smiled and replied: 'Yes, just fine.' Nobody mentioned the war, but they were in France and it was difficult to know the sympathies of anyone; it was unusual to see two young men relaxing in these circumstances. Most would be working, or in the Resistance. They decided to head for home as soon as he had gone, so carrying their poles they turned back to Écouviez. As they walked through the village in the middle of the road, they heard a car horn behind them and they stepped to one side to see an open-topped car with two members of 'Organisation Todt' riding in it. This could be dangerous.

The Todt Organisation had been set up in Germany before the war, under the leadership of a German engineer, Fritz Todt, to build some of the country's gigantic structures and motorways. They had built Hitler's 'Atlantic Wall' that, even then, the Allies were pounding their way through. The organisation also controlled the battalions of forced labour from occupied countries; Todt had built the giant stadium in Nuremberg where the Nazis had held their huge rallies. Their members all wore distinctive tan uniforms.

In the back of the car were two German Army officers. Jim thought: 'This is stupid. We had better get home and out of sight as quickly as we can.' They picked up another beer at the bakery and headed back across the bridge to Belgium. That night Germaine found out about their excursion and was livid with anger. Here she was risking her life, and that of her children, and the two men could have thrown them all away. Emile made his apologies, and Jim kept silent. He knew they had been stupid, but he had wanted the exercise. Instead of doing anything more risky, he kept busy helping Germaine with her beehives.

It was inevitable that Jim would have to return to the Maquis camp – with all the risks, especially to his health, that that posed – so he decided to ally himself with the Russians there, especially if they were going to make a run for the Swiss border. At this time one of Jim's main worries was his lack of identification. He had lost his 'dog-tags' months before, so the only 'ID' he had was his false papers in the name of Charles Lebrun. If he was caught by the Germans he would probably be shot, in which case the Canadian Air Force, or his parents, might never know what happened to him. So Germaine made a small purse for his money, on which he marked his name, rank and birth date in indelible pencil. When two men came for him he made his goodbyes, especially to Madame Germaine Autphenne, who had risked her life to help him, and to whom he would always be eternally grateful.

On return to the camp, he decided to make an effort to keep clean and bathe regularly. The local men could always return home for a few hours, but he and the Russians could not, so they made arrangements to visit a local stream. There, they dug a hole into the sandy bed of the river to use as a bath, and scrubbed themselves with the sand to keep the skin in good shape. Even though it was the height of summer the water was icy cold. Jim was still wearing the borrowed clothing from Étalle and the Autphennes, and the Maquis had given him boots and a cut-throat razor. He had not so far been on any raids, but one day he went with some of the resistance members to a grocery store in a nearby village, he thought presumably to scrounge some food. They asked the girl behind the counter for her father by name, but she said he was away for the day. Jim never found out if they would have shot him for being a collaborator, as he would not give them food. It was about this time the Maquis leader decided they would need some better victuals and decided they would kill a wild boar. They were tough animals so they made 'dumdum' bullets by cutting a cross in the head of the round so it would break up on contact. After three nights waiting on the edge of a potato field an animal turned up and was quickly killed. The boar was cooked that night over the camp-fire. The meat was dark and strong; it hit Jim's sensitive system badly, and started up his boils again.

Jim became worried that the risks were starting to increase. A lack of action was caused by the Allied leadership asking the Resistance to 'lie low' at this stage, until they could be given proper weaponry. Every few days a handful of men would go into a local village to scrounge food, and this increased the risk of being betrayed, so Jim decided to broach the idea of the run to Switzerland with the Russians. Conversation was difficult with Nikolai and the others, but he was beginning to make himself understood in a crude form of German. He suggested a plan and they readily agreed. The following day, the Russians approached one of the men and said, 'We will go for wood', and Jim offered to fetch water with a pail. Once they were out of sight of the camp the men ran for all they were worth, all day towards France.

Every so often they stopped to catch their breath, and it was on one of these rest pauses that Jim decided to get rid of his false identity, so he tore up the documents and buried the papers of 'Charles Lebrun' right where they were. If he had been seized he would have been shot as a spy, but without any papers at all he stood a better chance by using his Canadian name.

The evaders stayed away from farms and villages and kept to the woods, only crossing open spaces when they had no alternative. They had no food and were very thirsty and hungry. They had only crossed one stream, but had been able to take a drink of water. As one of the Russians – Nikolai's friend, Yenka – was still nursing a wound, he was having difficulty running so they decided to move at night when it was cooler, and try for the roads where it was easier to walk. They ate some cabbage-type plants from a field, as they had not eaten for three days, and were immediately sick. It was tobacco. After lying low under a bush in a soggy field, clinging to one another for warmth, they decided to risk making contact with a man they saw working one of the fields. 'We are on our way to Switzerland,' Jim said. He was Italian, and immediately helpful, and gave them a raw egg, which they shared, and broke his sandwich up into three portions for them. He also had some tea in a wine bottle, which they gratefully drank. 'I know someone who can help you,' he told them in French, 'I'll go and get someone.' As soon as he left, they retreated back to the edge of a wood and hid, just in case he brought some Germans. After an hour he came back with one man.

The farmer was excitedly gesticulating all the way. The other man was taller and well dressed. The escapees came out of hiding, and walked towards them. 'Je suis Louis Paul,' the tall man said. 'Je suis un Maquisard.' Jim was dumbfounded! Here was yet another member of the Paul family coming to help him. He explained he was an active member of the Resistance and he could help Jim get back to England. As he spoke fluent German, he offered to get the Russians to a Polish underground camp. It turned out, though, that Louis Paul was no relative of the family Jim knew, but it was still good news all round and Jim felt optimistic again.

After thanking their Italian friend, they made their way to a road where there was a small truck with a driver. As it happened, they had been walking west for about 30 kilometres rather than east towards Switzerland, and they were now at the village of Martincourt; the big river that now blocked their way was the Meuse. They climbed on to the back of the truck, and Louis told them they were to pretend they were foreign workers. As they drove along small back roads, Jim was scared they would be stopped, but their luck was in. After an hour they halted by a forest and there was a hurried consultation in German between Louis and the Russians. The Polish camp was up a track in the forest, and Nicolai and Yenka headed up the trail as Jim waved his goodbye. It was his last sight of them. After a further while, the truck pulled up at another wood, and Louis bid Jim to jump down and join him, and together they headed off down a track into a stand of tall maple and beech trees. It was Le Bois de Chenon near Baalon. Jim's confidence returned, as Louis seemed to know what he was doing, and in a short while they came to a clear glade where a group of young men were gathered, some armed and others not. They all seemed very relaxed and casual. This was Louis's band of fighters, and he was obviously proud of them.

After a while they retraced their steps back to the truck and made their way to the village of Baalon, France, where Louis lived. It was now becoming obvious to Jim that he had not travelled too far from Torgny, in Belgium. It appeared he had been going round in circles. As Madame Paul made some food for supper, they chatted in the living room, and Jim found out that Louis had been a lieutenant in the French Army until the occupation, when he had become involved in the Resistance. He told Jim of his resistance work, and how he hoped to get more weapons to continue the fight. There was now another plan for Jim's escape and return to England, better than anything he had heard so far. It involved possibly getting a British Lysander aircraft to pick him up. This was more fortunate than Jim could ever believe. He thought at last, 'I'm going home.' Then the screaming began.

'Les Boche, les Boche!' shrilled Madame Paul as she ran into the room.

'Les Boche sont ici!' Louis reacted quickly and said to Jim: 'There's a window out back. Get out of it and get lost. You don't know me. You never saw me. You've never heard of me, and don't come back. Jim didn't answer, and made for where some French doors opened out on to a patio. He ran out across a lawn beyond and started to squirm his way through a thick dense hedge, with a plan to cross the road. As he crawled on hands and knees he suddenly saw a pair of boots and a rifle butt. Hardly daring to breathe he stopped right there in the hedge, and tried to make himself comfortable without making a sound. There was no noise now, and he could not tell what was happening. Once again he was hiding in a hedge, with a German soldier within inches, just like earlier in Étalle. There was no yelling or shouting, and after a while a truck came by and there was talking between the soldier and those on the truck, then some movement, and the truck drove away with the German.

As soon as he considered the coast was clear, Jim sped across the road and through a field of livestock, consisting of rather shabby-looking horses and Friesian cows. They seemed to take an interest in him, but his mind was elsewhere. He was pumping with adrenalin. 'What now?' He decided his best chance was to make his way back to the clearing where he had seen the Maquis camp, if he could remember where it was. He knew it was the other side of the village, so he decided to wait until darkness fell. It was a moonlit night with no cloud, and he estimated it to be about midnight when he slowly walked through the village, keeping to shadows if he could and listening for the possible return of German trucks. After about 5 kilometres, sure enough he came across the trail, which looked obvious in the moonlight. 'Surely the Germans would spot that,' he thought. He found the glade and could see the men sleeping, but no guard. He called, 'Bonjour, je suis Charles Lebrun', in a soft voice. No movement. Then spoke again, but still no reaction. He leaned over one of the men and touched his skin. It was ice cold. He was dead. They had all been shot. Some had their heads caved in. These young, laughing and happy young men were all dead. It was the most horrifying sight and too much for him to bear. He turned back towards the path and ran. When he reached the road he kept running, not caring about traffic or where he was heading, until he dropped down behind a thick hedge and fell into an exhausted sleep.

Jim woke to the sounds of birds. It was a hot, sunny July day and he was very hungry. He had not had anything to eat or drink in four days except that sandwich and cold tea the old Italian farmer had given him. He also came to realise he had been running the wrong way, towards the north, back the way he had already come. His mind was now on trying to get on track towards Switzerland. He thought: 'The Germans will know there is someone around. They will still be on the lookout with patrols.' He headed back at a slow pace, keeping away from any villages or people. The roads were quiet. Then he saw someone in a khaki uniform, definitely not German. To suddenly dive for cover would look suspicious, so he strode on. They looked at one another, but said nothing, and he kept going, not knowing whether to make contact. Jim speculated: 'Was that man part of the Resistance? Was I right not to speak to him? I'll never know.' He kept walking all that day, his drive to reach Switzerland spurring him on, though he was ravenously hungry and thirsty. Eventually he curled up in the woods under some trees and got some fitful sleep.

The next day, his third alone again, he heard some voices just inside the woods; his hunger got the better of him and led him towards a clearing. Again there were young men, some with guns, tanning themselves and talking excitedly in French. As he strolled into the glade, he introduced himself with, 'Bonjour, bonjour', and was greeted with three guns shoved into his face. 'Je suis Canadien. Aviateur, aviateur!' They went silent and accused him of working for the Germans. 'We won't waste a bullet on you. We'll just hang you from the nearest tree,' they exclaimed. Jim was very frightened at this; he had no real proof of his identity except for the little purse that Germaine Autphenne had made for him. They fed him all right, but it was a basic mixture of few ingredients, which tasted like soggy cooked dough. It was dreadful, but he was so hungry he ate it gladly. He was kept under armed guard. After a while they started to become friendlier, still keeping a gun trained on him. There were eighteen of them, mostly in their early twenties, and the camp was similar to the previous one he had been in, just in the open with no real cover.

Their Maquis leader was Lucien Sibenaler, previously a French naval officer, with a striped t-shirt, and naval beret constantly worn at a jaunty angle. When the French Navy was disbanded by the Germans with the fall of the Vichy government, he took to the forests to join the resistance movement. He was older than the others and had an air of authority about him. One of the young men (they only used first names and Jim did not find out their surnames until after the war) had a mouth organ and kept them amused with soft, haunting melodies. This was James Grunenwald, and he was a good-looking chap. Jim offered to play, as he had learned some tunes as a youngster, so he gave a rendition of 'Irish Washerwoman' and a couple of tunes he had heard in the survey camps of Timmins. This may have helped him to be accepted, as he heard James say to one of the others, 'I think maybe he is Canadian.'

After three days the camp was visited by a tall, well-dressed man with an escort of two armed men with Sten-guns. There was a buzz of excitement, and Jim was taken to a clear area where an interview was conducted privately. He was asked by this anonymous man to give his details, including his hometown, squadron, names of crew, where had he flown from, and where he had crashed. He certainly seemed to be someone important, but Jim didn't tell him anything about his time with the Belgian Resistance, or what they had done for him. After about an hour he said, 'Fine. We will take care of you. It won't be long now. You will be going home.' Then the man whose name he did not know turned to Sibenaler and said, 'He's definitely a Canadian airman', and then he left the camp with his escort. The Maquis men all came up and shook his hand warmly, but the anonymous visitor was never mentioned again. Jim was now an official nineteenth member of the Maquis unit of La Fronte Francais de L'Interieur, and was issued with a carbine and signed on the payroll pay-book each week. James Grunenwald and Jim became firm friends and shared playing the mouth organ. James asked about his family and how old he was. Jim asked, 'What is the date?' '4 August' was the reply. In just two days he would be twenty-three years old. They gave him a celebration with some 'blancmange', and some rustled-up Calvados apple brandy.

The next night they were told a raid was planned, to bring in important provisions. The camp moved to another location closer to Torgny and the Belgian border. There was a village close by, with an enemy detachment consisting of an old First World War German officer and a small unit of six elderly soldiers in charge of a team of Polish forced labourers working the fields. Sibenaler briefed them: 'The "chief officer" is going to a nearby town for supplies, and we will raid the place while he is away. Be careful, he has a dog, which might be a problem as it will be guarding the house. No rifles tonight, only revolvers and pistols.' They gave Jim a revolver, and he took it to use with his left hand – from then on he was called 'Main Gauche' or 'Lefty'.

They moved stealthily up to the front door of the building, but it was locked. Jim sneaked round the back and pushed up the sash window, ready to crawl in, when the dog came up and licked his hand. Jim climbed in, patted the dog, and made his way to the front door to let his other three colleagues in. As they headed out of the door with their 'loot' of bread, ham, honey and other items, someone complained: 'How are we going to carry all this; it's heavy!' One of the men found a wheelbarrow to load everything into, and they headed back to camp. This was Jim's first Maquis operation, and here they were skulking away with a big soft dog following them. This was the 'vicious' dog they had been warned about. Just what they needed! Luckily, after about a kilometre the animal gave up and turned back.

The area was known locally as 'Le Bois d'Ire-le-Sec' and the track the 'Chemin Jaune' after the yellow sand. They quickly dumped the barrow and staggered off with their haul. It was altogether a good night's work that gave them some really good food for a number of days. Two nights later another similar raid was planned on the village of Jametz. This included a haul of cigarettes, a highly prized commodity that could be used for barter as well as consumption. Jametz was a two-hour walk away; the plan was to be in and out quickly, but Jim did have an unhappy moment when he was asked to guard the female cook in the kitchen. She was dressed exactly as his mother would have been, with apron and bun in her hair. 'I just hope she doesn't make any trouble,' Jim thought, 'I simply could not shoot her. Dear God don't let her move.' She did not, as she was petrified, and just stared at him. 'Voila les Boche', went up the call. They ran out of the village just as they could see some German soldiers were returning in the far distance. Jim thought this all great fun, like playing 'Cowboys and Indians'. They had not been shot at – yet!

They moved camp again, so as not to leave worn trails that could be followed; this time westwards to the Bois de Juvigny. It was easier for Jim to converse now, all the time in French, though his health was causing him concern. Lack of bathing meant the scabies had returned and the boils were back in abundance. At least they were doing some fighting now, although sometimes Jim was too weak and stayed back in camp. The next raid was to be the first fighting attack. The Germans were now retreating as the Allies advanced northwards from the Normandy beachhead, and this next raid would be an ambush, the aim being to harass the retreating soldiers heading for Germany.

They had no particular intelligence; they just picked a likely road and waited. Armed with only rifles and their one and only machine gun, which they mounted on an embankment by the road but hidden in the woods, they laid in wait. Jim was uncomfortable at being on the wrong side of the road, away from the woods and their line of retreat. After an hour a convoy of German cars and trucks passed, then after a short while a German staff car carrying three people in uniforms. Sibenaler shouted, 'Tirez!', and they all stood up and started firing. The car crashed into the ditch, and the occupants were immediately shot. They could take no prisoners. It was all hugely exciting and a great adrenalin rush for Jim, but he could not shoot in cold blood like the others. It was all so different from being in an aircraft turret, firing at an invisible target of an 'anonymous' aircraft. He was surprised at the feelings the adrenalin gave him, and the sort of emotion that took hold of him.

Grabbing any money, guns and ammunition that they could find, they ran for their lives. After they were back at their camp, the 'thrill' of the raid lasting four or five hours, a chap called 'Barbeau' rolled up with a beard and a pistol in a holster on his hip, and started showing off. He slapped his hip and the gun went off, shooting him in his leg. He screamed in pain and threw the gun and holster away. Jim asked, 'Can I have it?' 'Hell, yes', was the reply. It was a German copy of the .45 Browning issued to US Army officers. Jim had at last got his 'own' firearm.

The rest of that day was spent packing up and moving camp again, this time about 15 kilometres away, arriving as the sun went down. The Germans would undoubtedly be searching for them and it would have been stupid to stay in the same area. They settled into their new camp, with the ground crunching underfoot. 'What's that?' Jim asked. 'Oh, escargots', came the answer, and in the morning light Jim stared at the biggest snails he had ever seen. At night they came down from the trees to forage, and the Maquis were sleeping among them.

One day another raid took place, which became known as the 'cigarette hold-up'. Sibenaler told them to hide at the side of the road, as before, but not to fire until told to do so. They were in a more vulnerable position, with less cover than previously. After a while a closed van approached and, after a warning not to fire again, they jumped up in front of the truck to stop it. The occupants were ordered out, and then started laughing and shaking hands. One of them was the brother of a member of the Maquis. As the siblings caught up on the latest news about their families, the others unloaded some of the cartons of cigarettes. When the two men in the van reached their destination, Lucien Sibenaler instructed them to report right away that they had been held up by 'terroristes'. The Maquis melted away into the forest.

A few days later they were awakened at about three in the morning by the sound of gunfire. Jimmy Grunenwald had gone into the city of Longuyon, to pick up what information he could so they could plan another attack. Jimmy had accidentally cycled right through a German encampment at the edge of the wood. Everyone was instantly on the alert, guns at the ready as Jimmy ran into camp, having dumped the bike. 'The Germans have us surrounded,' he panted. 'They are all around us. They're all over. They shot at me. There are trucks and armoured vehicles at the edge of the forest!' Sibenaler immediately sent two men out in one direction, and Jim and a colleague in another, with orders to confirm the way to the road, check out 'les Boche', and hurry back. As they headed through the forest, they heard an engine and a jeep-type vehicle approached, with an officer standing at the front – hanging on the windscreen – and two other soldiers in the back. They hid behind a couple of big trees. The car stopped, and then moved on after a while, whereby Jim and his comrade left their hiding place and found about thirty vehicles on the road, and the Germans getting ready for breakfast. Jim thought: 'They're not looking for us but hiding during the daylight hours from the marauding Allied aircraft.' The Allies had planes such as American P-51 Mustangs and RAF Typhoons, that were strafing anything that moved on the roads. They went back to report to Sibenaler that the Germans were not looking for them, but hiding from Allied fighter-bombers. The others reported the same. For a while they had been hearing artillery in the distance. Surely Allied troops could not be far away now.

After some deliberating Lucien Sibenaler made his decision on what they were to do. As the sun came up he told them individually to make their way out into the wheat field and lie down in the crop away from each other, and wait for the Germans to leave. They cleared the camp so there was no sign of their occupation and did as he directed. At one stage an enemy half-track made its way across the field, luckily without running over anyone, and thankfully taking the exact same route back later. That night they could hear the convoy moving out, and when the coast was clear they retreated to their camp area. It was drizzling at the time and Jim suggested: 'Why don't we camp by the pine trees; it might be a little drier there.' 'Aha,' they laughed, 'the Indian from Canada.' But they agreed it was a good idea. However, they still had to go through the morning ceremony they had got used to, due to the blood-sucking 'ticks' in this woodland. Each day they had to drop their trousers and burn off the little insects that had dug their way into the skin in their groins each night; not a pleasant job.

On 20 August, the Maquis group had a new leader, Emile Randolet. James Grunenwald had decided to cycle to Longuyon where Randolet had been working as a professor of mathematics in the college before enlisting in the Resistance, where he and James had first met. The Allies were now advancing across the continent. General de Gaulle had rallied the Resistance in July, and had asked for all officers and NCOs to return to service. Lieutenant Randolet had been chief of a section in the 132 Regiment of Fortress, commanding two of the Maginot Line forts. He came to their company with a sergeant, Lucien Hennequin, who had been leading another resistance group of his own. They brought with them a military bearing, and they were now about to go out searching for trouble. Most of the rest of the gathering were young men who had escaped from forced labour working parties, or had even left school to fight. Some had even been caught and imprisoned by the Germans for short periods, so there was no love lost for the enemy soldiers.

One day Jim heard Randolet and the group discussing a German radar station. As it was still very secret, none of them realised its significance, so Jim – being the only one who knew about such things – had to explain about radar, and the threat it posed to Allied aircraft. It would be a good idea to knock the station out, but they had insufficient strength in their force, so Randolet decided to have Jim lead a party to cut the telephone lines to the unit. This they did in daylight, but a check a day or so later showed they had already been repaired. So when they reported this to their new leader, Randolet stated: 'Oh, we'll fix their clock!' He sent two men to cut the lines again, but this time in a place more difficult to find, then left three men, including Jim, to wait and watch. Eventually two soldiers came along on bicycles. They shot them both, in spite of the pleas of one who said he had a wife and family in Germany. The cruelty of it hit Jim with a shock. That evening they moved on to another camp.

Jim and James Grunenwald had become firm friends. James had another bicycle and would regularly cycle into his hometown of Longuyon to gather intelligence, assemble more arms, and visit his family. One day he had called at his mother's house when the woman living next door ran into the street screaming, 'Un terroriste, un terroriste!' The Germans gave chase and, as Jimmy was pedalling away as fast as he could, the soldiers shot him in the back. When he did not return, the group soon learned the full story. Randolet said: 'I want a volunteer to take care of that collaborator.' Jim thought: 'Although this is war, that man was my friend.' He put his hand in his pocket and touched the mouth organ they had shared. Jean Martin volunteered, and came back a little later and told them what happened: 'I went to Madame Grunenwald's neighbour and said, 'Madame you know what you have done', and then I put the gun to her head and shot her.' It was 24 August, Paris had just been liberated following a Maquis uprising, and French armour was paraded down the Champs-Elysées just two days later.

Randolet now set up lines of communication, their group using a boy of ten or twelve years of age. He would call every couple of days with messages and news of enemy troop movements. The sound of the artillery was slowly getting closer. The group continued its harassment of the enemy, with attacks on military vehicles. Now they stayed on one side of the road, close to cover, which made more sense. They would wait for a convoy to pass, and there would usually be a truck that followed. Sibenaler and his colleague would man the machine gun, and they would all fire in unison. On one occasion the truck was loaded with Wehrmacht soldiers; they kept firing until the truck hit the ditch and then caught fire and blew up, so there was not much in the way of a haul on ammunition and weapons on that occasion. All the soldiers died.

They kept up the pressure each day, finding different locations. Their adrenalin was running high, and they returned to the camp tired out, but yet excited. Jim still was not well. The boils and scabies were causing him terrible discomfort, and although he did not know it, he was again suffering from malnutrition as well. At this time they were all wearing 'FFI' (French Forces of the Interior) armbands. It didn't help much; if the Germans caught them they would be shot anyway, but it did encourage an 'esprit de corps'.

One day the boy came in with a message and Randolet said to the group: 'Ah, there are ten or fifteen Germans hiding in a village called Quincy. We are going to capture them.' The Germans did not want to surrender to the

French for fear of their lives; they were waiting for the Americans to arrive. Randolet was a regular officer soldier, who had been defeated and who had seen the atrocities perpetrated by the Germans, and he wanted his moment. There was a different feeling about this raid. Two of the group were of Italian extraction, Gino Norris and Roger Broggi, and there was considerable apprehension at what they were about to try. Roger stuck to Jim's side as they made their way to Quincy. As they approached it they could see down the tree-lined road into the town; Randolet put Hennequin in charge of half of the group, and they followed the hill to one side, crossed the river and cut off any retreat for the fifteen or so soldiers. As the main group went down the hill they came across a man pushing his bicycle up it. He told Randolet he was in the intelligence section of the Resistance. They must have looked like a scruffy group, carrying only side arms, rifles and one machine gun. 'Oh, it's good to see you guys operating in the daylight,' the man said. Randolet told him: 'Yes, we are going to capture the Germans. Where are they?' 'Ce n'est pas difficile. Over the hill there's about twenty. They have a mortar, and machine gun. And in the bushes there, about 200 metres down, there's a further machine gun. There is another similar group over the other hill, and over there ...' he said, pointing in another direction, '... and down in the city hall there are about 200 more Germans.' They looked on in horror. They could see their friends on the low land walking in innocence of what was really waiting for them. Randolet was frantic. Waving his arms he yelled at the distant resistance fighters: 'Let's get out of here – get away!'

The Germans opened up with everything they had. They probably thought the body of men was the forward party of a larger army. Bullets flew everywhere. The first blast Jim's group received was into an old Maginot Line bunker just up the hill behind them, where the enemy thought they were hiding. Roger and Jim hit the dirt. Jim looked up and saw Randolet running. He had a big black hat for protection against the sun, and a bullet whipped it off his head just before he dived behind the bunker.

Jim lay as flat as he could, but lifting his head a little he could see that everyone else had disappeared. Roger Broggi, still quite petrified, asked: 'What are we going to do?' They crawled about 20 metres away from the position, behind some bushes, and then started returning fire. Sibenaler's machine-gun loader appeared, with blood streaming from his nose and ears. The gun had taken a direct hit from a mortar bomb. 'We're the only ones here,' he shouted, 'they've all gone.' Jim could see his Maquis colleagues running away for all they were worth across the field behind the bunker. They decided to retreat, too, but along the road, as by that time the field was under fire. The sun was high and the Germans kept up their fire for about 20 minutes or so. Jim was suddenly very thirsty, and drank from a puddle in the road; it tasted cool and clear, although he doubted it was. Jim, Roger, and the machine gunner fled as fast as they could, and made their way back to the camp in the woods. The others in their group arrived during the course of the next few hours and into the evening, and eventually it became clear some were not coming back.

The whole raid had been a disaster. Their leader, Randolet, had taken a bullet in his leg, and was sufficiently badly wounded that some of the others took him to a safe house, from whence he ended up in the house of an army officer where a doctor treated his wound. Two others had hidden in a flour mill, and although the Germans searched it they were not found. Another of the forward party had taken refuge in the reeds by the river for hours, before he was able to make his escape. Hennequin, the army sergeant, was killed in the first round of fire. Two others, a young twenty-year-old René Warion, and older Joseph Pawlack – who had only joined the group a few days earlier, the latter being slightly wounded – were captured by the Germans and taken into the town of Quincy, where, along with about twenty of the most prominent townspeople, including the mayor, were held as hostages in case the Resistance attacked again. The following day the Allied guns roared once more. There was no room for prisoners, so before the horrified villagers the Germans hanged the two Resistance men on a hastily made scaffold. The 250 Germans continued the retreat northwards, without any loss from the assault.

After this the Maquis decided to lie low. Sibenaler was now back in charge. Three days later, one of their young couriers came from nearby Jametz with news: 'There are soldiers in the village!' However, when questioned he was unsure if they were Allied or German. Sibenaler decided to be cautious and sent Jim and two others to reconnoitre. 'You go with them. You'll know if they are Allied or not,' he said. They sneaked in the back way around the little building, and there in the town square was a US Army jeep, with an American sergeant leaning back with his feet up on the folded windscreen. 'That's got to be an American,' thought Jim, 'nobody else would act like that!' He led the party at a run into the square, and shouted to the 'Yank': 'What kept you so long?' That sparked laughter all round. The soldier was Sergeant William Ellis from North Carolina, in an American reconnaissance unit. The two others went back to Sibenaler to tell him the good news, and while Jim would have liked to have returned to say his goodbyes, here was his opportunity to reunite with Allied forces and Sergeant Ellis had asked him to report with him to his lieutenant.

In an upstairs room of a nearby house the officer was sitting alone at a table with a steak in front of him, and he bid Jim to sit and join him. Jim explained: 'I'm Flying Officer James Moffat of the Royal Canadian Air Force, shot down in March.' Jim refused a piece of the steak; the Maquis team had all just had goose at the camp, when the young messenger had arrived. After such a long time, almost six months, Jim found it hard to think and speak in English. 'How in God's name did you live?' asked the lieutenant. 'Oh! C'est la guerre!' was the reply. Jim must have looked a sight to the American: dressed in a German tunic, with hand grenades in his pockets, thick wide belt around grubby trousers and with his German pistol shoved down it; hob-nailed boots he had acquired at some time; and carrying a French carbine. His face was covered in a heavy growth of beard, and he probably was not too fragrant! 'We can't have you travelling like that,' said the lieutenant, and promptly issued Jim with a full US uniform: puttees, boots, helmet, the lot. Time for a bath later, and in the pockets of the tunic Jim found lieutenant's bars – so he put them on and promptly took the rank, and joined the US Army!

The reconnaissance column consisted of the lead jeep, with Jim, and five others, and an M8 six-wheeled armoured car with a 37mm cannon. They were tasked with finding bridges that had not been blown up, and then holding them, or dismantling any demolition charges found. They roared off down the highway. Jim had no time to think about his lucky break. Each village they passed through they were greeted with happy villagers offering fruit and drink. The Americans responded with chocolate and toilet rolls; liberation American style! The lieutenant asked for champagne and he got a rough prune 'whisky'. It burned its way down Jim's throat. Coming across a roadside inn, they stopped and, as Jim was now fluent in French, he was prompted to go in and ask the innkeeper about the Germans. He was friendly enough, and to the question, 'Are there any Germans around?', he answered: 'Mais oui, be careful. There are some at the bridge up ahead, and they have a machine gun covering it on the far side, and the bridge is mined. They will blow it up.' Jim reported the detail to the officer, who scoffed at the information. 'Ah. These "Frenchies" are all full of shit! Let's go!' Jim thought, 'My God!', and off they sped, with Jim and the officer's jeep in the lead.

Jim was very 'jumpy' after his experience at Quincy, and he had reckoned the innkeeper had been telling the truth. He estimated they were doing about 100km an hour (about 65mph) when shells started whizzing past them. They were under fire, but the Germans could not hit the column. The lieutenant ordered a quick turnaround, and they made their way back to the inn. The armoured car was pouring shells into the German position. They then decided to circumvent the enemy, but not before encountering a possible ambush. The location had been abandoned, possibly in favour of the position at the bridge. Eventually they came to a small town, Montmédy, where the bridge had been blown up into the River Chiers. As they stopped outside a large house, a lady came out to greet them. Jim was acting as interpreter still and he was told: 'Have the men bring shovels. I'll show you where the champagne is buried.' They found twenty-five bottles and, within a very short period of time, they were all very happy soldiers! However, something then occurred that somewhat sobered them up.

The lady returned and asked them to attend a service of thanksgiving in the local church. The day before, some local students on hearing the approach of Allied artillery and shelling decided to do something to help the liberation. They scattered nails all over the roads, and many of the tyres on German vehicles were damaged, and this slowed down the retreat. The German Army commander ordered as many of the youngsters as they could find to be rounded up, and then lined up against a wall while a firing squad was organised. Then a German Army doctor came to the rescue. 'These are not part of the Resistance,' he said. 'They are just young people. The war is almost over. It would be a waste of young lives.' The commander was eventually talked out of it, and the enemy fled ahead of the Allied advance. The lady's son had been one of those students, and what better way to celebrate his life being spared than to have some of the Allied troops at the service. In his alcoholic haze, the lieutenant agreed, and throughout the service – of which he understood not one word – he kept mumbling: 'Isn't that marvellous.' That night they slept in an apple orchard, Jim not really able to believe his luck was holding out.

They returned to the reconnaissance unit headquarters where the Americans had a field kitchen. Jim had his first really decent hot meal since staying with Madame Autphenne in Couvreux months before. Over the meal Jim chatted to the sergeant, Bill Ellis, about the lieutenant's 'gung-ho' attitude, especially on the road to the bridge. 'This is our fifth lieutenant since D-Day,' he admitted, 'the others were all killed. They don't know anything from beans! We try to save them, but we have a hard time.' That was the danger of being in a reconnaissance unit. The next morning an RAF Auster spotter aircraft landed in an adjacent field. Jim saw his opportunity to get back in the air and to the RAF. He was fed up of all this trudging around over the past months. But the commanding colonel vetoed his plans: 'Oh no. You stay with us. We'll take you back.' The Auster shortly flew off, the pilot having completed his communication duty.

The full reconnaissance unit of about 250 vehicles headed off north again, overcoming several obstacles left by the retreating enemy, and eventually Jim found the unit at a captured camp near Bastogne, later that winter to become the scene of an epic siege during the Battle of the Bulge. The Americans had brought here a group of about thirty evading Allied airmen. They were all gathered together, given blankets, and they slept on the floor of a mess hall, strewn with papers. The following morning they were given another hot meal with 'bully' beef, cheese and biscuits, washed down by lots of hot coffee. The airmen – including Jim, three Canadians, five British and the remaining American, all scruffy and bedraggled – were loaded on to jeeps, and over the following hours driven north, then west, ultimately arriving in Brussels in the evening. Jim could not believe it – here they were at the Metropole Hotel, one of Brussels's biggest, on the rue de Brouckèreplein. Life was looking up!

Jim strolled through the front door; the main bar was near reception, and there sitting at the nearest table was Canadian Army major, Ken Cross, the Laird crew's flight engineer Bill Cardy's brother-in-law. Last time Jim had seen him was at Leeming, when they had taken him for a flight in the Halifax, as part of the preparations for D-Day. Jim strolled over: 'Ken, what the hell are you doing here?' Ken was stunned. Jim's appearance in a US Army uniform, with helmet and pistol startled him. 'What are you doing in that get-up?' Jim said: 'I'll explain, just let me go up to my room and have a much-needed bath. Then I'll come down and we'll have a beer together.' Jim shared room 315 with an American bomb aimer, but when he returned to the bar, Ken and his colleagues had gone. At the time, Cross was acting as Canadian Army liaison officer attached to General Montgomery's army.

At the bar Jim met up with a member of the American army air force, also called Laird. Jim told him about his pilot of the same name and his crew, now all dead. It made Jim morose to think they had all gone, and now the war was coming to an end. After an abortive sortie to chat up some Belgian girls with Jim's French – they were all Flemish speaking – Jim and his room-mate headed downtown to a dance hall to celebrate the liberation of Brussels, officially commemorated by the mayor of the city and General Montgomery on 7 September.

After breakfast the next day the rescued airmen were shown into a room by a RAF wing commander. There was only a large table in the centre. 'I want all your guns, grenades and bombs on the table. I want all your souvenirs on the table. You will be searched afterwards to ensure you have left everything,' he said. Jim was shocked; he didn't want to give up his souvenir. He had his Walther automatic he had acquired with the resistance group, and his carbine. He had the pistol tucked under his armpit. The 'loot' from everyone stunned him. The table was soon loaded with big 'potato masher' grenades, pistols and revolvers, paratrooper-style folding stock machine guns, and other assorted items. Jim thought, 'If they search me, then so be it', but the threat from the wing commander did not come to anything.

He was also allowed one telegram home, so Jim sent a form-type telegram – 'I am alive and well, Jim' – but his mother never received it. Then a military bus took them to Brussels airport, now in Allied hands, and they boarded a US Army Air Corps C-47 'Skytrain' (Dakota). They were on their way home at last.

But even the flight home was not without incident. Fog had descended over southern England. The American pilot had turned to the navigator and asked: 'Where the hell are we?' The navigator said he had no idea, and was told to find out and be quick about it. Jim was amazed at the casual nature. 'Is this the American air force?' he thought. Eventually they landed at a base north of London (author's note – probably RAF North Weald) and trucks were organised to take them into the city. It was hard to believe he was back in England, as his mind was still thinking in French and about his time with the Maquis. Then he saw a roadside inn, and he banged on the roof to alert the driver. 'What's the trouble?' 'We haven't had English beer for many months. Couldn't we stop?' So in they went for a few drinks each. In London they were taken to a medical clinic for examination and delousing, and to be supplied with new British battledress uniforms.

Determined to keep his pistol, Jim hid it under his clothes and it was still there after the shower, though his other items had been removed. Along with a couple of others, he was then sent to a hospital in Watford, as he was still in pretty bad shape and badly undernourished.

In the hospital he was kept in bed in an officers' ward for a week. He still had over forty boils, and infected scabies. Most of the other patients present seemed to have inflicted injuries on themselves, in cars, accidents and suchlike. After three weeks Jim was considered strong enough to be discharged, and was told to report to an RAF intelligence centre, where he was quizzed about his six months behind enemy lines and a report filled in. Then he was asked by the officer in charge: 'Do you want to continue with another tour of duty?' Jim now well knew what the Nazis were up to, and confirmed most definitely that he did. He wanted to be in at the finish. It was autumn 1944 and before the German push in Belgium – the Battle of the Bulge – which was a setback for the Allies and occurred in the area where Jim had been with the Resistance. Before this he was posted on a week's leave in the UK, and a further week in Canada, before he would return to operational duties.

After a debriefing, he headed into the centre of London; first stop the bank – he hadn't been paid for six months. Then his plan was to head north back to Leeming, and his squadron. As he waited in the line he heard a row going on at a nearby counter. One involved sounded Canadian, and he recognised 'Rocky' Durocher, their gunnery leader in No. 427 Squadron. He was with his brother Ken, a navigator in the unit. After being served, Jim walked over. 'Hi Rocky, what are you doing here?' He was greeted with: 'My God, Moffat, you're supposed to be dead! How did you get here?' 'Well, I came back to life,' responded Jim. 'We'll have to do a "low-level" in town,' said Rocky, and they spent the rest of the day on a pub crawl, something at which Rocky was a legend in the squadron.

Eventually Jim made his way back to Leeming, where he found Ganderton doing his second tour, now a wing commander and this time leading No. 427 Squadron since late September. Jim had long talks with him, regaling his adventures and catching up with the news at Leeming, and then headed back to the London RAF officers' club to await his boat home. After a week's stay at a leave centre in Warrington – which he remembers as very wet as it never stopped raining – the Canadians boarded the *Queen Mary* at Liverpool for what turned out to be a stormy crossing. As the ship was considerably faster than the regular merchant ship, she always made the trip on her own. Because of the weather they were not allowed on deck, but it was still a comfortable journey. Despite having to cover himself every day with antiseptic cream from the neck down, to help deal with the boils and scabies, Jim was otherwise feeling great, and especially thankful to be heading home. The voyage took just over a week.

Their arrival in New York brought tears to Jim's eyes. They were met by the Red Cross with coffee and doughnuts, then the Canadians entrained for Ottawa, reaching the RCAF station at Rockliffe on the outskirts of the city on 22 October 1944. Jim immediately took the train to Colborne on the coast of Lake Erie, to where his family had moved while he had been overseas. He planned to take a taxi home from there, but as he walked into town in the morning, there was his brother Rob in his distinctive little yellow convertible 1930 Model 'A' Ford, so he could cadge a lift with him. But on the way there was a bit of a fright. Smoke was coming through the floorboards of the car and Jim instinctively ducked and yelled, 'Fire! There's a fire!' Jim was still feeling nervous after his wartime experiences, but Rob allayed his fears: 'It's only oil dropping on the muffler' [author's note: exhaust]. Jim climbed out of the car in the yard of his home and was greeted by their old farm dog, Buster. 'Oh Buster,' he cried, and the dog came to him as though he had never been away. Jim's mum, Elizabeth, wrapped him in her strong arms like she was never going to let him go.

Over the next few days, Jim found out that his mother had never received the telegram he had sent in September from Brussels. It had been a long six months for the family. Elizabeth had been called to the telephone at a neighbour's house to be informed that her son was missing in action, and his siblings had been taken out of school to be told the news. The official letter from the RCAF did not arrive until 10 April: '... with deep regret that Flying Officer James Moffat, RCAF has been reported missing ....' On 22 April, Wing Commander Bob Turnbull, CO of the squadron, had written a wonderful letter, saying how much Jim was missed. Then there was nothing else all through the long summer months. On 23 August, in response to a letter from Jim's father, the RCAF casualty officer wrote to say that '... no further information has been received on your son. Every effort is being made to trace your son, although due to the lapse of time, it is now felt there is less hope of locating him. ...' Exactly a month later, the same casualty officer wrote: 'I am pleased to advise that your son,

FO James Moffat, previously reported missing on Active Service, is now reported to have arrived safely in the United Kingdom.' That was the first time the family knew Jim was well. In October his father wrote asking for more news, and the casualty officer responded on 27 October, but not with any real information. By that time Jim was already in Ottawa. After all that, Jim's family were glad to have him home safe. While on leave he took the train to his hometown of Timmins. He felt the need to see Mrs Fournier, the mother of his old friend Roger, and part of a large close family. Mrs Fournier cried: 'Why did you come back and my Roger didn't? Why didn't Roger come back?' Jim had no easy answer to that.

Jim eventually returned to the RCAF in Ottawa at the end of his leave, and was posted to RCAF Rockliffe to the east of the city, where he volunteered for a posting to the Far East, most likely as a member of the planned 'Tiger Force'. Like other ex-Bomber Command aircrew in the spring of 1945, he ended up at the RCAF station at Aylmer, near London, Ontario, awaiting the posting. The policy of using tour-expired crew from Europe changed, and Jim was demobbed on 31 March 1945, returning to civilian life, with support from the RCAF, and entering what is now Ryerson University. After that he found employment within industry, and retired in 1984. He became a member of the Royal Air Force Escaping Society. Jim also found out what had happed to Albert Paul, who was so influential on the early part of his escape. Albert had been imprisoned by the Germans for several months; then on 14 August 1944 he was executed by the Nazis at La Citadelle in Liège. His body was returned to Halanzy in October of that year, and buried with great ceremony. Jim eventually returned to Belgium in the late 1980s where he met Cecile Paul once again, Monique – the baby he had once held in his arms – and many of his Maquis friends, and in 1990 was present to unveil a memorial in Rachecourt close to where his Halifax and the No. 622 Squadron Lancaster had come down. The names of the crew members who died on that fateful day of 31 March 1944 are inscribed on the monument:

Halifax III LV923 ZL-W 427 (Lion) Squadron, Royal Canadian Air Force
    S/Ldr G.J. Laird DFC RCAF   Pilot
    F/Sgt A.J. Stainton RCAF   Co-pilot
    F/O W.E.P. Soeder RCAF   Navigator

P/O J.C. Corbally RCAF — Bomb Aimer
F/Sgt W.P. Clapham RAF — Wireless Operator
F/O J. Morrison DFC RAF — Flight Engineer
P/O L.H. Smith — Mid-upper Gunner
F/O J. Moffat RCAF (Survivor) — Rear Gunner

Lancaster III ND767 GI-D 622 Squadron, Royal Air Force
P/O E. Picken RAF — Pilot
P/O J.P. Meritt RCAF — Navigator
Sgt R.J. Asplin RAF — Wireless Operator
F/Sgt C.J. Schmidt RAAF — Air Bomber
Sgt G.R. Collins RAF — Air Gunner
Sgt N.J. Coup RAF — Air Gunner
Sgt H.F. Page RAF — Flight Engineer

Jim Moffat was present at the unveiling of the Bomber Command Memorial in London in June 2012, representing those who evaded, where he and the author met, and where he gave his permission for his story to be told.

UNDER THE
MAPLE LEAF

PART III
PATHFINDER

Reg Lane.

Part III: Pathfinder

8. The Boy from Victoria

'We have a special job for you to do.' Squadron Leader Reginald Lane, DSO, DFC, had been called to RCAF headquarters, at Lincoln's Inn Fields, London, in July 1943. He was ushered into the office of Air Marshal H. Edwards, commanding officer of RCAF Overseas. Here he was told to proceed back to Canada. Edwards said: 'The first Canadian-built Avro Lancaster X, KB700, has been constructed at Avro's plant at Malton, just to the north-west of Toronto. You are to go and bring it back to England with a scratch group of aircrew from all over Bomber Command.' Staff at RCAF HQ in London informed him: 'Your crew will travel separately and meet you in Ottawa.' As Reg lay in the freezing bomb bay of the Liberator taking him back across the Atlantic to his homeland, he reflected on his career in the RCAF so far.

Reginald John Lane had been born in January 1920 in Victoria, British Columbia. His father, Gerald, had emigrated to Canada from London in 1910, and then fought with the Canadian Army in the First World War, returning to British Columbia with his British wife, Norah, a girl he had known before the war in London. Reg attended the local Victoria High School, was very studious and did well, but his parents were not in a position to afford a university education, so he entered the commercial world, joining the Hudson's Bay Company shop in downtown Victoria in 1937, working in the footwear department. He was a long-standing member of the choir at Christ Church Cathedral in the city as well as being a bell-ringer, and was very active in the Scouting movement, becoming Scout master in 1938. He remained in the Scouts until enlistment, confirming his leadership and management skills.

From August to October 1941 he served as a volunteer in the 13th Field Ambulance, RCAMC, until in October he was called up to join the RCAF, having had his first interview and medical in 1940. Reg had always wanted to be a pilot and on enlistment in October, after basic training, he went on to flying training on Tiger Moths at No. 8 Elementary Flying Training School (EFTS) of the British Commonwealth Air Training Plan (BCATP), at Sea Island, Vancouver. Proceeding then to No. 10 SFTS, at Dauphin, Manitoba, for advanced training on North American Harvards, he graduated first in his class. His commission to pilot officer came through the following day. Reg was lucky to be one of the few pilots at this time to be selected for overseas service, and after a short period of leave at home, made his way on the long trip across Canada by train to Halifax, Nova Scotia, for embarkation on a ship to the UK.

After staying in the reception centre at Bournemouth on the south coast of England, Reg was selected for bomber training and posted to No. 10 Operational Training Unit (OTU) at Abingdon, Oxfordshire, for instruction on slow, ponderous Armstrong Whitworth Whitley bombers. These lumbering twin-engined aircraft, with a strange flying attitude that looked as though they were tilting downwards, were almost the best the RAF had at the time, with a very long range, but poor bomb load of 5,300lb, and a tendency to be unforgiving on a bad landing. Reg's first flight was in a radial-engined Whitley III on 24 August, followed four days later with a flight in a Merlin-engined Mk V, P4132, the type becoming the regular training 'mount'. Reg progressed quickly and went on his first solo in a bomber on 7 September 1941, and by the end of the month had received his operational posting – to No. 35 Squadron based at RAF Linton-on-Ouse in the Vale of York. Reg would serve two tours with this squadron. This was a remarkably quick progression, indicative of how urgently Bomber Command required good multi-engined-trained pilots.

No. 35 (Madras Presidency) Squadron (motto *Uno Animo Agimus* – We Act with One Accord) was one of the RAF's earliest units, formed in the days of the Royal Flying Corps. Originally formed at Thetford in Norfolk on 1 February 1916, it then utilised BE2c biplanes. After further training at Narborough in Leicestershire, the unit was posted to the Western Front in February 1917, equipped with Armstrong Whitworth FK8s. The squadron had the distinction of having been specially trained for cooperation with the cavalry, and some of the cavalry officers attached to it during mobilisation accompanied it overseas. Soon after arrival on the Western Front it was posted for duty with the Cavalry Corps and remained attached until March 1918. After a ten-year period of disbandment at the end of the conflict, the unit was re-formed in 1929 as a bomber unit, being equipped with de Havilland DH9s, and later the Fairey Gordon. Much of the 1930s were taken up with operations in the Middle East and East Africa, and the squadron returned to the UK on the outbreak of the Second World War. After another period as a training unit the squadron was re-formed at Boscombe Down as the first of the RAF's Handley Page Halifax squadrons in November 1940, moving to RAF Leeming, and then to its operational base at RAF Linton-on-Ouse a few weeks later. The Halifax became the second of the RAF's 'heavies' to become operational, early in 1941, with their first operation to Le Havre the night of 11/12 March 1941, just a month after the first operation by a Short Stirling. No. 35 Squadron was to have a major part in Reg's life.

In October 1941 Reg was posted to B Flight with Flight Lieutenant G.L. Cheshire as flight commander, later to become one of the RAF's most distinguished bomber pilots, commander of No. 617 (Dambusters) Squadron, and holder of the Victoria Cross. (At this time the squadron had Squadron Leader J.B. Tait as A Flight commander, also later to become CO of the 'Dambusters'.) Reg's first flight in a Halifax was a circular cross-country to Kirkbride and Ternhill and back to base on 15 October 1941 in Halifax Mk I L9524 with Cheshire as captain. Reg found Cheshire a good teacher and easy to get on with. Along with other aircrew, they often socialised together; on a trip to York, they crashed Cheshire's Bentley into a hedge, all a little the worse for wear from Yorkshire hospitality. Cheshire was frustrated at this time, as he had completed his tour and was 'grounded' from operations. (He stayed with the squadron until March 1942.) To young Reg, Cheshire was his inspiration. This was followed with a period of working-up on this new aircraft. His first operation, as 'second dickey' pilot to Sergeant Williams, was on 7 November 1941, which was a long haul of 8 hours 25 minutes to Berlin and back, followed only a few days later with his next trip, this time to Hamburg, both in Halifax I L9600 TL-U. His third 'second dickey' trip, a 4-hour round trip to Cologne, was again with the Williams crew, but luck was on his side as this time he flew in Halifax I V9983. L9600, with Pilot Officer H. Buckley and his crew, was lost on this trip; it is thought to have come down in the North Sea, with no survivors. For Sergeant Williams, Reg and the crew there was a close encounter with a Me 110 night fighter, which made four passes at their aircraft near the Dutch island of Norderney before they made their escape.

Reg's next two operations, again with Sergeant Williams – with his own crew of Sergeants Sykes, Thorpe, Flint and Martin, in R9364 TL-M – were against a very specific target, the *Scharnhorst* battleship in harbour at Brest. This ship, along with the *Gneisenau*, was a serious threat to the Allied navies operating in the Atlantic, and to the supply lines to the Mediterranean theatre, via Gibraltar. For the first sortie, on 18 December 1941, their aircraft, R9364, made a three-engined landing at Boscombe Down, having been hit in one engine by flak, and they returned to base the following day. The first raid in company with Stirlings and Manchesters from the Lincolnshire bomber groups, and Halifaxes from No. 10 Squadron, was not a success, no hits on the ship being seen as there was a fair amount of cloud cover. The second trip to bomb the *Scharnhorst* was ordered on 30 December for Halifaxes from Nos 10, 76 and 35 Squadrons, this time in daylight, and escorted by Polish Spitfires. It was more successful and hits on the target were claimed, athough three Halifaxes were lost. One of those that went down was V9978 TL-A of Wing Commander Robinson. Hit in two port engines, the pilot successfully ditched the aircraft in the sea, and the crew were rescued by a Royal Navy patrol boat. Robinson was later awarded a DSO for this act. When the crew eventually got back to York, they were welcomed by their No. 35 Squadron crew mates, including Reg, singing 'The Wingco's in the drink!'

For Reg the following couple of months were taken up with consolidating his flying skills on the No. 35 Squadron Halifax Conversion Flight with various exercises, finally qualifying as first pilot on 18 February 1942. During this time he forged a close friendship with another skipper, Pilot Officer Don MacIntyre, a Canadian from the Maritime Province of New Brunswick. The squadron was stood down for a month to allow the navigation aid Gee to be installed in the aircraft. During that month, Reg was kept busy with night-flying training, and other duties that included his delivering of new aircraft from the factories at Radlett, Hertfordshire, and Samlesbury, Preston. It was also during this month the *Scharnhorst* and *Gneisenau*, accompanied by the *Prinz Eugen*, made their successful break through the English Channel to return to Germany, masterminded by Adolph Galland, who told this author in an interview, 'We just couldn't believe our luck!' Reg was back on operations on the night of 3 March

1942, with a raid to the Renault factory at Billancourt, near Paris, in R9425 TL-M. This was a big raid, and the first tactical use of flares from the leading aircraft to mark the target, something that was to be developed further, as will be seen.

Reg had two more raids to the Ruhr: Essen on the night of 8 March, and Cologne on 13 March, both in R9425 TL-M, on which Gee was used and target marking employed. However, poor weather meant the Krupps works were not that well identified, and the strike could not be called effective. Next the squadron was briefed for a very special attack, which meant they were to operate from Scotland. The *Tirpitz* was the heaviest battleship in the German Navy, and was on the top of Prime Minister Churchill's 'hit list'. The ship had sneaked out of port in Kiel and headed north, where it planned to attack convoys from the North American continent to the British Isles. (Later it became a threat to the Russian convoys too.) Because of the location of the ship so far north in Norway's Asen Fjord, near Trondheim, it was necessary to operate from RAF Lossiemouth in Morayshire. In January a mixed force of Stirlings and Halifaxes raided the target without success. Another attempt was left to Halifaxes of No. 4 Group, and on 27 March 1942 No. 35 Squadron with Reg in Halifax II W1019 TL-U, in company with No. 10 Squadron, was armed with some drum-shaped bombs, and No. 76 Squadron was armed with conventional bombs. They were tasked with attacking the supporting infrastructure and flak positions and made their way up the east coast, flying low to confuse enemy radar. In a series of interviews Reg said: 'I believe the drums were filled with some sort of incendiary chemical designed to attack the metal of the ship. We were not briefed on the actual content, just told to drop them at low level. They looked like five-gallon paint tins, set into containers of about eight to ten at a time, on each bomb rack.' It was a total force on the raid of twenty-two aircraft.

They left Lossiemouth on 30 March for the flight across the North Sea. Unfortunately the cloud and fog cover meant the target was obscured, and as the area was at the extreme range of the Halifaxes, they could not stay long. Reg continued:

> It was a long haul in a Halifax, and there was a layer of low cloud in the area. The fjord was about 400 yards wide, very narrow, and a valley off at the end, which was our way out. We were briefed to go in at mast height. I knew the masts on the *Tirpitz* were 125 feet high, so I

approached at 200 feet for bombing accuracy. On our estimated time of arrival I could see a hole in the cloud so I let down through that in tight circles, to maintain sight of the sea. If I had gone into cloud it would have been very risky. I could see the ship nestling against the side of the fjord, but as we let down, every gun in the area opened up at us. Our navigation had been perfect. We were told the best way to avoid the defences was to approach down the fjord at low level. They were using searchlights and plenty of tracer rounds. We could see it bouncing off the water. My second pilot, another Canadian, Sgt Hammond, stood alongside me to take over if I was hit. He looked through the window, saw all the mayhem and ducked down again. He did this several times bobbing up and down, and I broke out laughing; probably through hysteria. We could see ahead the low cloud obscuring the sides of the fjord in the darkness on our planned route ahead. We were not going to get anywhere near the *Tirpitz*, and would have probably flown into the hills if we did. These decisions were all being taken very rapidly in a matter of seconds, so I decided to abort. We saw a wide clear snowfield and dumped our weapons there, and started our journey home.

When they arrived back at Lossiemouth there was great disappointment, and Reg found he was the only one to discover the hole in the cloud, locate the ship and be shot at. The rest of the force never saw the target, mainly due to navigation and weather, so the bombs were jettisoned and they returned to the UK. However, the operation was to prove costly as six aircraft failed to return, no doubt due to the above influences.

Another attempt was planned quickly, but poor weather both in Scotland and Norway stalled any prompt plans, and the squadron returned to Linton-on-Ouse after five days. After a wait of almost a month, the raid was on again, and Reg and the squadron flew back to Lossiemouth on 23 April. After waiting for a couple of days, the force, including the No. 35 Squadron aircraft led by their CO Squadron Leader Jimmy Marks, left for Norway at 20.30 hours on 27 April, and on this occasion the conditions were better and the attack went ahead. This time they were all armed with special 1,000-lb spherical mines. The Lane crew were in W1019 TL-U. Reg commented: 'They were round balls and looked like sea mines for shipping. I think we had four aboard each aircraft. We would drop in a salvo as the target was only the length of the ship.'

The plan was for the 'mine-armed' Halifaxes to drop their weapons on the hillside, intending to have them roll down and explode under the vulnerable underside of the vessel. 'This time it was clear and we could easily see the island we were to use as an approach marker,' continued Reg. 'We had flown in loose formation across the North Sea. My friend Don MacIntyre, in "S for Sugar" was in the same group. By the time we arrived the Germans had started the smoke generators, and the fjord was rapidly filling up. Our timed run from the island would be important. I watched Don go in, and he was hit immediately.'

Ian Hewitt, navigator on W1048 TL-S told the author: 'We had to approach at low level, the climb steeply toward the side of the fjord, effectively throwing the mines at the hillside so they would roll down under the *Tirpitz*, exploding beneath the weaker under hull of the vessel. It was very difficult with all the flak around. The whole experience was very unpleasant.' 'Sugar' was hit in the port outer engine as they left the target. Ian Hewitt continued: 'It was burning and we looked for somewhere to put the aircraft down as we could not gain height to bail out. Ahead of us was a lake [Lake Hocklingen]; we could not be certain if it was frozen, but it seemed right for us.' The crew all managed to step out on to the partly frozen surface, although the flight engineer, Sergeant Vic Stevens was injured. He was taken prisoner, but all the others evaded, and with the help of some Norwegians managed to make their way to Sweden, eventually arriving back in the UK. (The aircraft 'S for Sugar' also returned to the UK in 1973, and is now on display in the RAF Museum, Hendon – the only example of an early Mk II Halifax in existence. However, at the time of writing, another No. 35 Squadron Halifax has been found at the bottom of a fjord near Trondheim, and consideration is being given as to whether it should be recovered.)

As for Reg, he could not worry about his friend as he had his own troubles to contend with. There were gun emplacements everywhere, mostly 20mm light flak, even on the tops of the hills, firing down at the aircraft. 'We were being clobbered, with the aircraft being hit all over. I was expecting us to blow up as one shell in the fuel tanks would take us out. Bill Sykes, the Navigator, timed the run and as we dropped the mines I pulled up over the hills to get away from the murderous flak. One of the engines was losing coolant, so I had to feather that propeller once we were out of the immediate danger. I checked all the crew and amazingly no one was hurt, so I gave thanks.' So it would be a long slow flight back to

Scotland on three engines. When they touched down at base he inspected W1019. 'There were holes all over it including several big ones in the fuselage on both sides. The most serious had been one that went through the main spar, almost shattering it. A few inches either side would have hit the fuel tanks and it would have all been over.' Reg noted in the squadron ORB record: 'Mines dropped in position believed between land and ship. Target obscured by smoke.'

The following day seven aircraft returned to Trondheim. Reg had volunteered to go but the engineering officer said the aircraft was too badly damaged: 'The wing might fold in severe manoeuvres', he was warned. So Reg was not tasked with this raid, but after two aircraft failed to return, he was sent on a sortie of over 6 hours in W7658 to search for survivors, which was unsuccessful. The missing aircraft were W1053 TL-G of Pilot Officer J.R. Roe, and W7656 TL-P of Flight Lieutenant D. Petley. Another aircraft lost on that 27 April raid was that of the new CO of No. 10 Squadron, Wing Commander Don Bennett, who also evaded via Sweden and returned to resume command of his squadron. Bennett was to have a major influence on Reg's life later as the founder of No. 8 'Pathfinder' Group of Bomber Command. The crews returned to Linton-on-Ouse on 30 March; out of twelve aircraft that had left Linton only four returned. They did not know if they had hit the ship, and with so many losses the airmen were very dejected.

About six weeks later, Reg was in the officers' mess when Don MacIntyre strolled in. Reg thought he was seeing a ghost. The last time he had seen Don's plane it was going down in flames, now Don was able to recount his story to his squadron chums, of the long hike over the snow-covered hills, being lost and then discovered by a local farmer who was a 'quisling' (in this case a Norwegian collaborator), escape from him and eventual arrival in Sweden, and the flight home in the bomb bay of a civilian BOAC Mosquito. Having been shot down over Europe, Don was now posted away from No. 35 Squadron to duties in the Middle East, but he remained firm friends with Reg for the rest of their lives.

At this time Reg was quartered in a building that was a half-size Nissen hut, sharing it with another officer, Peter Cribb. They got on well, but there was little privacy, except for a sheet hanging from the ceiling as a crude divider, and the only illumination being a single light bulb they shared, hanging in the middle of the hut. One night when they came home in a jubilant and 'well-oiled' state after a mess party, they climbed into bed as quickly as possible; these huts had a terrible reputation for being damp and freezing and the 'last up' was never keen to get out of bed and turn off the light. So when it became obvious that neither could persuade the other to get out of bed and switch the light off, Peter, a man of great resource, decided the best thing to do was to pull out his service revolver and take pot-shots at the bulb. But in his inebriated state, and shivering from the cold, he kept missing, even emptying the chamber of the gun. Reg thought, with typical Canadian overstatement, 'I'm a better shot than him – I'm Canadian!', and proceeded to empty his revolver too, also without success. On hearing their racket, their 'batman', a chap with much experience of rowdy officers, strolled into the hut resplendent in a silk dressing gown, and offered the comment, 'Sir, have I your permission to reload?'

Part III: Pathfinder

9. Tirpitz and the Ruhr

On 4 May, the squadron was briefed for Stuttgart, with Reg in his new role of acting flying officer, a second dickey, and his regular crew of Sykes, Thorpe, Haxby, Williams and Phillips, in R9483 TL-C. However, the aircraft had mechanical problems, and they turned for home at Ostend. Two days later Reg did a 'bullseye' exercise around the Irish Sea in W7676 TL-P. This aircraft, 'P-Peter', was to become the regular mount for him and his crew, and they were to complete sixteen operations together in it. Eventually it was lost on an operation being flown by another No. 35 Squadron crew after Reg had completed his first tour. Reg told the author this was one of the most reliable aircraft on the squadron. A few days later, on the night of 8/9 May, they took it on their first raid together to the port of Warnemünde on the Baltic coast near Rostock, a trip of 7 hours 20 minutes, followed by an attack on Mannheim on 19 May, carrying a 'second dickey' pilot, Pilot Officer Dobson. The next two raids were to be quite different.

However, on the afternoon of 19 May, before the Warnemünde trip, Reg was told to do some formation flying in 'P-Peter' W7676 with Pilot Officer K. Reynolds in W7749 TL-F. The plan was they were to fly off the North Yorkshire coast and meet up with an RAF Anson. The Anson duly appeared and Reg could see the windows on the starboard side of the fuselage had been removed and several plate cameras on tripods installed. There was a figure crouched inside, all wrapped up in flying clothing and moving from one camera to another. It was the well-known staff photographer for *Flight* magazine, Charles E. Brown, and the colour images he took that afternoon became some of the best wartime photographs of a Halifax in flight ever known. Even today they are reproduced widely and used as posters, book covers and on many museum souvenirs, and even on a brand of beer in Yorkshire. During a visit to his home in Victoria in 2001, Reg commented to the author that he could see his new light-grey flying gloves on the controls, and we managed to date this important photograph. He vividly remembered being asked to fly in front of various cloud formations, that were reproduced in some of the black and white photos also taken at the time. He had no idea his Halifax was so well publicised. The author believes they are the only known surviving colour photographs of an early Halifax Mk II in flight. W7676 was eventually lost on the night of 28/29 August 1942, failing to return from an operation to Nuremberg.

On 28/29 March 1942 Bomber Command had carried out a major attack on the city of Lübeck, leaving much of the medieval city in flames. It was a target selected by Bomber Command's chief, Air Marshal Arthur 'Bomber' Harris, known to his crews as 'Butch', for the ease of identification, and to see if a large force could totally destroy a town. In this case 234 aircraft were sent out, dropping 144 tons of incendiaries and 144 tons of high explosives. Some 13 aircraft were lost. At this time Bomber Command, which was – in the summer of 1942 – still the smallest of the RAF Commands, was being expected to produce fully successful results, with still only a modicum of navigational aids.

This raid to Lübeck, and the follow-up to Rostock, and the Heinkel factory in particular, were very successful and provided a morale boost for the Command. Harris thought by amalgamating the training units with the operational units he could muster 1,000 aircraft. The plan, called Operation Millennium – not a name Harris favoured – was approved by Churchill in a meeting at Chequers, the prime minister's residence, late on a Sunday afternoon. The moon would be full by the end of May, and the weather could be expected to be reasonable, though there might be cloud over the North Sea. The target selected was Cologne; it was not too deep into Germany, and the weather in the area at that time of year would be good. Harris noted in his memoires that ' ... the organisation of the force involved a tremendous amount of work throughout the Command. Training units put up 366 aircraft, and No. 3 Group put up 250 aircraft, No. 4 Group 146 aircraft and the balance coming from Nos 1 and 5 Groups. Apart from a very few aircraft from Flying Training Command, the whole force of 1,047 bombers came from Bomber Command.' Army Co-operation and Fighter Commands put up aircraft to carry out diversionary raids, and attacks on enemy airfields. The Halifaxes of No. 4 Group would be in the final phase of the attack.

TIRPITZ AND THE RUHR

So on 31 May at 00.05 hours, Reg took off in 'Peter' with his crew of Pilot Officers Dobson and James and Sergeants Thorpe, Richmond, Williams and Haxby, together with the other twenty aircraft of No. 35 Squadron. It turned out to be an uneventful trip, Reg noting ' ... bomb bursts observed on target, incendiaries seem to be spreading. 'Nickels' [author's note – leaflets] dropped eleven minutes before target. Me 110 seen over target – no encounter.' The results were devastating, nonetheless. Over 600 acres of Cologne's built-up areas were destroyed. Being part of the later phase of the operation, Reg remembered the large conflagrations of fire spreading through the city, a memorable sight from the bomber stream. As the Halifaxes were in the third phase of the attack their losses were less, only 1.9% as opposed to 4.8% in the leading phases, probably because by then the enemy defences had been overwhelmed. The raid had been a huge success and a great morale booster for the Command and the British public.

With the weather favourable, and the 'Thousand Bomber' force still in place, Harris decided to go again on the night of 1/2 June, this time against Essen. Not quite the full 1,000, 956 bombers made the trip. Some 138 Halifaxes from No. 4 Group, including the Lane crew in 'P-Peter', left Yorkshire late that night, but the results were not as good. The regular Essen haze was a contributory factor, and daylight reconnaissance revealed little damage in the city. It was to be the last 'Thousand Bomber' raid until the end of June. No. 35 Squadron put on a follow-up raid the night after, 3 June, and Reg with crew in 'Peter' returned on an uneventful trip of some 4½ hours.

By this time, due to his survival, Reg was now becoming one of the more experienced pilots on the squadron. Having already been promoted to acting flying officer earlier in the year, he was now quickly promoted to acting flight lieutenant, confirmed soon afterwards, and within the month he was raised to acting squadron leader on taking control of the squadron's B Flight. Following raids on Bonn and Osnabrück on 16 and 19 June respectively, the momentum for the squadron switched to another priority. At this stage of the war Bomber Command was working to support the Navy in the Battle of the Atlantic, with regular raids on German naval targets and U-boat pens. The raids on Emden and Bremen became known as 'milk runs'. Reg went to each of these targets in W7676 three times in June and July. The first one to Bremen was another 'Thousand Bomber' raid. This was followed by Duisburg on three consecutive nights from 21 July. After a raid on Hamburg on the night of 26/27 July, the Lane crew went to Saarbrücken on a raid against a rail marshalling yard. When they arrived over the target they found almost no flak. Reg remembered: 'We dropped flares and identified our target, then flew back and forth dropping our bombs one at a time. It was like being on a practice range. When we got back we found we had misidentified the target and hit a smaller town nearby. There was a great "ruckus" about that. Saarbrücken was a well-defended target and we should have realised.' After one more operation to Düsseldorf, Reg's first tour of thirty operations was complete. It was at this time he was awarded a Distinguished Flying Cross, the citation being as follows:

> Throughout his tour of operations, this officer has displayed unshakeable determination to reach his target. His skill, together with his coolness under fire, whatever the weather, has inspired his crew with extreme confidence. Some of the targets he attacked include Berlin, Brest, Cologne and Bremen. His splendid captaincy and outstanding courage have set a splendid example.

After some leave, Reg's posting was to be to a heavy conversion unit (HCU) instructing bomber crews. There were now sufficient Halifaxes and Lancasters for the RAF to set up these units, rather than initiate a training unit within a squadron, such as Reg had been through earlier that year. However, he really did not relish going to the HCU, and as luck would have it a new squadron commander had been posted in to No. 35 Squadron, Wing Commander Jimmy Marks. Reg knew him from his days at the OTU at Abingdon, and remembered: 'He was a very popular chap, with a DSO and DFC, tall and affable. Within a couple of weeks he got to know his crews and their family responsibilities very well. I pleaded with him not to go training. I really didn't fancy that.'

The raid on Saarbrücken had proved there was a need for a proper marking system, and at this time Don Bennett's pleas to assemble a dedicated group to carry out the task had been accepted. 'Butch' Harris was set against the formation of an 'elite' group, preferring to have 'raid leaders' (Harris's description) within each squadron. On 14 June 1942 he received a directive from the Chief of Air Staff to select a squadron from each group to form a new Pathfinder unit, numbered No. 8 Group. Accepting the inevitable, Harris pressed ahead with its establishment, under the auspices of No. 3 Group, to be led by Don Bennett, promoted to group captain. Eventually, when the group was elevated to a separate organisation, Bennett would be promoted to air commodore, and then to air vice marshal. The No. 4 Group squadron allocated to this new group was No. 35 Squadron at RAF Linton-on-Ouse. Jimmy Marks was a great leader to take the squadron into the pathfinder role.

On hearing about the transfer to the HCU, Reg went to Jimmy and told him: 'I don't want to be an instructor. Is there any chance I can stay with the squadron? I understand one can do two tours, back to back, if you are in the Pathfinder Group?' Jimmy Marks agreed to look into it, and in a couple of days came back and said: 'Yes, I have the authority. You can stay with the squadron and come to Pathfinders. However, you should take a good rest after being on 'ops' since November, so take three weeks' leave after we move the squadron to its new base at Graveley.'

So on 15 August 1942, Reg and his crew flew W7676 to Graveley, in Cambridgeshire, the county where the new group would be based. For the next few weeks he busied himself in the job of bringing the squadron south, flying between Yorkshire and Cambridge. After his leave, spent with relatives in London, on 27 September he was attached to the No. 1502 Beam Approach Flight (a technique of blind landing using opposing radio beams) at RAF Driffield, Yorkshire. Employed there flying Oxford trainers, he arrived back with the squadron at the beginning of October. While he was on leave Reg had missed the first couple of raids of the Pathfinders, the first being on Flensberg on the night of 18/19 August. Reg continued: 'On return to the squadron I was shocked to find we had lost the CO Jimmy Marks in my Halifax, TL-P W7676, with another crew on the raid to Nuremberg on the night of 28/29 August. His loss hit me and the squadron hard; he was such a great leader. For his replacement we had W/Cdr B.V. Robinson, DSO, DFC, back in charge; the exact opposite of Jimmy, and not at all popular.'

Being a new station, Graveley had opened in March 1942, and passed to No. 8 Group in August that year; it had been built fresh on a farmer's fields. Graveley was a shock for the men of No. 35 Squadron, far different from the comforts of the pre-war station of Linton-on-Ouse. The men were accommodated in Nissen huts, and there was mud everywhere. It did have one advantage – it was one of the first operational airfields equipped with FIDO (Fog, Intensive, Dispersal Of). This was a system whereby the main runway was lined with petrol-burning pipes to clear the area of fog.

First tested in February 1942 by Don Bennett, it proved its worth later in the year, on 19 November, when four of No. 35 Squadron's Halifaxes made use of it, and landed safely.

In the early days the living conditions at Graveley were very poor. Gastro-enteritis was rife among the crews, causing all sorts of problems. Reg remembered one crew's experience that was symptomatic of the times. The Halifax was only equipped with an Elsan bucket-style toilet, at the rear of the aircraft. To use it at altitude was very cold and uncomfortable. One pilot, who shall not be named, decided: 'I'm not going to use that thing. It's so cold I might stick to it!' He chose to use the newspaper they had their snacks wrapped in, placed it on the floor, did the necessary, and then in a matter of poor judgement, instead of placing it in the Elsan, opened a hatch and threw it out of the aircraft. As he opened the hatch the stream of air took the contents of the paper, being mostly liquid, and distributed it all over the interior. He returned to his cockpit, and the entire crew were subject to the aroma permeating the fuselage. 'Switch on oxygen was the cry!' On return to Graveley, as the crew left their aircraft the sergeant in charge of the ground crew put his head in the entrance and asked 'Everything all right?' Then he cried, 'Oh S**T!' 'Exactly,' said the pilot, and trooped off leaving the ground crew to clean up the mess, and bring the aircraft back to an acceptable standard.

'This is how conditions were,' said Reg. 'We should not have been flying. We had a really excellent likeable doctor, a West Indian chap, and he took a sample of the water supply to the Adjutant, a chap called Bingham, a staid Englishman. I happened to be in his office at the time. The "Doc" offered the sample to Bingham with an offer to make a cup of tea with it. "No way, there are bits floating in it," said Bingham. "Then swear to me you will see to the matter straightaway," said the "Doc". The episode lasted three to four weeks. It was not a happy time.'

Part III: Pathfinder

10. Pathfinder Force

It was now the beginning of the battle to destroy the German industrial powerbase. On the night of 13 October Reg was off on a raid to Kiel with some new crew members in his new Halifax II, TL-N W7866: navigator Flight Lieutenant Mack, bomb aimer Flying Officer Webster, wireless operator Pilot Officer Thorpe, flight engineer Flight Sergeant Haxby and gunners Sergeants Tullock and James Scannell. Two nights later it was Cologne again. At this time they were still experimenting with marking methods initially developed by the squadron earlier in the year. The technique at this time just consisted of the Pathfinder bombers releasing marker flares at the appointed location, usually designated by the Gee navigational aid, a method whereby two radio beams from two points in the UK coincided to provide a release point. The disadvantage of the system was its range – a maximum of 400 miles – and the ability of the Germans to jam the signals, once they had figured out the system. The technique, developed by No. 4 Group, was known as 'Shaker'. This involved breaking the bombing force into three sections: the 'Illuminators', the 'Target Markers' and the 'Followers'. The 'Illuminator' team, all equipped with Gee, would arrive over the target first, dropping bundles of flares at 10-second intervals, backed up by high-explosive bombs. The planned result would be that the target would be indicated by lines of flares to guide the 'Target Markers', which would drop maximum loads of incendiary bombs. This would cause a conflagration clearly visible to the 'Followers' who would finish the raid with high explosives.

On 24/25 October the Lane crew flew across the Alps in W7866 TL-N to bomb Turin, without any incident. After a raid to Hamburg on 9/10 November, Reg was detached to the Handley Page factory at Radlett, missing a later raid on Turin on 18/19 November when the CO, Wing Commander Robinson, had a rough trip. Four flares had failed to drop and caused a fire in the fuselage. Fearing the aircraft would break up he told his crew to bail out, but before he could leave the aircraft the fire abated and finally extinguished itself. By using the navigator's log and flight plan, he managed to bring the aircraft, DT488 TL-S, home alone, crash-landing at RAF Colerne in Wiltshire. Robinson eventually received a bar to his DFC.

On 22/23 November it was back to the Ruhr and Stuttgart, in 'N-Nuts' a trip of just over 7 hours. After this, over the next couple of months, Reg's time seems to have been taken up on training flights, many of them 'bullseyes' around cities in the UK, improving navigation techniques. His next operational raids were on 30 January and 3 February when the Lane crew flew to Hamburg in W7874 TL-D, the aircraft he had used over the past months for the 'bullseyes'. On the first raid he had to return early with engine trouble, but the second was completed with no problems. Reg was now commander of No. 35 Squadron's C Flight, and confirmed as squadron leader.

This would now be an opportunity to review Reg's thoughts on Pathfinder techniques. Much of the material this author has received, in addition to personal conversations, is from interviews with Reg Lane in May 1978, after his retirement from the RCAF. As explained earlier, Gee was the only navigational aid available to the bomber crews in the early days; later this was joined by H2S, which was an omnidirectional radar-based system allowing the navigator to gain a picture on a screen of the topography below the aeroplane. Aircraft using this system were distinguished by a distinctive radome under the rear fuselage. In Reg's words: 'It was a map-reading radar, and a good operator with a good set in good working condition could pick out the target area quite accurately blind over cloud. It could pick up land topography, or built up areas, but not any specific building. An operator would check maps when planning the trip, and identify relevant features, and that would help approach. Then by offsetting the features he could know when they were at the release point and release the bombs. He was in the same sense as a bomb sight.' One advantage of H2S was that it was difficult to jam as it was based on an emission from each aircraft. However, later the Germans did develop a system using the bomber aircraft's H2S signals to home in on by a night fighter. H2S became operational in Bomber Command, just as the year turned, but it was only fitted in a few aircraft, and it would take a while to train up effective operators.

There was another more compact system for marking, called Oboe. This was the most accurate system used in the war. The bombing aircraft, usually a de Havilland Mosquito, flew at a constant arc from a beam transmitting from Trimingham on the Norfolk coast. When it was at the correct range from the ground station at Walmer, on the Kent coast, a second operator there would indicate the time of release for the markers. Reg remembered: 'Oboe was incredibly accurate. The Mosquitoes were operating at heights of 30,000 feet, and yet their accuracy was often within 100 yards of the aiming point.' Reg told the author: 'After the Lancaster, the Mosquito is my favourite aircraft. I did get to fly one later in the war.'

As already explained, in earlier times crews dropped their flares, coloured differently, supposedly on the city. For cloud-covered targets, forecast by the met. officer, 'sky markers' were developed to drop on clouds, aircraft then following up by dropping their bombs as the markers came into view in the bomb-sight. The probability of the sky markers drifting, particularly in high winds, could be a problem. Also there was a risk of 'creep back' when the following aircraft started to bomb short of the target; this was due to the earlier markers being slowly carried away from the target. Eventually this led to the allocation of a 'master bomber' (and deputy master bomber in case the former was shot down). Reg continued: 'His job was to come in behind the "Illuminators", and those who had bombed on radar, to the conflagration, in the middle of which theoretically was the aiming point. They would have gone in at H minus 7 mins. He was to drop markers, say red in colour, exactly on that aiming point. "H-Hour" would be the time the main force was to arrive; he would go in at H minus 5. After dropping he would do a circuit to check his accuracy. Was he accurate? It might be if he was inaccurate he had to go around and drop more markers, which he hoped would be more accurate. At the same time other Pathfinders would be coming in dropping markers of different colours. If he was accurate on the first run he would reinforce those markers with more.' The master bomber would then transmit on VHF radio to the main force the location to drop their weapons using the colours of the markers to help with precision. He would say, 'Bomb on the red markers', or if inexact use the other markers, such as, 'Take the northerly flares', or 'Bomb to the south-west of the greens', for example. It was a decidedly dangerous role for the master bomber, which is why there was always a deputy. Often on a big raid the master bomber would be circling the target for up to 30 minutes, just circling and giving instructions.

Reg clarified the situation: 'There was no air traffic control up there, flying upwind into the main stream could be dicey. It was often safer to drop down to a lower height, and take your chances with bombs coming down, than dodging the incoming bombers. The chances of being hit by a falling bomb were less than colliding in mid-air. In situations like this, it could be that the Master Bomber was incapacitated, either by damage to the aircraft or coning by searchlights. He would then call to his deputy, "You go in and take over, I'm having difficulty." In the case of the inability to transmit by radio failure, the deputy would take over on his own initiative. If the deputy was not required, he would turn for home taking his bombs with him.'

The Luftwaffe's night-fighter operations were now building up to a peak, and also taking a heavy toll of the bombers. With the installation of the Lichtenstein airborne radar systems – in Messerschmitt Bf 110s and Junkers Ju 88s – and, later on, the Schräge Musik upward-firing cannons – mounted mostly in Ju 88s and Heinkel He 219 Uhus (Owls) – the fighters were now regularly mixing with the bomber stream. In addition the Wilde Sau (Wild Boar) single-seat fighters vectored on the bombers by ground controllers, a scheme devised by Oberst (Major) Hajo Hermann, was also brought into use in time for the 27/28 July 1943 raid on Hamburg. Reg had completed his second tour by that time and luckily was not involved.

As part of the counter to these operations, Bomber Command came up with the 'Diversion Raid' tactic. The German radars would start to track a sortie as it built up to fly across the North Sea. The fighter controllers along the defensive 'Kammhuber Line', named after General Josef Kammhuber who had been designated in charge of night-fighter operations by Goering, would then plan their defence and fighter deployment accordingly. So the RAF devised 'spoof' raids whereby an alternative force, or forces, was sent in a diverging direction from the main force to try and fool the fighter controllers. Reg remarked: 'Often there would be more than one raid in one evening. Mostly the others would be conducted by No. 5 Group, which was now a big Group fully equipped with Lancasters. They gained authority from Bomber Command to carry out their form of very low level marking, as perfected by Cheshire. This irritated Don Bennett, OC No. 8 Group, who hated anyone getting ahead of him, or coming up with an idea that he had not come up with. He took a very much "dog in the manger" attitude that he would continue with high level marking for his Group. Bennett also came up with the code names for the markers, using Antipodean names such as "Wanganui" for sky markers.'

During this second tour, all with No. 35 Squadron, Reg's operations were all against the might of the German war machine, with the exception of an operation to Turin on the night of 4/5 February 1943. On that trip, in W7808 TL-P, he remembered: 'The target was covered in cloud, but we knew Turin was in a relatively flat area, and the Italian defences were not that good. So I dropped through the cloud. Silly, really, but it was the "press on" attitude. We dropped our bombs on the target – I think the aiming point was the station – and then returned.' In the first four months of 1943 he flew to Berlin three times; Stuttgart, Cologne and Nuremberg twice, and Kiel. All these raids were carried out in Halifax Mk II aircraft. On the raid to Cologne on 14/15 February, Reg and his crew, in W7874 TL-U, had their first direct attack by a night fighter. In his interview he recalled:

> It was our first real 'tangle' with a night fighter. We had seen the odd fighter, but never so far exchanged shots with one. We were on our way home; it was a lovely clear night, when my rear gunner, Sgt Jimmy Scannell, who was an Irishman, shouted, 'We have a fighter coming up, Skipper. It's a 110 [Messerschmitt Bf 110]. I've got him. Be ready for directions.' The fighter approached from one beam, and one had to turn into the fighter, just before he fired. At the right moment, Jimmy said 'Turn!' and we did. The enemy pilot's shell went right over the top of us. A few moments later Jimmy called, 'He's coming back. I've got him again, get ready to turn – turn!' This time the Me 110 'clobbered' us, his shells going through the port wing. One of the port engines was hit. In the cockpit we were having a busy night. I had to feather one engine [author's note: he could not remember which one] as he had hit the header tank. Jimmy then said, 'Here he comes a third time, Skipper.' I asked, 'What are you doing, Jimmy?' 'I can't fire my guns, Skipper. They are frozen, and I can't shoot back. Just give me a direction.' 'Holy Crow!' I called and I literally stood the aircraft on its nose and dived for safety. We were getting close to the coast, and there were cloud tops about 2,000ft. So I headed for them to escape another attack. Jimmy had tested his guns on the way out to Cologne, and

they had been fine. It turned out we had been through a temperature inversion with high cold air, and he had picked up some condensation which had frozen the breech blocks of the machine guns. It was brave of Jimmy Scannell to sit there, knowing the German pilot would realise something was wrong with no return fire, and calmly give me directions.

They got home safely after a flight of 3½ hours. Being a rear gunner was a tough job. Often they were the first crew member to perish in an encounter with a fighter. When cannon shells hit the turret, and the unfortunate occupant was killed, there was little left, and back at base all the ground crew could do was hose the turret and rear fuselage out, as we learned in an earlier section of this book.

There was an interesting end to the story of that raid. Reg continued: 'When the ground crew were inspecting the aircraft to check there was nothing left inside, they found that one of the cannon shells had gone through all five fuel tanks in the starboard wing, and lodged in the wall of the end one. It was an incendiary, but hadn't gone off. They removed it, but as it was being disarmed it exploded, badly injuring an armourer, and blowing his hand off. If that shell had gone off it would have taken the starboard wing off and we would have gone down. It just made you feel your "number wasn't up" and that is all there was to it. It was an incredible bit of luck for us.'

On a further comment on the Halifax defences, Reg pointed out that the mid-upper and nose turrets were ' ... a bit of a waste of time. The only time the upper turret was useful was on daylight raids when fighters came from above. Night fighters came in from behind and below. The belly of the Halifax was the most vulnerable spot, and they developed a system with cannons mounted firing upwards [author's note – the Schräge Musik mentioned earlier], usually in a Ju 88. If the cannon shells hit the fuel tanks in the wings, or the bomb load – that was it!' Reg added: 'The only time our front gunner became useful, I remember, was on a return trip and we were over Denmark, probably after a raid on Berlin, on a beautiful clear night, bright moonlight. I could see what looked like an airfield ahead. I got the engineer to go into the nose turret, and warned Jimmy Scannell over the radio. We were down about 500 to 1,000ft, you could see for miles. It was too late to change course, so I said to the two of them, "It's up to you. Shoot at anything you see." There were aeroplanes parked in lines, and they just let go with everything they had, spraying machine-gun bullets everywhere. They had great fun! There was no return fire or flak – we were lucky again. We never knew the results of that episode, but we sure hit some aircraft.'

Berlin had always been a problematic target. Firstly there were the long distances involved and, secondly, with no clearly visible geographical features, such as an estuary or hills, it was a struggle for the H2S radar to recognise features. These were early days for this radar, and operators were still learning. Reg went to the city three times in March 1943, as recalled, initially on the night of 1/2 March, in W7874 TL-U, with the squadron CO Wing Commander Robinson as second pilot, when Reg and the other Pathfinders had difficulty spotting the exact aiming point and bombs were scattered all over the city. The second two trips to Berlin were at the end of the month, on the 27th/28th, when the raid was a spectacular failure, the Pathfinders dropping their flares well short of the target. Interestingly, one concentration of bombs hit a secret Luftwaffe stores depot at Tetlow in the suburbs, destroying a large quantity of valuable radar and electronic equipment; the Luftwaffe were impressed by the accuracy of the raid, which they thought was the main target and not knowing it was a 'fluke'. Two nights later, on 29/30 March, the squadron returned, with Reg in DT806 TL-Z, but he came back early after only 5 hours in the air. The raid brought to an end the first part of AVM Arthur 'Bomber' Harris's campaign against the German capital.

After a raid to Kiel in DT806 again, Reg finished the last operation of his second tour. This was to the Škoda works at Pilsen, Czechoslovakia, in Halifax JB787 TL-Z. By this time some of his crew had completed their tour but Jim Scannell, Haxby and Thorpe were still in the crew. However, he had as navigator Squadron Leader Bob Trickett, a Canadian, who was also on his last sortie. Reg remembered:

> It was a long trip – the longest I had been on, almost eight and a half hours. The target was covered in heavy cloud, and as we went lower it became industrial haze, like 'smog'. I don't think anyone else dared venture below the clouds. We dropped some flares but did not see any point in dropping markers because of the haze. As we climbed out I said to Bob, 'Let's head back.' It was one of those nights when there had been two raids, and the other was on Mannheim, just slightly

to the north of our track home. As we had not been shot at or seen any flak, I suggested to Bob, 'Why don't we go and have a look at the other target and we might be able to give a report if it's clear?' As we left the Czech border the cloud suddenly cleared, like a wall disappearing, and Fl Lt Michael Mack, our H2S operator, said, 'We are getting terribly close to Mannheim.' We had strayed too far north and were right over the other target planned for that night, with no bombs. The previous raid had gone home. Suddenly we were locked into searchlights. 'Bob, you S.O.B! You've got us right over the target; I only wanted to fly nearby!' I decided to dive the aircraft, and for that reason the flak was above and behind us. We didn't pick up any damage, but it had been a 'hairy' moment. My final words to Bob Trickett: 'Bob, this was your and my last trip, and you nearly got us killed!' Luck had been on our side again.

Back at Graveley, Squadron Leader Reg Lane was 'screened'; he had completed fifty-one operations. His next posting came through on 11 May 1943, when he was transferred to the Pathfinder Force Navigation Training Unit at nearby RAF Gransden Lodge, just a few miles from his previous base. Gransden Lodge was a wartime-built airfield, on the Cambridgeshire/Bedfordshire border and had been opened in 1942. It became a base in the Pathfinder group in April 1943 and was to figure strongly in Reg's story. His experience was much needed to train pilots and bring his expertise to bear on them. Over the rest of the month, in addition to more Halifax training flights, he at last got to fly a Lancaster on 15 May. On the first flight in an aircraft that was to become synonymous with his name, he took Avro Lancaster W4162 aloft for just over an hour, completing three more familiarisation flights over the next two days. The next month he had a flight in his declared favourite aircraft, a de Havilland Mosquito, DZ409; it was to be his only flight in the type, which had such an effect on the efficiency of No. 8 'Pathfinder' Group. During this time Reg was gazetted for a Distinguished Service Order medal. The citation read: 'Squadron Leader Lane has been engaged in operational duties for a long period over a wide range of targets. His missions have been marked by unvarying success. As a Flight Commander he has rendered most valuable service and his leadership and example have been inspiring to all the aircrew with whom he has come into contact. This officer has recently been on operational sorties to such targets as Berlin, Stuttgart, and Munich, and by his courage and devotion to duty has achieved many outstanding successes.'

Further training continued until the end of July when he was called to RCAF HQ in Lincoln's Inn Fields in London. He was to be sent to Canada on his very special 'operation'. During the meeting in London he was introduced to a 'scratch' crew, none of whom he knew. The crew consisted of Pilot Officer Steve Boczar and Sergeant Bill Wright, DFM, both from Saskatoon, Saskatchewan; Pilot Officer John Carere of Cochrane, Ontario; Sergeant Ross Webb of Glenevon, Saskatchewan; Flight Sergeant Reg Burgar of Biggar, Saskatchewan; and Sergeant Mike Baczinski of Brandon, Manitoba.

The story of the Canadian Lancasters is interesting. No. 6 (RCAF) Bomber Group had come into operation on 1 January 1943 after the insistence of the Canadian prime minister, William McKenzie-King's pleas with Churchill to have a Canadian-funded organisation within the Allied war effort, in return for Canada's commitment to the British Commonwealth Air Training Plan. Based north of the city of York, the group had been initially equipped with Wellingtons, then later supplied mainly with Halifax bombers, although four squadrons had Hercules-engined Lancaster IIs. Air Vice Marshal George Brookes, the commanding officer of the group, born a Yorkshireman but now a committed Canadian, repeatedly pleaded to his boss, Air Marshal Arthur 'Butch' Harris, to have the group provided throughout with Lancasters. In fact most of the Canadian crews preferred the Halifax, because of its better survivability record. The capacity to move easily about the fuselage of the Halifax was a big advantage, and it could absorb punishment well.

However, Brookes was convinced, like Harris, that the Lancaster was the 'gleaming sword'. The deal brokered by Rolls-Royce for the American Packard Company to manufacture the Merlin engine in the USA was the 'clincher'. The Aircraft Division of the National Steel Corporation – stirringly renamed by the government 'Victory Aircraft Corporation' – at Malton (author's note: Malton is the northern part of today's Toronto airport), would build the Lancaster under licence from Avro, powered exclusively by the American Merlins. A standard aircraft, R5727, from the first production batch made at Avro Woodford, was sent over to Canada, along with two Avro engineers to assist in the appraisal of the aircraft in January 1943 to act as a pattern, and the government set the date for the release of the first aircraft as 6 August 1943. Victory were not happy; they were convinced the rush would mean the aircraft would not be fully ready, especially the electrics, but the date had been set in stone by the politicians.

Reg took Lancaster W4126 up to Prestwick, having had extra experience on the type on some cross-country exercises at Gransden and, as related earlier, departed to Canada on Liberator AL590 to Gander, Newfoundland. Then it was on to Dorval, Montreal, arriving on 10 July 1943. The flight left a lasting impression; he told the author in conversation:

> It was a freezing cold flight of about 11 hours, even though it was July, and I was accommodated lying on one of the bomb doors. I was glad I had been told to take all my bomber flying kit with me. I was continually nervous the pilot, Captain Bowen, would accidentally pull the 'open' lever, and didn't sleep much. I did get a chance to fly the aircraft for a short time; it was not as responsive as the Lancaster in my opinion. After a quick refuelling stop at Gander we were off on another four hour cold flight to Montreal. It was a hot July day at Dorval, and we quickly dived to the bar to cool off. I was wearing the usual British kit in Barathea material. Almost immediately, I was rushed off to Ottawa, caught up with the rest of the crew at Air Force HQ, and was called in to the office of the air force chief, Air Marshal Lloyd Breadner, an ex-WWI fighter pilot and a big man with a booming voice – a great chap. He said, 'I suppose you are going home to meet your families. You have ten days before you need to be at Victory Aircraft in Malton.' He had no idea we were mostly from the west of Canada.

Breadner then 'pulled rank' and called his executive officer, and demanded five places on an executive flight across Canada. The officer went white. Outside the office he said to Reg: 'Do you realise these flights are in Lockheed Lodestars, they only have fourteen seats, and they are usually full with priority diplomatic personnel? I don't know what is going to happen. It's going to be very difficult to get you guys on this flight!' Reg and the four crew members from western Canada followed him down to the Movements Centre, where the executive officer addressed a squadron leader by his first name and told him the problem. The other officer gulped, 'What tonight?' 'Yes, just get on the phone to Trans Canada Airlines and organise it.' The squadron leader held the phone up as he made the call, and they could hear the commotion at the other end of the line. 'Yes, I know you have priority customers but this is what the Chief wants.' Leaving him to sort matters out, Reg and his colleagues went to lunch, and when they came back, there were the travel warrants for the flight to Calgary and Vancouver.

Reg took the opportunity to go over to Victoria and see his parents. He had phoned from Ottawa, and they knew he was back in Canada, but the trip home was a big surprise. By the time he was back, the city had organised a civic reception and lunch, where Reg was presented with a silver salver by the mayor. There were speeches and publicity interviews, all to do with the war effort and Reg telling of his experiences, even though he did not like that too much. He told this author: 'It was all about "line shooting" and in Bomber Command we were not really happy about that, when so many of our friends were being lost. I was never really easy with it. We preferred to keep emotion out of the stories, and tell the facts about the good operations, and that is what I did through most of my interviews. The RCAF and government wanted as much publicity as possible as the war in Europe was so far removed from life in Canada.'

All too soon it was back to the east, and a long flight to Ottawa, in another Lodestar. They started a relentless round of publicity interviews and visits to the factory to meet the workers. There were more speeches, especially to the workers, telling them how important their contribution would be to the bombing effort. He got the chance to meet E.P. Taylor, the financier who was the moving force behind Victory Aircraft. 'We went for dinner at his house, a mansion on the edge of Toronto, a grand building with servants. It was a very grand affair,' Reg continued, 'and he was a great guy who just fired lots of questions at us, and made us feel at ease.'

The roll-out date of 6 August came and the Lancaster, KB700, was duly named 'Ruhr Express' by Mrs C.G. Power, wife of the air minister, with much celebration and a bottle of champagne 'cracked' against it. Although there had been a test flight by Avro personnel, it was not really ready to fly. In front of the assembled media and cameras, with the occasion announced by one of Canada's major actors, Lorne Greene (later to be known in the TV series *Bonanza*), the crew boarded the aircraft. The day was committed to film by the Film Board of Canada in *Target Berlin*, a truly 'jingoistic' epic recounting the day's events and subsequent flights.

Reg had this to say: 'When we climbed aboard in front of the cameras, and the engines started, none of the engine instruments worked – not one!' Contrary to press reports, the aircraft was not flown that day. According to Reg's log book he did not take the aircraft up until 12 August on a local familiarisation flight of 1½ hours. He told the author:

The aircraft was in a dreadful state. Not many of the cockpit instruments and few of the engine instruments worked. It was clearly dangerous, and I decided not to take it further. I felt I could not land it back at Malton, so we had discussion among us in the crew, and we flew it to Dorval, where the aircraft was quickly rolled into a hangar out of sight of prying eyes. There I told the manufacturer's personnel [author's note: including Ken Molson, later to write a history of Canadian aircraft manufacture, who had been on the project from the beginning, and was now brought in as 'troubleshooter'], who met us a day or so later, including the Rolls-Royce chap scrounging a lift back to the UK, 'Put it right and I'll come back when it's ready and see if it's safe to fly across the Atlantic.' The problem was with the wiring, and the aircraft had to be completely re-wired. As far as I know the aircraft never went back to Malton for repairs.

Further flight tests were carried out over Quebec, during one of which an engine failed at 22,000 feet. Molson had to go back to Malton to get a replacement engine and more tools. One of the crew, Reg Burgar, brought along a little poodle dog, Bambi, which was very popular at Malton, especially with the press, but Reg regarded as '... a bloody nuisance!' After quite a few more adjustments to the instrumentation and the engines, carried out by Rolls-Royce, they flew to Gander on Canada's east coast.

Reg continued: 'At Gander we met an experienced "Transatlantic Ferry" pilot, called Clangbourne; he was a very experienced pre-war pilot. The RCAF wanted nothing to go wrong, so he was seconded on to the crew for the trip across the ocean. We waited several days before the bad weather cleared and left on 15 September.' On arrival at Prestwick after a 10-hour flight, the dog was whisked away into quarantine, and they flew down to Northolt, to a more muted UK reception. Reg's place in Canadian air force history had been sealed. The Lancaster itself was flown away by Avro to Woodford, Manchester, for a full inspection. According to Avro historian Harry Holmes: 'The aircraft was never fully cured of all its faults. We did remove the belly twin machine gun mounting, as that was not wanted by the RAF.' However, the 'Ruhr Express' did eventually complete forty-nine successful sorties. It would figure again in Reg's story later in the year.

Reg was invited to a reception in London with the RCAF 'top brass', including C-in-C RCAF Overseas, Air Marshal H. Edwards, who asked

PART III: PATHFINDER

35 Sqn Halifax Mk.II W7676 TL-P being flown by Reg Lane on 12 May 1942 off the east coast of Yorkshire. One of a famous series of black and white and colour images taken at the time.
Charles E. Brown. photo, RAF Museum

Official 35 Squadron photograph taken March 1942. Reg Lane is seated front row 8th from the left. Taken at the time of handover from W/Cdr Whitworth to W/Cdr Jimmy Marks - both seated centre.
RAF Linton on Ouse Museum

PART III: PATHFINDER

Staff officers at 6 (RCAF) Group HQ Allerton Park. Grp Capt Lane is seated fourth from right, on his right Grp Capt Johnny Fauquier, and centre OC 6 Group, Air Vice Marshal 'Black Mike' McEwan.
Author's collection

KB700 during engine test run autumn 1943. Interesting to note the rear under twin machine gun mount is quite clear. This had been removed before the aircraft entered squadron service.
Bomber Command Museum via Karl Kjarsgaard

Ground Crew servicing the Merlin engines 35 Sqn Halifax Mk.II.
Charles E. Brown photo via author's collection

Crew of Lancaster X KB700 'Ruhr Express' on arrival at RAF Northolt. (Note the presence of the dog indicates that this might actually be at UK landfall at RAF Prestwick.)
RCAF Archives via R. Koval

PART III: PATHFINDER

Close up of 'Ruhr Express' artwork during service with 405 'Vancouver' Sqn.
RCAF Archives via R. Koval

Avro Lancaster Mk.VI DV170. This aircraft, one of only seven built, has Merlin 87 engines of higher performance, and annular radiators. This aircraft retained by Rolls Royce for testing. Reg flew JB713.
Avro Archive via Harry Holmes

PART III: PATHFINDER

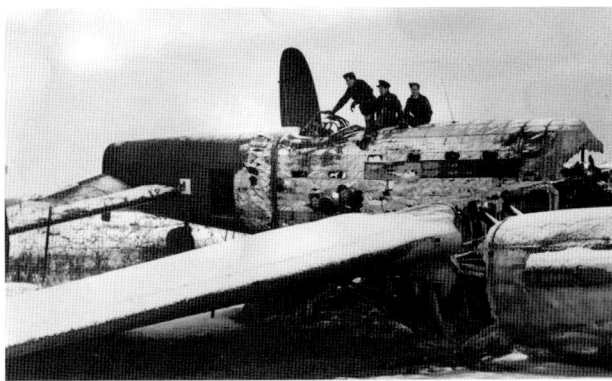

The end of the 'Ruhr Express' crashed after landing after an operation with
419 'Moose' Sqn 2 January 1945 at RAF Middleton St. George.
Avro Archive via Harry Holmes

KB700 at Avro factory during pre service inspections at Woodford October
1943. Note the guns have been removed from the under belly mounting.
Avro Archive via Harry Holmes

Halifax Mk. II W7710 LQ-R 'Ruhr Valley Express' of No. 405 'Vancouver'
Sqn. This aircraft failed to return from Flensburg 2 October 1942.
RCAF archives via Author

PART III: PATHFINDER

Reg and Barbara Lane's wedding at St. John's Church, Alwoodley, Leeds, 3 December 1945.
RCAF Archives via Lane Family

Roll out of the first Canadian built Lancaster X, KB700 'Ruhr Express' at
Victory Aircraft Co, Malton, Ontario. 6 August 1943.
Avro Archive via Harry Holmes

PART III: PATHFINDER

Reg in the cockpit of 'Ruhr Express' on roll-out 6 August 1943.
Author's collection via Lane family

Reg Lane after his DFC.
Author's collection via Lane Family

Group Captain Reg Lane after investiture of Distinguished Service Order, in 1944 which was awarded in December 1943.
RCAF Archive via R. Koval

PART III: PATHFINDER

Official photograph of Air-Vice Marshal R. J, Lane DSO, DFC*, CMM, CD. taken just prior to the amalgamation of Canadian Forces in 1968.
Lane Family

PART IV: SCOTTY

Bill Gracie with his cousin Jean Muir in Crossford, Lanarkshire on his last leave in June 1944.
Author's collection

'The Aircraftman' a periodical published by the Galt Aircraft School during the Second World War.
Author's collection

Bill aged 19 during his training at Galt Aircraft School during February to July 1941. Bill is third from left, second row from top.
Author's collection

Bill's pilot, PO Gerry Philbin (right) shares a tea and a chat with No. 431 'Iroquois' Sqn CO W/Cdr. Bill Newson.
RCAF Archives via Author's collection

PART IV: SCOTTY

SS Westerland was the ship in which Bill sailed for the UK and his overseas service in the RCAF.
Launched as the SS Regina for the White Star Line, her service before the Second World War
was plying between Liverpool and Canada.
Author's collection

RAF Croft near Darlington 1944. Halifaxes can be
seen on frying pan style dispersal points.
This airfield is now a racing circuit.
RCAF Archives via R.Koval

RAF Tholthorpe soon after initial construction
before paved runway - circa 1942.
After the Battle magazine archive

PART IV: SCOTTY

RAF Tholthorpe in late 1943, after the Canadians had taken over the airfield. Halifaxes can be clearly seen on the dispersals. Bomb dump to the lower right of the photo.
Author's collection via G. Wood

The disused Tholthorpe airfield in the 1970s looking towards the west. The later Watch Office can be just made out in the distance and one of the two remaining 'T-Type' hangars to the right of the photograph.
Author's collection via G. Wood

PART IV: SCOTTY

Halifax Mk. V LK640 SE-Q 'Queenie' of No. 431 'Iroquois' Squadron at dispersal at Tholthorpe. This aircraft was lost on the 18/19 November 1943 raid to Mannheim, in which the Philbin crew took part.
RCAF Archives via R.Koval

Evocative photograph of No. 425 'Alouette' Sqn Halifax LL596 KW-U running up its engines. Taken in November 1944, after LL594 was lost, it is typical of daily activities on a wartime bomber airfield.
Author's collection via RCAF Archives

PART IV: SCOTTY

10 December 1943. WAAF's wave farewell to the Philbin crew in LK991 SE-U as they leave Tholthorpe for their new base at RAF Croft.
Author's collection via R. Koval

The crew very relaxed at Croft in 1944. Standing left to right Les Stamp, 'Scotty', Tom Lee and Al Brooks; lower left to right, Gerry Philbin, with Lloyd Barker over Irwin Klein.
Author's collection

The crew in the Autumn of 1943, at Tholthorpe; Standing left to right bomb aimer Tom Lee, pilot Gerry Philbin, wireless operator, Les Stamp, navigator Al Brooks, below gunners Irwin Klein, and Lloyd Barker, and the flight engineer, Bill to the right.
Author's collection

September 1943 and the crew 'bus' heads across Tholthorpe airfield taking the crews to their Halifaxes for another operation.
Author's collection

PART IV: SCOTTY

Three countries are represented in the group of Iroquois Squadron airmen pictured as they relaxed after returning from an attack on Mannheim on the night of 18/19 November 1943. Shown are (left to right) front row - Pilot Officer John Morton, an English lad in the RAF, navigator; P/O George Rich, from Berkeley, Cal., U.S.A., air gunner; F/O George Milner, also English. Standing - F/O Douglas Wiley, London, Ont. air gunner; F/Sgt. Malcolm McMillan, Edmonton, Alta. pilot. Doug Wiley flew with the Philbin crew on several ops as mid-upper and under gunner.
RCAF Archives via R. Koval

The St. Leu raid in progress on 5 August 1944. This target token was taken by a No.420 Squadron aircraft, A-Able flown by P/O Johnson and his crew at 13.15 hours, about the time 'Scotty's aircraft went down.
Author's collection via Lt. Gen A.C. Hull

Two of the entrance to the caves at St. Leu. The heavy concrete sliding blast door can just be seen behind the shrubbery. This photo taken in 1994.
Author's collection

PART IV: SCOTTY

RAF reconnaissance photo of the 'Noball' target at St. Leu D'Esserent, prior to the major attacks of July and August 1944.
RAF archive via Author's collection

Reconnaissance photos of the St. Leu D'Esserent target after the initial raids in July. Items marked with a letter 'D' are the cave entrances.
RAF archive via Author's collection

Taken in 2014, gun pit above the cliffs at St. Valery on the channel coast. This was the target for the No.431 Sqn. operation on 7 May 1944.
Author's collection

PART IV: SCOTTY

The crash site of No. 433 'Porcupine' Squadron's Halifax II MZ828 BM-H at Skipton on Swale - taken the day after the crash 6 August 1944.
Jim Kinder via Author

V1 Storage buildings at Renescure. These were typical of the type of buildings used; often hidden in deeply wooded areas, and difficult for the bombers to locate. Targets such as those at Sautrecourt, Foret de Nieppe, and Bamiere were all hit by the Philbin crew. Taken in 2008.
Author's collection

The 'Allan Cup' Canadian Hockey League trophy. Gerry Philbin had been a striker in the team that won the cup in 1941. This was painted on the side of Halifax LL594 just under the Pilot's cockpit side window.
C. Simonsen

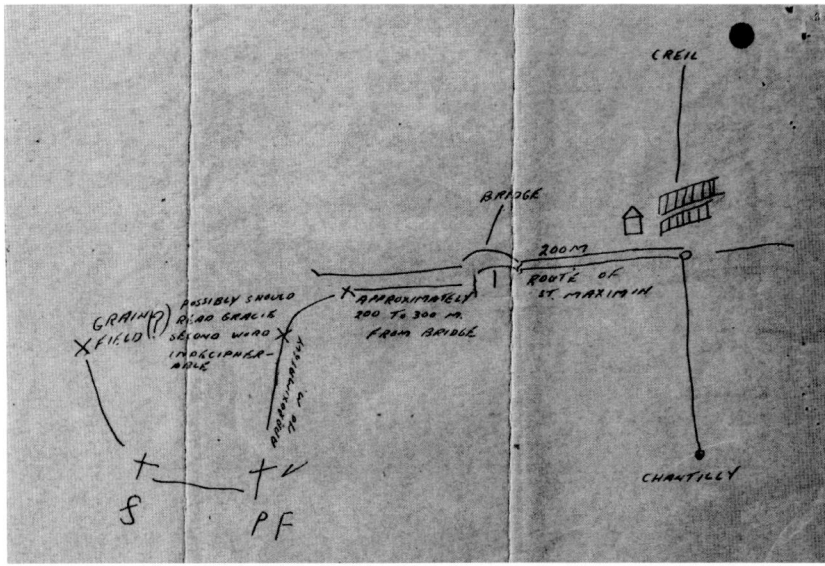

Map drawn by the Patriotic Guards' of the Communist Resistance showing where the bodies of the Canadian crew of LL594 had been found and buried – clearly identifying the temporary grave of Bill 'Scotty' Gracie, near the village of St. Maximin.
Author's collection

Reg what he would like to do now. 'I had thought that it would be a good idea to attend the RAF Staff College at RAF Cranwell,' Reg remembered. 'I suppose I was thinking of staying in the air force after the war, so I asked if that would be possible? "That should be easy," Edwards replied, and it was left at that.' After all the excitement, Reg was back to the routine of the Pathfinder training unit, as commander of A Flight tutoring pilots on the Lancaster I and II and the Halifax II, through September and October. Then he was called to the office of the AOC 8 Group, Air Vice Marshal Don Bennett. Bennett said: 'I hear you want to go to the RAF Staff College. I've had a communication from RCAF Overseas HQ. They want you to start the next course in October. I don't want you to go. The bombing campaign is picking up and I want you to go to 405 Squadron, and eventually take over the squadron from Johnny Fauquier.' 'Fine,' Reg replied, 'I'm OK with that.' In his interview, Reg said that life in his night training unit was beginning to pall and he had now been off operations since the spring and therefore relished the thought of getting back into action.

So in November came his posting to No. 405 (Vancouver) Squadron at Gransden Lodge. Reg had been marked out as a future squadron commander on joining the Pathfinder training unit. In his service report, endorsed by Group Captain Boyce as he joined the squadron, compiled on 26 October 1943, it was noted: 'He is an exceptionally keen and efficient officer, and will make an excellent squadron commander.' On the 4th of the month he was awarded a bar to his DFC, again not for a specific event but for displaying fine leadership and 'a fine fighting spirit and inspiration to his crews'.

No. 405 (Vancouver) Squadron was the first of the 400 number series Canadian bomber squadrons to be formed in Bomber Command, becoming part of the Yorkshire-based No. 4 Group at RAF Driffield, East Yorkshire, in April 1941, initially flying Vickers Wellingtons, like so many bomber squadrons at that time. On 12/13 June it carried out the RCAF's first bombing operation, only ten weeks after formation. During this time it was also based at RAF Leeming. However, in spring 1942 it converted to the new four-engined Halifax, becoming the first Canadian squadron to do so. It carried out the first RCAF four-engined bomber raid to Cologne on 30/31 May, from RAF Pocklington, east of York, as part of the 'Thousand Bomber' raid, an operation in which Reg had taken part. The squadron had transferred to No. 8 (Pathfinder) Group in April 1943, and had become very much the 'elite' bombing squadron of the RCAF. By now No. 405 Squadron was an all-Lancaster squadron, having relinquished all their Halifaxes by the end of September.

Reg joined as officer commanding B Flight, bringing with him one of his old Halifax crew, Flight Sergeant Jim Scannell, and some new members, and on 17 November they were off on their first sortie together (Reg's fifty-fourth operation) to Mannheim in Lancaster III JB374 LQ-X. On 22 November he was asked to give a briefing to the press at the end of the first operation to Berlin by the 'Ruhr Express', under the command of Flight Sergeant Harry Floren of Weyburn, Saskatchewan (Floren and his all-Canadian crew of JA974 LQ-V failed to return from an operation to Brunswick in January 1944.) This was followed by operations for Reg and his crew to Berlin and Frankfurt on 16 and 20 December, both operations in JB374 LQ-X.

The raid to Berlin was particularly memorable for Bomber Command, and became known as 'Black Thursday', as twenty-nine aircraft were lost on returning to England. The weather was quite awful, with mist and low cloud rolling into the eastern counties from late afternoon, and some crews were forced to bail out whereas others crashed into high ground or on approach to an airfield. Three of No. 405 Squadron's aircraft were written off trying to land, with Flying Officer B.A. McLennan in JB369 LQ-D crashing near Graveley airfield and the village of Yelling, Cambridgeshire, and Flight Lieutenant Allan's crew in JB477 LQ-O on approach to Graveley. There was only one person rescued, the rear gunner, Warrant Officer S.N. 'Clare' Nutting, DFM, on McLennan's aircraft, surviving when the turret bounced clear of the wreck. Three of Allan's crew died in the crash, Allan succumbing to his wounds later in hospital. The third Lancaster from the squadron, JB481 LQ-R with Flying Officer E.B. Drew, crashed near Marham in Norfolk with only the pilot surviving, but badly injured. There are discrepancies on official records, but it is estimated that over 150 Bomber Command aircrew were killed on their return from this operation.

Most of January 1944 was taken up with administration in preparation for Reg's next role. By this time Lancaster X KB700 'Ruhr Express' had left No. 405 Squadron and been sent to No. 419 (Moose) Squadron at RAF Middleton St George in 6 Group, where it met its demise on 2 January 1945, crashing into an airfield vehicle on return from a raid and completely burning out. Reg commented to the author: 'It really was a bit of a problem aircraft for us at Gransden. All the other Lancasters were British-built, and its idiosyncrasies were a problem for the ground crews. We were glad to see it go.'

On 22 January Reg was promoted to wing commander, and finally took charge of the squadron after his fifty-seventh operation to Magdeburg in Lancaster ND412 the previous day. His predecessor, Group Captain Johnny Fauquier, was promoted to air commodore, and moved to No. 6 (RCAF) Group headquarters at Allerton Park in Yorkshire as senior operations staff officer (SOSO). He was later to drop a rank to take over command of No. 617 'Dambuster' Squadron in December 1944, which he led until almost the end of the conflict; he was bitterly disappointed not to be with the squadron on the last Dambuster raid of the war on 28 April 1945.

Reg found the airfield a good one, with a well-coordinated team. There was a large palatial house close to the airfield that had been the home of King Peter of Yugoslavia and his family, as refugees from the conflict, and had been specially equipped for them by the Foreign Office. The King and family had moved out due to the increased noise of the aircraft. The base commander, Group Captain Gordon Dunlop, said to Reg: 'Why don't we take it over?' Reg recalled: 'It was beautifully furnished by the British, and we were actually closer to the flight line than the RAF Officers' Quarters. We were able to entertain the senior Group Officers, and when the King and Queen came to visit the station we were able to entertain them at the house after the formalities. It was quite beautiful.'

Life for the crews at this time was tough. The accommodation in the Nissen huts was not the best, as this was a wartime station with none of the refinements of the pre-war bases. During the winter it was always cold and damp, and the huts were unheated if no one was around, so it was not uncommon to come off a raid, sweaty with the exertion, and to get out of flying kit and lie on a damp bed. Food was lacking, and alcohol in short supply. Crews used to wander around the hostelries in the area to get a few beers, and hard liquor was almost unattainable.

It was also the time of 'Bomber' Harris's Battle of Berlin; a long trip usually well over 7 hours to a target that was difficult to find as there were few distinguishing geographical features, such as lakes or a coastline. Reg remembered the crew coming into the mess and seeing the map and operation notices, and saying, 'God, Berlin again – oh no!' Reg felt that 'Harris lost that battle.' When asked by the author, 'What were the reasons?', he responded: 'Distance mainly – the greater the distance the greater the problems of navigation, and change in wind directions. We knew little about the "jet stream" in those days. With the attrition rate taking its toll of experienced crews, inexperienced bomber captains found it difficult. They were getting "hacked" out of the sky. Also there were few recognisable features for the H2S operators to latch on to; not like a target with a coastline or big river to work with.'

In February Reg completed two operations – on the 16th/17th and 24th/25th – to Berlin and Schweinfurt, both in Lancaster III, ND412 LQ-X. Over Berlin there had been 10/10ths cloud, and the target had to be identified by using the H2S radar, after confirmation taken on bearings of nearby turning points.

The squadron Operations Record Book provides a good account of Reg's other trip to the Schweinfurt ball-bearing factories. Bomber Command split the bombing force into two parts, separated by a 2-hour interval, the first time this tactic had been employed. The ORB says of Reg's part in the raid: 'The weather was clear over the target, and the target identified visually. Many adjacent towns and countryside identified. Load released on aiming point at 23.05 hours. Ran up river from south-west, and TIs of white flares, and greens over woods to south. Circled to starboard and made second run south-east along railway. Identified one red marker on aiming point, another red marker marshalling yard, and another in the new town. Own TI undershot 600 to 700 yards to south-east. By 23.10 whole town area well covered by incendiaries with three very good fires, but some TIs and incendiaries were spreading up to five miles to west of town. Good route marking.' Reg was back at Gransden by 01.30 hours after a sortie of 6½ hours.

Then after two familiarisation flights on 22 and 23 March, he had the opportunity to take up a new experimental Lancaster, JB713. It was a Lancaster Mk VI, one of only seven built, all converted by Avro from standard Mk III airframes, having higher-rated Merlin 85 or 87 engines installed, really designed for use in fighters. The visual difference on the aircraft was the fitting of 'annular' radiators, which wrapped around the nacelle, such as would be common on the Lancaster's successor, the Lincoln. Reg told this author: 'It handled beautifully, just like a fighter.' He took it, as LQ-Z, on his next raid to Berlin on 24 March.

'Most important of all,' he continued with his interview, 'by this time the Luftwaffe had perfected their night operations with their "Wild Boar" night fighter plan, and more effective control and warning systems.' Reg told of some of the shortcomings:

> There was one Berlin raid and I was 'Master Bomber', I think it was the raid of 24/25 March 1944. We had been routed out over Denmark then to come south to Berlin, over the target, then south over central Germany and out to the north of the Ruhr on the flight home. It was one of those nights when we encountered strong winds. There was a system now, an improved Pathfinder technique, whereby the lead aircraft would calculate the wind speed and any revised direction, and transmit back to the weather centre at Bomber Command HQ, and they would in turn transmit the revisions to the crews in transit with times they should use the information during the flight. Remember VHF aircraft radio was in its infancy. Each squadron had its own frequency, and VHF could not be used until the Master Bomber had started transmitting. The system of codes used did not allow for a wind speed over two digits, say 100 mph plus. ... It was crazy really. This particular night my Navigator called me to say, 'I don't believe it. I really don't believe it, Skipper! I have a wind speed of 115 mph.' Well, of course we were in what we now know as the 'jet stream'. The Nav. continued, 'It gets worse, Skip. We are 90 degrees out from what we were given at briefing.' We were up at the front of the bomber stream, and I knew this was going to play havoc. The Nav. told the Wireless Operator to transmit that high figure, but the W/Op. said, 'I can't do that, and duly transmitted the code for 99, and that was relayed to the stream. By the time we got to Berlin, and I had dropped my markers, aircraft were all over the place. I was over the target for well over half an hour, and eventually when we made our way home I told the Nav. to come up to the cockpit with me and said, 'We'll map read our way home' which we did. We knew most of the heavily defended areas, and could find our way between them, but we could see others being shot out of the sky because they were so scattered; the enemy was well prepared for them. We couldn't warn another aircraft that they were in the wrong place, or there was a fighter on their tail, because we didn't know their frequency. It was another bad night for the Command.

In conversation with the author, he later said he owed his life to the power of that Lancaster Mk VI – 'Its performance outclassed the other Lancasters' – but unfortunately those engines were required for fighters, so the aircraft was returned to Avro. (Author's note: it did actually also fly on operations with Nos 7 and 635 Squadrons.)

The Lancaster VI was taken by Reg on his next two operations; on 18 April it was to Paris, the marshalling yards at Noisy-le-Sec. The target was well covered and delayed-action bombs continued to explode for a week after the raid. Sadly, as these types of targets tended to be surrounded by residential property, over 450 French civilians lost their lives. With Reg were seven other aircraft from the squadron. A further eight were sent to another rail target at Tergnier.

This type of split of the Pathfinder squadron resources was typical at this period. Two days later they were off to Lens, another rail target. Reg's crew included his regulars, long-time gunner Jim Scannell, now a pilot officer; Squadron Leader Langley; and navigator, Squadron Leader Ellwood. (Author's note: see section on 'Scotty' for more details on this raid.) For this strategic target, like the previous ones, Reg acted as master bomber, using the performance of the Mk VI Lancaster to maximum effect. It was a full squadron effort, with fourteen aircraft detailed, and it proved an effective strike. The initial Pathfinders were Mosquitoes, the green TIs of which were accurately dropped centrally on the target, followed up by the No. 405 Squadron Lancasters bombing on H2S radar through patchy cloud. These raids were part of the dedicated plan issued by Churchill to Air Marshal Sir Charles Portal, as Chief of the Air Staff, to wreck the enemy transport infrastructure in the build-up to D-Day. At the same time, raids were continuing on the German cities, both to destroy the enemy's will to carry on, and to detract from the specific nature of the transport targets.

The sortie to Montzen on 27 April was Reg's sixty-third and penultimate operation. This time he was in Lancaster III ND855 LQ-V. Another rail target, and Reg was master bomber again, as eight No. 405 Squadron aircraft were detailed on the raid. This time it was not as straightforward as the previous trips. The force was attacked by German fighters that were waiting for them; in total fourteen Halifaxes and one Lancaster were lost. However, the Lancaster was JA976 LQ-S, that of the deputy master bomber, Reg's friend Squadron Leader E.M. Blenkinsop, DFC, who was blown from the aircraft and the only survivor of the crew. He subsequently made contact with the Belgian Resistance, and fought with them until he was captured in December 1944 and sent to a forced labour camp. He eventually died in Belsen concentration camp of 'heart failure' and has no known grave. Reg told the author he felt his loss deeply, as he much admired his colleague, whom he regarded as the best pilot in No. 8 Group.

The next couple of months were taken up with the administration required as squadron commander, but Reg did get the chance to fly another Lancaster, VI JB675, on 12 and 23 May. There was much to do in the planning of operations as this was the final run-up to D-Day. Yet he did have the opportunity for one more final operation, a key raid in direct support of the Allied troops in Normandy. The sortie was to the area around Caen, to bomb five fortified villages through which the British Second Army Corps was to advance during Operation Goodwood. Reg in Lancaster III PA129 LQ-A was deputy master bomber on this occasion, the main role appointed to Squadron Leader E.K. Cresswell. Three of the targets were successfully marked using 'Oboe' and the others by visual identification, the raid being carried out at dawn. There was subdued flak, after being shelled by naval gunfire, and there were no fighters. Elements of the 16th Luftwaffe Field Division and 21st Panzer Division were badly affected, and the Allied operation had got off to a good start. Reg could not miss out on the chance to help the Allied armies.

A couple of weeks later, in early August, details of his next posting – to No. 6 (RCAF) Group headquarters in Allerton Park near Knaresborough, Yorkshire – came through, and his last flight in an RAF Lancaster was to RAF Linton-on-Ouse on the 7th of that month. Group Captain Reg Lane, DSO, DFC and Bar, had completed 64 operational sorties and 996 hours flying, of which 386 hours were as first pilot and 352 hours at night. Apart from a couple of attacks by night fighters he had come through unscathed; his closest call, he told the author, was 'a piece of a flak fragment through my flying jacket on an operation over Berlin'. He had certainly earned the nickname 'Lucky Lane'!

Reg's wartime flying in the RCAF was now over, and he took the senior staff post of senior operations officer (air 1) at the headquarters of the Canadian bomber unit 6 (RCAF) Group at Allerton Park. It was about this time Reg began the relationship with the lady who would become his wife, Barbara Andrews. Barbara, a Leeds girl, was a dancer with a wartime entertainment group, and was introduced to Reg at an event at the Queens Hotel in Leeds by a friend who was working at 6 (RCAF) Group headquarters. Barbara had been a part-time member of the Royal Observer Corps (ROC), working as a plotter at the area ROC HQ in Leeds. Initially she thought him too young to be a group captain (he was twenty-four – one of the youngest of such rank in the RCAF), but after Reg got to know her family and enjoyed their active social life, their relationship blossomed. One night Reg and Barbara were leaving a ROC dance at the Capitol ballroom in Leeds when a police officer came over and asked Reg about his use of petrol and his coupons. Petrol was strictly rationed in the UK, and Reg was asked to prove the right to use it for social reasons. It took a phone call to the adjutant at Allerton Park to confirm his visit was an 'official' one.

Reg stayed in his post at Allerton Park until March 1945. As the war in Europe wound down, a new bombing force was proposed to take on the Japanese in the Far East – 'Tiger Force' – and a new headquarters for the organisation was set up at Bushy Park. The plan was to form a combined bombing force of Lancasters (and later Avro Lincolns), and USAF Liberators, operating out of the Japanese islands. Reg was to be Tiger Force Senior Group Staff Officer in charge of Operations, but as he was about to fly to Okinawa, news came through of the release of the atomic bombs, and the organisation was deemed to be unnecessary. In short order the victory celebrations got under way, and Reg and Barbara got married in Leeds. He was asked to stay in the UK, and became station commander at RAF Odiham in Hampshire as part of 120 (Transport) Wing with C-47 Dakotas, helping to supervise the Dakota force bringing relief to a shattered Europe and repatriating Allied prisoners of war. On 3 April 1946 he was one of the VIPs – along with British fighter 'ace' Air Vice Marshal James 'Johnnie' Johnson, who had led the Canadian fighter wing – waving off a large batch of Dakotas taking their passengers home to Canada.

In June 1946 he was recalled back to Canada, his young wife following on the SS *Aquitania*, and they met up at Halifax, Nova Scotia, and stayed a night in the area with a friend of Reg's, George Stevenson. The following day they took the train across Canada, stopping for a night in Winnipeg, before heading for Vancouver and eventually across to Vancouver Island and the city of Victoria; the journey took about a week in all. Reg was then posted to the RCAF staff college for six months and went back east, leaving his wife with his parents. This would be the life they would get used to, moving from one place to another. Barbara told the author that from the time they began their married life (she aged twenty-one), she was always the 'wife of the CO' so she had to learn to be the perfect hostess. It was a steep learning curve.

Reg remained in the Royal Canadian Air Force (from 1968 to 2010 known as the Air Division of the Canadian Armed Forces during a unification programme) until his retirement in 1974. During that period he became involved in the post-war planning of the RCAF, and became air force liaison officer on a round-the-world diplomatic trip devised by the Secretary of State for External Affairs, Lester B. Pearson. The Canadair North Star aircraft (a Merlin-engined Douglas DC6) became the first RCAF aircraft to fly around the world. During the tour, from 2 January to 8 February 1950, Reg could not resist taking the controls on the 'legs' from Fayid, Egypt, to Karachi, and Fairfield, California, to Canadian Forces Base (CFB) Rockliffe.

After this Reg was made commanding officer of CFB Edmonton in Alberta. In 1952 he had been 'aide-de-camp' to the governor general of Canada, the Hon. Vincent Massey, then was promoted to air commodore, and made air officer commanding Air Transport Command, including overseeing the introduction of the C-130 Hercules into the RCAF. By this time his entries in the log book are finished. When asked, 'Why?', by this author in conversation, Reg said: 'I didn't have any reason to enter all the flights. I had been given a B-25 Mitchell to use as I pleased, and there was nobody senior to me to check and sign off the book!' On 1 April 1964, Air Commodore Reg Lane, DSO, DFC and Bar, took the salute at Rockliffe air base near Ottawa on the retirement of the Avro Lancaster in RCAF service. Canadian Lancasters FM104, KB839, KB882, KB976, and all of No. 408 (Goose) Squadron were present, and three performed a final flypast in what would be the last multiple formation of Lancasters for fifty years, until FM213 (now operated by Canadian Warplane Heritage) flew to the UK in 2014, to fly alongside the RAF's Lancaster, PA474.

By 1966 Reg was back in Europe, promoted to air vice marshal, and took control of No. 1 Air Division at Metz in France, at a time when the CF104 Starfighter was being deployed, followed by a three-year stint as director of Mobile Command in St Hubert, Quebec. In the summer of 1972 he received his final promotion to lieutenant general (a changed designation of rank due to the amalgamation of the Canadian Armed Forces) and became deputy C-in-C of the North American Air Defence Command headquarters in Colorado, USA, from where he retired after thirty-five years of service to live in his home town of Victoria, British Columbia.

During the 1990s he became patron of the Yorkshire Air Museum, Canada branch, and the big 6 (RCAF) Group reunion held in London and York in June 1990, and subsequently the 6 (RCAF) Group Bomber Command Association. In 2000 he was inducted into Canada's Aviation Hall of Fame, an appointment of which he was particularly proud. In the summer of 2003 he brought his family over to the UK, and in company with this author, visited many of his old haunts, including Gransden Lodge and the Canadian Lancaster KB889 at the Imperial War Museum site at Duxford, Cambridge. He passed away peacefully in his beloved Victoria on 2 October 2003.

UNDER THE
MAPLE LEAF
PART IV
SCOTTY

'Scotty' (standing 2nd from left).

Part IV: Scotty

11. The Young Volunteer

It was a sunny day when the White Star Line SS *Regina* docked at Pier 19 in Halifax, Nova Scotia, after its voyage from Greenock, Scotland. Aboard, among the many passengers and immigrants to Canada was Mrs Christina Gracie with her three young children – William (just under eight years old), Jean (six years) and David (eighteen months) – who had left Lanarkshire in the middle of the Depression. Mrs Gracie remembered: 'It was a tough time. We were a poor family, and we had not had a hot meal for some time. A kindly Jewish gentleman took sympathy on us, and bought us hot food during the trip. That was the first hot food we had for three months!' They eventually landed at Montreal on a sunny 'Canada Day', 1 August 1929, and made their way to Peterborough, Ontario, to join father, William Sr, who had come over earlier. He had arrived at the immigration depot in Halifax on the SS *Athenia* (later to achieve notoriety as the first British ship to be torpedoed by a submarine, U-30, in the forthcoming war) on 1 April 1929, and had managed to gain employment as a local gardener, so he could send for his family. Settling in the town, the family became well known in the community, Christina working as a cook at the nearby YMCA, and in the local gardening club. David Gracie told this author: 'During the war when the YMCA was full up, I often came home from school to find Canadian servicemen sleeping around our house, even on the stairs!'

Years afterwards, as the clouds of the Second World War darkened, and the ramifications of what was going on in Europe became obvious to the world at large, William (Bill) Brown Gracie, the eldest son of the family, volunteered for the RCAF. He had a great interest in 'things mechanical' and had several motorcycles. He worked at the neighbourhood cereal factory and was a well-liked lad locally, although known to be a bit of a daredevil – once jumping off the huge lift-lock on the Trent waterway about 65 feet into the canal below. His brother David told the author: 'You never "dared" Billy to do anything, as he always would do it!' Bill was much involved in the local church and Scouts, and spent many of the pre-war summers on the nearby lakes of Ontario. He was keen to join the air force, especially to fly, and, having an aptitude for such things, he enrolled in an aircraft mechanics course at the Galt Aircraft School, between February and July 1941, moving to a flat in the town.

On 10 July 1941, and still only nineteen, his final enlistment papers came through, and he was enrolled into the Royal Canadian Air Force to become a member of No. 6 Squadron RCAF Manning Depot, Toronto, eventually passing the standard entry exam with 'above average' classification on 17 July. For his basic enlistment training, he was sent at the end of November to No. 2 SFTS at Uplands Air Station, and then to the technical training school at St Thomas, near London, Ontario, then in the charge of Wing Commander J.H. Keens, AFC, a First World War RCAF pilot.

Bill's classification was moved up to aircraftman first class, just before he was sent to No. 14 Depot, Yarmouth, Nova Scotia, where he was promoted to leading aircraftman on 25 February 1942. It was while he was at Yarmouth that he met and befriended another young airman, Tommy Lee from Sarnia, Ontario, and they became firm friends. Tom was training to be a bomb aimer and was to feature prominently in Bill's service life. It was here Bill got his first experience of flight, in a 'Canso' flying boat (known as a Catalina in RAF service). Bill eventually received notification he was to be sent to Europe, and the chance of becoming the aircrew he so much desired became a possibility. The next stop was No. 17 Depot and Halifax, Nova Scotia, on 11 January 1943 and embarkation for the UK, leaving the port on the SS *Andes*, a fast troopship that made the Atlantic crossing alone on 26 January. The *Andes* had been built for the Royal Mail Lines in Belfast by Harland and Wolff and was one of the finest liners of her time, but war intervened. She survived the war, though, and eventually became a cruise liner, but sadly ended her days as scrap in 1972.

After a fast crossing during what was a very dangerous time in the North Atlantic, the vessel arrived in Glasgow on 4 February, so Bill had returned to his native land. But not for long; he and the contingent of aspiring airmen who had docked with him were immediately shipped down south to Bournemouth. The seaside town, well known as a summer holiday resort, had been taken over by the air force as a reception centre for incoming airmen, which included not only those from the Commonwealth but also other Allied airmen. Hotels and boarding houses were commandeered for accommodation and cinemas and halls around the town for messing facilities. Here in between copious amounts of 'square bashing' and parades, and long runs along the shore, the Commonwealth airmen were sorted out into their planned courses, prior to issue of their final squadron or unit assignments. Even though it was a fairly relaxed regime in the town, it was not without its dangers. Fred Davies, another Canadian, remembered: 'The Germans knew it was a "staging place" for airmen, and every now and then Luftwaffe fighter-bombers would fly in from the Channel and spray cannon shells and bullets right up the main street, which led from the sea. Sometimes their output would go straight into a hotel [author's note – he thought it to be the Metropole], which was at the big intersection of several streets. We never went there in daytime. You might drink your last pint if you did!' All who went through Bournemouth recall the beaches being mined and out of bounds.

After ten days Bill was posted up to the 6 (RCAF) Group in North Yorkshire, to the RAF station at Topcliffe, near Thirsk. By now, with his qualification as air engineer second class, he was most likely used as ground crew for the old Merlin-engined Mk II and Mk V Handley Page Halifaxes of the No. 1659 Heavy Conversion Unit. The conversion units were designed to train and bond crews together, and get them used to flying the aircraft that they would later use in action, before being allocated to operational squadrons. Aircraft assigned to the conversion units were 'war weary', and generally had seen better times. Those that had been used in operational squadrons were sent to the HCUs as new aircraft were delivered to the active units. The practice was unfortunate, but sadly necessary, as Bomber Command was still building up its strength and replacing operational losses.

No. 6 (RCAF) Group had two HCUs at this time: No. 1659 at Topcliffe and No. 1664 at Croft, near Darlington. This part of the country, close to the Pennines, a hill chain known as the 'backbone of England', would claim many an inexperienced crew unused to the rapidly changing weather in the UK. This was a constant problem for the Canadians, not used to the variations of an island climate like Britain's, as opposed to the continental climate of Canada where they had trained. Such airfields in Canada were mostly located on the flatlands to the east of the Rockies, and west of mid-Ontario, where weather was more settled.

It was while at Topcliffe that Bill formally volunteered and applied for aircrew duties. He was sent before a selection board, where he was assessed by a Squadron Leader Potter as 'Fit and well educated – Keen to be a flight engineer – Intelligent, quick type.' Then, while still attached to No. 1659 HCU, Bill was transferred to No. 4 School of Technical Training (SoTT) at RAF St Athan in South Wales. With a sprawling area that included thirty-six large hangars, it was here that the initial training of flight engineers for the RAF was carried out. The base was also home to a sizeable No. 32 Maintenance Unit, and this gave access to a number of different types of aircraft. Here Bill learned the vagaries of the Rolls-Royce Merlin, and later Hercules, engines and bomber aircraft fuel systems.

On 1 December 1942 he was promoted to leading aircraftman. It was also while he was at No. 4 SoTT that he was sent to Rootes Securities in Speke, Liverpool, from 17 to 23 July 1943, for detailed initiation into the aircraft he would be operating – the Handley Page Halifax, which were being built at the plant. At the outbreak of war, the government had brought into operation the 'shadow factory' scheme whereby aircraft production was scattered around the country. It was proposed by the Ministry of Aircraft Production (MAP) that Halifax construction was increased during January to December 1940, and after that three more manufacturing units were brought into the picture: the London Aircraft Production Group (including London Passenger Transport) with final assembly at Leavesden, near Watford; Fairey Aviation at Stockport, with final assembly at Ringway; and Rootes Securities, a car manufacturer in Speke, the location of Liverpool airport to the south of the city on the Mersey estuary. Rootes had quickly been utilised by the MAP for the production of Bristol Blenheim light bombers, so it had been relatively straightforward to switch to the building of the four-engined heavy bombers instead. Another manufacturer, already constructing Hampden twin-engined bombers for Handley Page – English Electric of Preston – also went into Halifax production, their final assembly being at Samlesbury between Preston and Blackburn. At the time of Bill's visit to Speke, Rootes were producing the Merlin-engined Halifax Mk V, which would be the aircraft Bill would eventually crew when posted.

It was while he was at Rootes, in July 1943, that Bill met a Wallasey woman who was working as a 'progress chaser' on the production of the nose sections, Emma Murray. She was a widow living in the Wirral across the River Mersey from Liverpool, having already lost her husband – local fisherman John Murray – on an armed trawler to a U-boat action in the Irish Sea in 1940. According to fellow British flight engineer, Bill Sparkes, who was with Bill on the course, one day they were in the canteen at the plant when they noticed a striking redhead, Emma, and Bill obviously was immediately attracted to her. This author was told by another on the course, Eddie Collyer, an Englishman from Slough, that Bill's colleagues bet him that he would not ask her out for a date. As earlier recounted, Bill was always one for a challenge, and did ask, with the result they embarked on a relationship. Later in the year, over the Christmas period, he spent a nine-day leave with her in Southport – the result of which is your author!

While at Speke, towards the end of his course, Bill was detached to No. 7 Air Gunnery School, at RAF Stormy Down in nearby South Wales, for training in armament. It was necessary for all aircrew to have at least the minimum instruction in operating the guns of the aircraft they would be using. Bill passed out with an above-average report. All of his training was done on a gunnery simulator, and no flights are noted in his log book.

Completing his course at St Athan, with a result of 69%, Bill was promoted to sergeant on 23 August, as by this stage in the war it was the minimum rank for all aircrew. On 28 August, Bill's posting came through, and he left for No. 1664 HCU at RAF Croft, near Darlington. It was during this operational training period that airmen mustered together to make up a crew. Normally this was by gathering together in a room or hangar those joining the unit; by conversation and friendship individuals eventually united to form a crew of seven for a Halifax, the type of aircraft they would be flying. As already recounted, Bill had made firm friends with bombardier Tom Lee from Sarnia, Ontario, with whom he had spent time in Canada before embarkation. Tom had arrived at Croft at the same time.

They teamed up with the French Canadian pilot, Pilot Officer Gerald 'Gerry' Philbin from Quebec. In the late 1930s Philbin had played ice hockey for the Trenton Flyers team, and that town and nearby airfield had a long association with the air force, which continues to this day. This influenced his decision to join the RCAF. After receiving his training and pilot's wings, Gerry was posted to RCAF Rockliffe, and this allowed him to play full-time for the Ottawa RCAF Flyers, and he was a key defender and star of the winning RCAF team in the Canadian national ice hockey league cup – the Allan Cup. This made him quite a sporting celebrity.

The other members joining the Philbin crew were Flying Officer Al Brook, of Boissevain, Manitoba, who joined as navigator; gunners Sergeants Irwin

Klein, of Esk, and Lloyd Barker of Kildeer, both from the wide Canadian flatlands in Saskatchewan; and RAF Londoner Sergeant Les Stamp as wireless operator/air gunner. In conversation with RAF flight engineer Sergeant Bill Sparkes and Canadian gunner Sergeant Doug Wiley – the latter later to join the Philbin crew – this author learned that it was about this time that Bill was given the nickname 'Scotty' because of his strong Scottish-Canadian accent.

Bill's crew training commenced with flying instruction on 9 September 1943. This was the beginning of an intense period, firstly flying as a flight engineer with A Flight commander, Squadron Leader Kenney, then with his regular pilot 'Gerry' Philbin. To take off, the engineer would move from his position behind the pilot under the astrodome, to a drop-down seat by the side of the pilot. The skipper would hold the aircraft on the brakes with his left hand and with the right advance the throttles, then the flight engineer would put his hand over his on the throttles, and the pilot would then release the brakes. As the aircraft built up speed, he would push the control column hard forward to get the tailwheel off the runway. When the tail was up the control column would be centralised to counter any swing. When the ground speed had built up to ½- or ¾-throttle, Gerry would take his hands off the throttle levers and Bill would push them full forward, and lock them in that position. It would require both hands on the column to get the aircraft into the sky, as there were no servo-assisted mechanisms to help with the movement of controls, outside the trim tabs. In order to get airborne 30 degrees of flap was used to assist lift, then when stabilised in the climb, the undercarriage and flaps would be raised.

For Bill it was a close, friendly relationship, the crew bonding together well, and it was at this time he would have been encouraged to take the controls of the Halifax, a procedure recommended by the RCAF in case the pilot was injured in action. His first chance to fly the Halifax came on 16 September, with Squadron Leader Kenney as training pilot. By 25 September 1943, Bill's hours in the air totalled over fifty-eight. In operational circumstances it was not unknown for the flight engineer to fly the aircraft, especially on the return flight.

The crew were posted to No. 431 (Iroquois) Squadron at RAF Tholthorpe, 12 miles to the north of York, on 26 September. The squadron had been formed at RAF Burn, just south of Selby in Yorkshire on 11 November 1942, the eleventh bomber squadron of the RCAF. Tholthorpe airfield was to be a major part of Bill's life when on operations. The land was low lying, and situated just to the west of the main rail line from York to Edinburgh, which ran across the end of east–west runway. The airfield was given the nickname of 'Tholthorpe in the Mud' by the Canadians, the damp weather and poor soil quality of the Vale of York combining with foggy weather to make the place somewhat miserable in the autumn and winter months. It had opened as a grass airfield in August 1940 as part of No. 4 Group, used by Armstrong Whitworth Whitleys of No. 77 Squadron, RAF. In December of that year, it was closed for major development, including paved runways, and reopened for the Canadians in June 1943 with No. 434 (Bluenose) Squadron forming there on 13 June. Unusually it had a pre-war watch office – with brick structure on top and exterior panels marking runway information – before the new watch office and control tower was built for the Canadians further out on the airfield. The old watch office continued to be used as a briefing room. Most surprisingly, both still exist as this book is written.

The Philbin crew went on operations after three training flights around the UK, on cross-country expeditions, in LK640 SE-Q and LK 632 SE-M (both these aircraft being lost on a raid to Ludwigshafen on 18 November) and again in LK640 'Q-Queenie' on a 'bullseye', which was a long-distance flight around Britain simulating the time and navigation required for operations over the continent and the North Sea. They were off on 8 October for their first operation together to Hanover, flying Halifax V LK898 SE-O. The crew included a 'second dickey' pilot, Australian Sergeant A.G. Craig. The No. 431 Squadron aircraft were among the early ones at their destination. All aircraft bombed on target, and there were reports of large explosions; a glow from fires could be seen from over 100 miles away. The operation was successful, with all aircraft bombing the primary target; the post-operation assessment showed the city centre receiving massive damage, and an important rubber factory and a machine works were knocked out. However, the force were attacked by defending German fighters, and damage meant that the Philbin crew had to divert on the way home to the US Army Air Corps base at Shipdam, returning to Croft the following day. Bill noted in his log book: 'Good trip for first.' This raid was also notable as it was the last operation carried out by Vickers Wellingtons of Bomber Command in the European theatre. Two Halifaxes of No. 431 Squadron, LK657 SE-K of Sergeant Ryan, and DK265 SE-C of Flight Sergeant

Chambers, an Australian serving with the squadron, failed to return.

The weather closed in over the next ten days, so at Tholthorpe operations were scrubbed for a while. After more training flights, including a 'fighter affiliation' exercise with a Hurricane from the Group Affiliation Unit at RAF Dalton, their next operation on 22 October – another night trip of 6 hours 20 minutes' duration – was to Kassel. After briefing at 14.00 hours, twelve aircraft from the 'Iroquois' squadron departed for the target. This time the Philbin crew were in LK952 SE-K. Pathfinders found the target at 20.48 hours and, weather clear, 'K' bombed at 19,500 feet. According to Bill's log book, on the return trip they diverted to the nearby 6 Group headquarters base of RAF Linton-on-Ouse, but in the Tholthorpe flying control log, a handwritten book recently discovered in Canadian archives, they actually landed at RAF East Moor, further east.

November 1943 was a busy month for 'Scotty' and his crew, completing five operations. On the second, the crew took Halifax V DK185 SE-S on an hour's flight test, prior to using the aircraft for an operation to Düsseldorf the following day. This appears to have been a bit of a 'rogue' aircraft, having returned prematurely from the earlier Kassel operation, and this time they got as far as 52.10N 03.18E, off the Dutch coast before having to turn back. Again, according to the flying control log, the problem was that the aircraft could not attain bombing altitude of over 16,000 feet. Bill wryly noted in his own log: 'A/C – U/S – DNCO (NBG).' Not completing an operation was hated by the bombing crews, feeling they had let down their comrades. Bill's observation of the aircraft being 'No Bloody Good' was correct. DK185 had suffered engine problems before and was taken out of operational squadron use and sent to No. 1664 Heavy Conversion Unit, by then at RAF Dishforth. It eventually flew into high ground on Ilkley Moor in bad weather on 31 January 1944, taking with it Pilot Officer D.G. McLeod and his all Canadian crew.

Part IV: Scotty

12. Iroquois Squadron

From 4 to 9 November the weather closed in again, affecting operations for the next week or so, and the crew were kept busy with ground courses and some local flying until training recommenced with several cross-country exercises, although bad weather meant an early return on the 10th. They also had trouble with the undercarriage on 'U-Uncle' on the 17th, but managed to land at base safely. Their next raid was on 18 November when an operation to Ludwigshafen, across the Rhine from Mannheim, was detailed. Taking off at 16.49 hours and flying their regular aircraft LK991 SE-U, they bombed the target yet did not see any red or yellow TIs from the Pathfinders, but did encounter some heavy icing at the French coast. It had been a long trip, too, nearly 7½ hours. However, their engines cut out and stopped on landing back at Croft; another lesson learned by Bill who noted: 'Good Prang. First mistake as F/E. Engines cut – no fuel.' Two 'Iroquois' aircraft, LK640 SE-Q of Flying Officer Carefoot and LK632 SE-M of Flight Sergeant Burge, failed to return, the former sending a message they were ditching in the North Sea, but they were never seen again.

The following night it was over to Leverkusen in LK991 SE-U again, where the target indicator markers were difficult to identify, and Bill wrote: 'Bags of Flak – circuits in Ruhr.' Obviously it was not a good operation, not aided by the problem with Oboe on equipped aircraft. Three nights later on the 22nd it was the crew's first trip to the 'Big City', Berlin, a round trip of almost 7 hours, again in LK991 'U-Uncle'; this Halifax Mk V was to become their regular aircraft. This was the most severe of the heaviest raids on Germany's capital city in 1943. In fact the aircraft were only over the target half an hour, from 19.55 to 20.25 hours (local time), and there was thick cloud. However, the Pathfinders were accurate and most of the bombing was done on the glow seen through the cloud. It caused serious damage to many public buildings, including Albert Speer's office and the War Industry ministry, as well as the fire and rescue services. Over 1,730 Berliners were killed, almost 7,000 injured and more than 180,000 displaced from their homes, a figure that would not be repeated until much later in 1944. For the Philbin crew it was a little 'dicey'. They were holed by flak on their port wing near the port inner engine, and had to return on three engines, Bill 'juggling' with the resources of the three remaining power plants.

The crew missed the next two operations to Berlin, while Bomber Command Lancasters visited the capital again on 23 and 26 November. They were due to be tasked with a raid to Frankfurt, but according to a recently discovered handwritten Operations Record Book, they were 'washed out' for that raid. Their next sortie was on the night of 26/27 November to Stuttgart, when they manned LK963 SE-H. The squadron put up eight aircraft, although one failed to take off, so seven set forth at 17.20 hours led by the squadron commander Wing Commander Bill Newson, DFC. The Philbin crew were the last of seventeen aircraft in total, from Nos 431 and 434 Squadrons, to take off from Tholthorpe. Again the target was obscured by cloud, but Pathfinders identified it well and the aircrews reported a good glow from fires. A shortage of fuel due to strong headwinds meant that SE-H had to land at Thorney Island on the south coast to refuel before returning to base, but low cloud at Tholthorpe delayed the Philbin crew for 24 hours before finally taking off at 12.35 hours on the 28th. They landed at their home airfield after a flight of just over 1½ hours. Tholthorpe, in the meantime, had been busy coping with six Lancasters of No. 467 Squadron and three of No. 106 Squadron, diverted in from their operations.

Bill and the crew's last operation together in 1943, and their seventh, was the first of two trips they would take to Leipzig, with thirteen other aircraft from the squadron. It would be their final trip from Tholthorpe, until summer 1944. It was a long flight deep inside enemy territory, with the average flight time being 8 hours 40 minutes; Philbin's LK991 took 8 hours 10 minutes. The target was hit well and good results were seen, but it had been a bad night for the group. Four 'Iroquois' aircraft were lost, including the bombing leader, Flight Lieutenant Lister in SE-F of B Flight. Overall, more than 50% of the twenty-four aircraft in total were lost due to being over the heavily defended southern section of the city on the return trip. It may be interesting for the reader to know that the well-known American broadcaster and journalist, Ed Murrow, was aboard a No. 619 Squadron Lancaster for this raid, and his report was relayed throughout the USA. A total of 527 Halifaxes and Lancasters took part, and 4.6% were lost. It was the Philbin crew's last operation in LK991, as Bill noted in his log book: 'First aircraft wrecked in accident 22.12.43.' In fact the aircraft was damaged by Halifax BB251 RV-V of No. 1659 HCU, although the plane must have been repaired as it eventually ended up at No. 1667 HCU at Sandtoft. There it stalled and crashed on take-off on 13 May 1944, and was written off. Bill recovered a small piece of plywood from the undercarriage doors, and mailed it home to his mother. Sadly none of his letters home have survived.

On 10 December 1943 the 'Iroquois' squadron left Tholthorpe and flew their aircraft to RAF Croft, replacing No. 1664 Heavy Conversion Unit, which had moved out to RAF Dishforth further south in Yorkshire, next to the A1 Great North Road, a few days earlier. RAF Croft was to be the squadron's base for the rest of the war, and March would see them re-equipping with Hercules-engined Halifax Mk IIIs over the next couple of months. Within 24 hours of arriving at Croft, the unit was detailed for a 'special mission', but this was scrubbed, and for the next seven days Bill and the rest of the squadron were kept busy with tuition, the flight engineers receiving training on the workings of the sextant.

The date of 18 December appears to have been Bill's only opportunity for instruction on the 'Link Trainer', of 1½ hours; this machine was an early flight simulator. Apart from local flying, training in aircraft handling and a long cross-country night exercise of nearly 5 hours on 10 January, the Philbin crew and Bill did not fly on operations until the night of 20/21 January, when they were tasked with their second trip to the 'Big City', although the rest of the squadron had flown there at the end of December. On that January night fourteen crews were briefed to go, including the Philbin crew with Sergeant M. Sonshine as 'second dickey' pilot. Berlin was again covered in 10/10ths cloud. However, the Pathfinder's red and green TIs were seen and the force, including Bill's LL152 SE-U, bombed on them, though no proper assessment of the damage was available afterwards. It must have been a bit of a 'milk run' for Bill as he noted: 'Good trip all the way.'

On the night of 21/22 January, the crew were briefed for an attack on

Magdeburg, but 'U-Uncle' let them down and they could not take off. No. 431 Squadron lost only one aircraft on that raid, that of Flight Sergeant H. Krenz and his crew in LK680 SE-E. So their next operation was seven days later, on the night of 28/29 January, when the crew were back over Germany's capital. There was less cloud, and damage could be seen to the city. However, the Philbin crew, in LL152 SE-U, must have had a tough time on the trip of over 8 hours, as Bill noted in his log book: 'Pretty shaky trip – predicted flak came damn close!' It must have been taxing for many, not just the Philbin crew. Out of a total of 673 heavy bombers dispatched, 46 were lost, of which 9 were from the Canadian group. Generally the No. 6 Group crews reported a 'good trip' and, for a change, with mixed cloud cover, they could see the results almost from the Baltic coast on their return trip home via Denmark. It would be the Philbin crew's last visit to Berlin and, unlike so many Bomber Command aircrew, they had survived the 'Battle of Berlin'.

Part IV: Scotty

13. Alouettes and a Date with Destiny

February was a quiet month for the 'Iroquois' squadron, with only two operations carried out, mainly due to a long moon period early in the month. Civilian contractors arrived at Croft to carry out modifications to the tails of the Halifaxes, replacing the triangular fins with the square slab type, later to become familiar with the type. Also, aircrew personnel thought of this as an opportunity for rest and reinvigoration. Bill's crew were thankfully not tasked with the trip to Berlin on the night of 15/16 February. And it was the final trip to the 'Big City' for the other 'Iroquois' crews, and ended their participation, too, in the so-called 'Battle of Berlin'. It had been a campaign that had taken its toll of 607 aircraft from Bomber Command, with 3,347 fatalities. No. 431 Squadron's losses of 9.8% were the second highest in No. 6 Group during the attacks on Germany's capital.

After a couple of weeks of no flying activity, Bill's only operation during February was to Leipzig on the night of the 18th/19th. According to post-operation reports, fighters were with the bomber stream all the way to the target, but the Philbin crew in LL258 SE-W apparently were lucky enough not to be bothered by enemy action and returned to Croft after a trip of 7 hours 45 minutes. However, although the Philbin crew had been fortunate, it was a bad night for the Halifax, with a loss rate of 13% of those dispatched. Among those who perished were Sergeant Murray Sonshine – who had been on a 'second dickey' trip with the Philbin crew only a month before – with his crew in Halifax LK905 SE-D.

Bomber Command's chief, Air Marshal Arthur 'Bomber' Harris, decided it was time to withdraw the Mk II and Mk V Halifaxes from operational service immediately and speed up the arrival of the much-improved Hercules-engined Mk IIIs. The opportunity was also taken to replace the

H2S radome in the belly of many of the Halifaxes with the 'Preston-Green' cupola, equipped with a 0.5-inch-calibre machine gun, a fitting very popular with the Canadians.

The rest of the month Bill's time was taken up with trips within the UK. One was with B Flight commander, Squadron Leader H. Dow, to Upwood, Wittering, and a US Army Air Corps base at Wendling, and a second took him to RAF Upwood to recover Flight Lieutenant Hill's SE-O, which had diverted due to loss of oil pressure and a runaway propeller. As the weather closed in Bill, along with some of his colleagues, experienced wonderful hospitality from the Americans, and even though quarters were cramped, their hosts did everything to make their visit as comfortable as possible. The Canadians commented: 'The meals there were excellent, most notably canned fruit with every meal and passable coffee.' Some of the crew, though not Bill, even had the experience of a flight in an 8th Air Force 392nd Bomb Group B-24 Liberator.

The first raid of March 1944, on the second day of the month, was to Meulan les Mureaux, an aircraft factory just to the north of Paris supplying aircraft components. It was selected by Bomber Command as a priority target. As the factory was near a residential area, an attack at low level was called for, to minimise civilian casualties. No. 431 Squadron sent eleven aircraft, and the Philbin crew were in LL152 SE-U again. The target was identified by red TI flares and a number of large explosions were seen. Bill noted: 'Low level – good prang!' The squadron ORB camera log file shows clear results from photos taken by the participating aircraft. The following day, Wing Commander Bill Newson was informed he would be stepping down as the squadron's commander, taking up a post as CO of No. 1664 HCU at Croft. He was a much-respected leader, often seen heading his aircraft on operations; not for him sitting behind a desk unless he had to!

Missing an operation to marshalling yards on 6/7 March, another French target – a railyard at Le Mans – was tasked for the Philbin crew in LL151 SE-P on the night of the 7th/8th. It appears from Bill's log book that the Pathfinder Force bombers were late, but altogether the operation was considered a success. On the 15th of that month 'Gerry' Philbin, with 'second dickey' pilot, Flying Officer R.W. Harrison, took Halifax Mk V LL152 SE-U on a raid to another rail target, the Amiens marshalling yards, but disaster happened on returning to Croft. Just as the aircraft taxied off the main runway, a 500-lb bomb that had 'hung up' in the bomb bay fell off, and blew the aircraft in two, the rear of the plane being totally destroyed. Luckily, Bill himself was not aboard; he had been confined to the station's sick quarters. He had been replaced as engineer by Sergeant J.L. Roche. Two of Bill's close friends were killed – gunners Warrant Officer Second Class Irwin Klein and Sergeant Lloyd Barker – though thankfully the rest of the crew, including Philbin, and 'second dickey' pilot Harrison, escaped as the aircraft became a mass of flames and were later admitted to the base hospital for treatment for shock. Sadly both Klein and Barker had just been recommended for a commission; both are now buried together in the Commonwealth War Graves Cemetery at Stonefall in Harrogate. Also at this time Flying Officer Al Brook – who had teamed up with the crew as they joined the squadron – was screened, having completed his tour of operations.

Throughout March the squadron was steadily re-equipping with the Halifax Mk III. On 19 March an official signal came through from No. 6 Group headquarters at Allerton Park telling the squadron to switch to Halifax Mk IIIs only, '… a signal received with joy by all air crew!' quoted the ORB. Bill's first flights in the type were on 24 and 26 March. The Hercules Mk XVI radial-engine version of the aircraft had a considerably improved performance over the older Merlin-engine type. Initially the Mk Vs had arrived on squadron with the triangular-shaped rear fin and smaller rudder. This had caused some directional instability, resulting in crashes, and over the winter of 1943/44 the majority of Mk Vs had those fins replaced by the 'slab' fin during routine maintenance periods as mentioned earlier; this was a great improvement. Now with the more powerful Bristol Hercules XVI and de Havilland 55/18 propeller, the Canadians could at last keep up with the Lancasters of Nos 3 and 5 Groups.

Bill's concluding operation in a Mk V Halifax on 23 March to Laon, northern France, was as part of the CO's crew in LL231 SE-J with squadron commander Wing Commander Newson on his final operation before leaving Croft for his new posting. This was part of Bomber Command's continuing strategy to destroy the enemy's transport infrastructure, in the months before the forthcoming D-Day landings in Normandy. The Canadians were in the second wave, and no TI flares were seen as the Pathfinder Force (PFF) aircraft were not present, and, due to the close proximity of French civilians, not all crews dropped their bombs. Bill recorded: 'PFF boob – Poor show.' Bad weather precluded operations at the end of March, and on the 29th all the engineers, including Bill, were given a lecture on the Bristol Hercules radial engine by a Mr Tomlinson, a representative of the manufacturer.

Throughout the end of March and into April, the switch to targets on the enemy rail and transport infrastructure came into force, as Bomber Command ranged far and wide over France, reducing the enemy's capacity to move their troops and equipment around the front. This was especially important to limit the Wehrmacht's ability to reinforce the Normandy area in the light of the forthcoming invasion of the continent. On 24 March the squadron commander, Wing Commander Newson, and Bill's B Flight commander, Squadron Leader Dow, along with some navigation crew, took charge of one of the new Halifax IIIs for the first time.

On 9 April, Bill was airborne in Halifax III SE-O, with Flight Lieutenant Hill and Gerry, on a local flight to RAF Linton-on-Ouse to pick up a new Halifax from Fairey Aviation, this one being a Stockport-built Mk III, LK884; this aircraft was destined to become 'X-Xray'.

After some more familiarisation flying, including fighter affiliation and a sea search lasting just over 5 hours, Bill's first raid in a Halifax Mk III, MZ522 SE-U, was on 18 April 1944 to Noisy-le-Sec just to the north-east of Paris city centre (noted in his log book as 'Le Bourget'). The whole squadron was using the Mk III aircraft for the first time. This was also the first trip with Philbin's new crew members: navigator Warrant Officer Second Class Ray Reed from Alameda, Saskatchewan, and Yorkshiremen Pilot Officer Sam Beresford and Warrant Officer Brian Clark from Harrogate and Bradford respectively. Bill had known Ray from training at No. 1664 HCU the previous year, and he had been posted to No. 431 Squadron at about the same time. Also joining them, when needs required an eighth member of the crew, was Flying Officer Doug Wiley from Toronto, operating mid-upper and rear turret positions, occasionally manning the Preston-Green mid-under position with a single machine gun. (See also 'Pathfinder' in Part III for more details on this raid.)

The mid-under gun's use was almost unique to the No. 6 Group Halifaxes. This replaced the H2S topographical 'radar' and its radome on many Canadian Mk III Halifaxes. It was very popular with the crews. The Canadians had been badly mauled when the Luftwaffe first introduced the Schräge-Musik upward-firing cannons into night fighters, and this was their way of combating the situation. This cupola (it was not a turret as it did not rotate) was fitted with a large 0.5-inch-calibre heavy machine gun, used to deter attacks at the weakest point of a bomber – the underside. The gunner sat on a canvas sling mounted in the lower fuselage, with the gun on a 'gimbal', allowing a wide field of fire; this author was told by Sergeant Ted Lewis, a gunner on No. 420 (Snowy Owl) Squadron that they were often allowed to use up the ammunition strafing ground targets if on their way home at low level, especially from a daylight raid. He once hit a line of enemy trucks behind the D-Day beaches!

On this operation to the Paris area, Bill recorded: 'Good Prang – encounter T/E A/C', which the author believes probably means they were attacked by fighters. The squadron ORB, noted that the 'primary' was well hit and that large fires with a lot of smoke indicated strikes on oil storage units. Several aircraft landed away from base for various reasons, but all eventually returned safely.

Strangely, Bill left two log books, though the author has been unable to establish why. The 'second' book confirms there were fighters on this raid, but then operations in April 1944 – just before the crew's posting to 425 (Alouette) Squadron – are missing completely, and flight listings recommence in June 1944, with the entries in the log being in a quite different hand, and definitely not Bill's writing. Also the 'second' book has none of the monthly annotations by the flight commander. Meanwhile, this author has used the 'first' log book as a document for these writings; possibly this second book was kept by Bill for personal record, and then lost for a while in the move back to Tholthorpe, which was to come soon, but more of that shortly.

Back at Croft and No. 431 Squadron, only a few days after the operation to Noisy-le-Sec, on the 20th they were off to Lens, again targeting marshalling yards in the enemy's transportation infrastructure in advance of the planned Allied landings. On 14 April Bomber Command had come under the direction of Supreme Headquarters Allied Expeditionary Force (SHAEF) in preparation for the forthcoming landings in Normandy. 'Bomber' Harris was not very happy and wanted to continue his campaign against the German homeland, but he was ordered to comply by General Dwight D. Eisenhower, supreme commander of the Allied forces, and Prime Minister Churchill. In MZ522 SE-U the Philbin crew were over the target at 23.43 hours and although the TIs were just to the north-east of the target, it could be visually identified, and good strikes and large fires were seen. They also encountered fighters on this operation, though no comment about if they were hit, and they were back at Croft after a flight of almost 5½ hours. On this operation, the station commander Group Captain Edwards, AFC, had been airborne as 'second dickey' with the squadron commander, Wing Commander Newson, who was 'sneaking in' another sortie, although he should have stopped operational flying. Just before midnight a tremendously large explosion was seen, thought to be fuel and explosives going off, with a brilliant flash and smoke rising over 2,000 feet.

On the 24th of the month the Philbin crew were again heading to Karlsruhe in Germany in MZ520 SE-Q, but had to abort the operation over enemy territory as Warrant Officer Brian Clark in the rear turret was taken ill. Returning, they jettisoned their bombs in a safe area over the North Sea. They landed back at Croft after a flight of 4 hours and 15 minutes. Two days later, with a replacement rear gunner, Flying Officer D.M. McArter, they were back in 'Happy Valley', the Ruhr, in MZ522 SE-U, the target being Essen. They were over the target at 01.30 hours on the 27th and had clear visibility, and the camera log noted that most aircraft had clear photographs of the target. Bill recorded there had been 'bags of flak!' A day or so later Bill was up with Gerry, and the station CO, Group Captain Edwards, in LW385 SE-M, just on a local flight. At the end of April, Flying Officer Gerry Philbin was promoted to flight lieutenant. The crew missed the last operation of that month, on 27 April, to rail yards at Montzen.

The following month was to be Bill's and the Philbin crew's final month with No. 431 (Iroquois) Squadron. On 7 May, they took MZ602 SE-U to Saint-Valery-en-Caux, and a heavy gun battery on the French coast just west of Dieppe. They were 'softening up' Rommel's 'Atlantic Wall'. The gun pits were situated high on cliffs either side of the harbour of the coastal port, and controlled by a bunker set deep in the cliffs about 30 feet below the top of the escarpment. This was a relatively low-level operation; they were bombing the target at only 5,500 feet and they hit the centre of the green TIs, although one stick of bombs from another aircraft was observed falling into the sea. However, a large explosion was seen by Flying Officer Doug Wiley in the rear turret. During a visit to the site in July 2014, bomb craters could still be viewed.

After another 'fighter affiliation' exercise on the 9th, the crew took MZ602 SE-U to Boulogne, just over the English Channel from Dover, but they encountered strong winds that had not been forecasted by the met.

officer. At this time the 'jet stream' was still unknown. That made it impossible to reach the target on time, so they turned back, and brought their bomb load home. They had better luck the following day, and the crew were off to Louvain, near Rennes in central France. There is a discrepancy on official records on this operation; according to the 'Raid Schedule', a 'tasking' list issued before the event, the crew should have been in their regular Halifax, MZ602 SE-U, and yet the squadron ORB tells that they were in LW576 SE-O. It is likely that 'U-Uncle' was unfit for the operation at the last minute and so they transferred to the other Halifax. In fact, MZ602, still marked as 'U-Uncle', disappeared after take-off just after D-Day and was never seen again, taking with it Pilot Officer J. Artyniuk and his crew. Whatever happened, on that night there was only light haze over the Louvain target, another marshalling yard, so the Halifaxes bombed from 7,500 feet just after midnight on 13 May, and a large explosion was seen, lasting at least 30 seconds, giving a column of black smoke; obviously a good strike. It was Bill's nineteenth operation.

On 23 May 1944 Bill Gracie was promoted to flight sergeant. A few days later he was airborne with a new pilot to the squadron, Sergeant Aldred, on a daytime 'fighter affiliation' exercise and a 'bullseye' practice night mission of almost 5 hours. At this point his log book is signed off by Wing Commander H.R. Dow, the 'Iroquois' squadron commander, and the whole crew 'en block' was now posted to No. 425 (Alouette) Squadron back at Tholthorpe. Only Flying Officer Doug Wiley did not transfer, staying with No. 431 Squadron. Having spoken to others, including Doug Wiley in the 1990s, Gerry Philbin, being from the Quebec area, and therefore French Canadian, was instrumental in their posting to 'Alouettes', the only French Canadian squadron in 6 Group and Bomber Command. After a seven-day leave, the crew reported to their new unit at the airfield they knew so well on 9 June 1944. It was during leave on 12 July that Bill took the opportunity to return to his 'roots', and he travelled up to Lanarkshire in Scotland to visit his mother's sister, Aunt Jean Muir, and her daughter, also Jean, in the village of Crossford, at a little cottage on the banks of the River Clyde. The photographs taken with a teenage Jean, by Craignethan Castle, are the last-known images of 'Scotty'.

This author was told by Real St Amour, the 'Alouette' squadron's wartime adjutant, at a reunion in Toronto that the squadron had experienced a bad time in May with quite heavy losses, and they were looking to increase the numbers of French Canadians in the unit. They had requested Gerry Philbin, from Montreal, because of his French-Canadian background and his experience. He was quickly promoted again, this time to squadron leader, and appointed commander of B Flight No. 425 Squadron. A few days later, after a test flight and bombing practice in Halifax III LW538 KW-V, the crew were off on their first raid with the new squadron. On 16 June they took Halifax LW680 KW-U to a V1 storage depot in the Pas de Calais area called Sautrecourt. This type of target was notoriously difficult to hit, comprising scattered block buildings in wooded areas. The author visited this site in September 2008 and found clear damage on some of the buildings. Their bomb load of 14 x 500-lb GP bombs, and 2 x 500-lb LD bombs were dropped from 14,900 feet, and bomb flashes were seen around the TIs, but no damage could be observed; not surprising seeing there was dense woodland, and the dispersed nature of the buildings.

A couple of days later Bill flew to the English Electric factory at Samlesbury near Preston with Flying Officer Henry in LW381 KW-B to pick up a new Halifax Mk III, MZ590, and return to Tholthorpe. As often happened, flight commanders had to carry out test flights within a squadron, so the next couple of days were taken up with that and training new crew personnel. The aircrew's next operation in LW680 KW-U was on 23 June to Bamieres, just to the north of the River Somme. This was a V1 flying-bomb launch site, also known as a 'ski site' due to the design of the final storage building, and one of six such locations targeted on that night. Bill's aircraft was one of forty Lancasters and sixty-five Halifaxes tasked to hit the target between midnight and 00.15 hours. Heavy cloud obscured the target, and Gerry Philbin commented at the debrief that if the TIs were on target the concentration of bomb bursts should have produced a good result. Bill noted, 'Very little flak.'

After a trip with Flight Lieutenant Jaques Cote, a diminutive jolly French Canadian (whom the author met in 1990), to RAF Linton-on-Ouse and back on 29 July, Bill's next operation with Gerry was a daylight operation to Amayé-sur-Seulles, in the Villers Bocage–Caumont area, on the American side of the Allied advance, which Bill noted was '2,000 yards ahead of our lines'. In all 692 aircraft were involved, and No. 425 Squadron were led by their commanding officer Wing Commander L.H. Lecomte in MZ620 KW-T. The post-operation debrief showed the squadron bombed from only 1,800 feet and the target was obscured by smoke from the very beginning, with the master bomber asking for bombing south of the smoke, although some bombs did 'creep' north towards the Allied troops. Lieutenant General (retired) Chester Hull, within a few days to be CO of No. 428 (Ghost) Squadron remembered: 'This was the third time we [author's note – No. 6 Group] had been out supporting the invasion troops. The Master Bomber instructed the bombers to go below the cloud and drop their bombs and, although some did not hear his instructions, most of Canadian crews came down and bombed accurately, aided by flares sent over by the ground forces. It was a successful attack, and produced good photographic results of a severely pock-marked target area. Thankfully there were no fighters, but it was altogether a difficult raid.'

The next outing, on 3 August, was back to bombing Operation Crossbow targets of the German missile offensive. Another problematic target deep in the Forêt de Nieppe, in the Oise Valley, this storage area was again a scattered site, and even today is hard to locate. The Philbin crew were flying LL594 KW-U, now named 'Allan Cup' after Gerry's success in ice hockey with, as the eighth crew member, Sergeant Gilbert L. Milliard, another French Canadian from Montreal, manning the mid-under position. This evening raid, the aircraft taking off at 18.30 hours, produced mixed results, with areas of the target being difficult to identify even though there was little cloud. At this point– the post-invasion period – this area of France was the most bombed region in the country. In 1994 Daniel Lesobre, chairman of the ANACR (the Resistance veteran's organisation) told the author that more French souls were killed and wounded in the Oise Valley during these raids on the V1 weapon sites than in any other part of France in the Second World War.

Just 24 hours later, one of only three aviation Canadian Victoria Cross awards was won by Squadron Leader Ian Bazalgette of No. 635 Squadron, RAF. On 4 August the distribution area in the woods of Trossy St Maximin (now known as St Maximin) was targeted, and it was during this raid that Bazalgette won the VC, for staying with his damaged Lancaster in an attempt to save two of his injured crew, bomb aimer Flight Lieutenant I.A. Hibbert, DFC, and mid-upper gunner Flight Sergeant V.V. Leeder, RAAF. The aircraft came down just outside the village of Senantes, with those left on board being killed. The site of the crater where the Lancaster III, ND811 F2-A, of No. 635 Squadron came down is still visible in the field, just to the north of the village, and the event is marked by a memorial plaque in the nearby hedgerow. Bazalgette is buried in the Senantes village churchyard in a grave immaculately maintained by the locals.

The next day, Saturday 5 August 1944, was to prove fateful for Gerry Philbin and his loyal crew. LL594 KW-U 'Allan Cup' took off from Tholthorpe airfield, about 11.00 hours and headed south. The flak was heavy over the target, again in the Oise Valley; this time the limestone caves of St Leu d'Esserent. The caves had been utilised by man from prehistory, mostly for mushroom farming, but during the late 1930s they had been extended and used by the French aviation industry for aircraft manufacture. In fact the target had been visited before, twice in July 1944 by Bomber Command, the attack including the use of 'Tallboy' bombs. It was known to be a tough target and well protected by anti-aircraft batteries. The area was heavily marked by the Pathfinders with aiming point indicated by TI daylight flares from H-Hour minus 4 minutes to H-Hour minus 2 minutes. An aerial photograph was taken during the raid from Pilot Officer Johnson's 'A-Able' aircraft of No. 420 Squadron at 13.15 hours. The main stream bombed from 15,000 feet, increasing to 17,000 feet at 160 knots indicated air speed. Over the target several No. 6 Group aircraft were hit, including No. 415 (Swordfish) Squadron's LK766 'V-Victor' flown by Flying Officer B. Roberts, and MZ 828 BM-H of No. 433 (Porcupine) Squadron from Skipton-on-Swale.

At about 13.18 hours, LL594 KW-U received a direct hit on the wing root of the starboard wing. Navigator Flying Officer Jim Kinder, who was in the cockpit of MZ828 with his pilot, was watching the raid progress. In a letter to the author he said: 'It was then I saw the aircraft (KW-U) ahead of us and slightly below, lose its starboard wing – my estimate was that it was 150–200 yards in front. The wing literally fell off – I doubt it would be any other reason but flak – must have been an explosion where the main plane joins the fuselage. We didn't see anyone bail out, but then we were hit, and we lost our starboard outer. This was the beginning of our problems.'

In fact, two members of the crew of 'Allan Cup' did manage to get out: Pilot Gerry Philbin, who found himself hanging under his parachute; and Sergeant Gilbert Milliard, who presumably slipped out of the gap where the gun was located in the Preston-Green cupola under the fuselage. Milliard was eventually captured and made a POW (No. 608 at Stalag Luft camp 7); Philbin came down in a field about 1½ miles from Chantilly. In his report for the No. 425 Squadron Operational Records Book he commented: 'The Halifax must have exploded in mid-air, as I was wounded in the face and had two broken ribs. Also my legs were black and blue as if having been knocked against something very hard. Immediately on landing I was surrounded by Germans. One of them pulled me away from the fires of the aircraft, and so saved my life.' In truth he landed among the bombs being dropped by his squadron, and one of the German gunners pulled him into a foxhole. The Halifax came down in woods near the village of St Maximin, close to where a railway bridge crosses the present-day D44 road.

The bodies of 'Scotty' Gracie, Ray Reed and Tommy Lee were found nearby, as can be seen in a drawing made by resistance fighters in the area. An RCAF letter to the Gracie family dated 30 April 1945 states ' ... that about 10 August 1944 one of the French "Patriotic Guards" [author's note – probably communist resistance fighters] found the bodies of three Canadian airmen which the Germans had obviously searched. Certain papers had been over-looked, however from these it has apparently been able to establish the identity of your son (William) and Pilot Officer Lee. These Canadian airmen were buried by the French who made a sketch location of the graves. The third Canadian is assumed to be Pilot Officer Reed, whose death has been confirmed by an American burial return form.' There is no reference to the British members of the crew, Les Stamp, Graham Beresford and Brian Clark in the RCAF correspondence, but their bodies must not have been far away. Beresford left a young wife of only six weeks, Marjory, back in Harrogate. All the Canadian and English crew of LL594 were eventually reinterred together in the Canadian cemetery at Hautot-sur-Mer at Dieppe, in October 1945, with the exception of Tommy Lee who was (in 1994) cared for by a French family in Chantilly cemetery along with one of their 'Resistance' family members, but is now buried alone with a standard Commonwealth War Graves headstone.

In a letter to the author in 1990, Gerry Philbin admitted he owed his life to having the pilot's seat of his aircraft modified to accept a fighter-pilot 'bum' parachute; he didn't remember leaving the aircraft, only 'coming to' under the canopy. His life was also saved by a German soldier who pulled him into a foxhole and defended him against his colleagues. Gerry had some broken ribs and fractured ankles. Later that day he was taken to a German field hospital, and the following day he was driven to the Beaujon Luftwaffe hospital in Clichy, Paris, where he stayed for nearly two weeks. He was then transferred to another hospital, with some USAAC B-17 crew from the 100th Bomb Group who had been shot down on a raid on 11 August, where they were told by the SS commander they would be transported to Germany that evening. Gerry and American airman Chuck Nekvasil decided to lead an escape attempt, both being fluent in French.

They were able to enlist help from the French and, as the Maquis attacked the Germans, they overpowered and killed the only guard on their seventh-floor rooms, grabbed the keys and made off; the group managed to make about 9 miles in the first 24 hours. On 3 September, after being strafed by an enemy fighter, they came across some motorcyclists from the French 2nd Armoured Division, and they were finally in Allied hands. Eventually, after survivor's leave, Gerry Philbin returned to the RCAF and a desk job in the UK.

LL594 KW-U was the only aircraft of the 742 Bomber Command aircraft – 469 Halifaxes, 257 Lancasters and 16 Mosquitoes – on the joint raids to St Leu d'Esserent and Trossy of 5 August to go down over the target, and so is listed as 'Missing on Operations'. In fact, as mentioned earlier, MZ828 'H' was badly damaged and managed to limp back to Yorkshire, but as it came in on approach to its home base of Skipton-on-Swale, it crashed in the centre of the local village of the same name, killing five-year-old schoolboy Kenneth Battensby, as well as the pilot Flying Officer Jim Harrison and flight engineer Sergeant David Whitbread. The other members of the crew survived, but it would be many weeks before they, including Jim Kinder, would be back on operations. This aircraft is listed as 'Crashed in UK'. There is a memorial on Skipton-on-Swale village green, unveiled on 19 May 1984, to the Canadian crew lost on operations from RAF Skipton-on-Swale.

In the Oise Valley in the centre of the village of St Maximin there is a children's kindergarten school next to which is a Canadian maple tree. By the tree is a memorial plaque to the crew of LL594. On Tholthorpe village green, next to the RCAF memorial – unveiled by Air Vice Marshal Donald 'Pathfinder' Bennett on 17 June 1986 – and close to where LL594 took off on its fatal sortie, is another maple tree, also with a commemorative plaque. Both trees were plucked as tiny saplings from the ground at the Gracie family house in Rogers Street, Peterborough, Ontario, in 1992, and brought to the UK by this author. As these became strong enough they were planted in those locations as memorials to a brave RCAF crew, in an aircraft that had a date with destiny. Why? Because Flight Sergeant Bill 'Scotty' Gracie was my father. A father sadly never known, as this author was born in Wallasey, Merseyside, seven days after his plane crashed – almost to the hour that the Halifax went down.

Mrs Christina Gracie, my grandmother, never really accepted that her eldest son had been killed in action, in spite of receiving correspondence from the RCAF, Bill's medals and his operations winged 'O' badge in 1947. The family told me: 'It was only when you came on the scene in the late 1970s that she fully accepted his death.' She admitted to me: 'I thought he would survive and was living in France, possibly with a French girl. Until I received your letters in 1977, I had no idea he had made a girl pregnant in Liverpool, or you existed! However, I now know his sacrifice was not in vain.' I got to know my grandmother well, until she passed on in 1992, and it was her inspiration that encouraged me to tell these stories.

Such were the changes in people's lives that came about because of the Second World War, a conflict that covered every continent and part of this planet. Canada's participation in the Allied cause was higher than any other Commonwealth country. The Canadian Navy became the third largest in the world. The country's contribution to the battles in the sky was huge, with Canadians being involved from the very earliest sorties, to the end in the Far East. Friendships made between the Canadians and the people of Britain during the hostilities endure to this day, and make the relationship between Canada and Britain as strong in the twenty-first century as it was over seventy years ago.

Appendix

Headquarters, bases and squadrons

Headquarters

No. 6 (RCAF) Group, Bomber Command, RAF Allerton Park, near Knaresborough, North Yorkshire. Formed October 1942. Operational from 1 January 1943.

Bases

No. 61 Base	Dishforth	Callsign 'Martex'
	Topcliffe	Callsign 'Goodfriend'
	Dalton	Callsign 'Holdtight'
No. 62 Base	Linton-on-Ouse	Callsign 'Dogbark'
Satellite	Tholthorpe	Callsign 'Fishzone'
Satellite	Eastmoor	Callsign 'Singer'
No. 63 Base	Leeming	Callsign 'Mustwe'
Satellite	Skipton-on-Swale	Callsign 'Briarwood'
No. 64 Base	Middleton St George	Callsign 'Strapper'
Satellite	Croft	Callsign 'Bigtree'
	Wombleton	Callsign 'Chicken Leg'

Nos 62, 63 and 64 Bases and their satellites were all 'operational' airfields, 61 Base airfields were used sparingly for operations, for dispersal and for maintenance and training. Dalton was the base for the Group Fighter Affiliation Unit and communications aircraft. Wombleton was the last

Yorkshire base to be constructed, opening in late 1943, and only ever used for No. 1666 HCU.

Squadrons of No. 6 (RCAF) Group

No. 405 (Vancouver) Squadron	Formed 23 April 1941 (only in No. 6 Group 1 March to 18 April 1943)
No. 408 (Goose) Squadron	Formed 24 June 1941
No. 415 (Swordfish) Squadron	Formed 20 August 1941
No. 419 (Moose) Squadron	Formed 5 December 1941
No. 420 (Snowy Owl) Squadron	Formed 19 December 1941
No. 424 (Tiger) Squadron	Formed 15 October 1942
No. 425 (Alouette) Squadron	Formed 22 June 1942
No. 426 (Thunderbird) Squadron	Formed 15 October 1942
No. 427 (Lion) Squadron	Formed 7 November 1942
No. 428 (Ghost) Squadron	Formed 7 November 1942
No. 429 (Bison) Squadron	Formed 7 November 1942
No. 431 (Iroquois) Squadron	Formed 11 November 1942
No. 432 (Leaside) Squadron	Formed 1 May 1943
No. 433 (Porcupine) Squadron	Formed 25 September 1943
No. 434 (Bluenose) Squadron	Formed 13 June 1943

Glossary

Units

ANS	Air Navigation School.
BCATP	British Commonwealth Air Training Plan.
B&GS	Bombing and Gunnery School.
CFB	Canadian Forces Base.
EFTS	Elementary Flying Training School.
HCU	Heavy Conversion Unit.
MU	Maintenance Unit.
OTU	Operational Training Unit.
PRD	Personnel Reception Depot.
RAAF	Royal Australian Air Force.
SFTS	Service Flying Training School.
WTS	Wireless Training School.

Awards

AFC	Air Force Cross (not on operational conditions).
CGM	Conspicuous Gallantry Medal (non-commissioned ranks – equivalent to DSO).
DFC	Distinguished Flying Cross (officers only).
DFM	Distinguished Flying Medal (NCOs only).
DSO	Distinguished Service Order (officers only).
VC	Victoria Cross (all ranks).

Other

Ack-ack	Slang for anti-aircraft fire.
Bullseye	Navigational exercise over UK simulating an operation.

DNCO	Did not complete operation.
E-boat	Coastal attack motor launch of German Navy.
H2S	Ground-following radar operated from aircraft.
HE	Heavy explosives content for bombs.
H-Hour	Designation time of attack for operation.
IFF	Indentification, friend or foe system.
LMF	Lack of moral fibre – failure to do the job during war.
Lord Haw-Haw	Englishman working for German propaganda broadcast network – William Joyce.
Nickel	Raid in which leaflets are dropped – not bombs.
ORB	Operations Record Book, completed daily by each squadron on the day's activities.
Pundit Light	Large beacon on airfield flashing identification letter in Morse code.
Ski-site	Concrete V1 flying bomb launch site – so called because of the layout of the building seen from the air.
SS	*Schutzstaffel* – Nazi secret police enforcement service.
Sten gun	Small lightweight sub-machine gun used by British Allied forces and supplied to the Resistance.
Tallboy	12,000-lb heavy penetration bomb designed by Barnes Wallis. Carried only by Lancasters.
TIs	Target indicator flares dropped by Pathfinders.
Tiger Force	Planned bomber force for Far East theatre of war. Commonwealth participation planned to be mostly from the Canadian bomber squadrons. Not operational.
U-boat pens	Large concrete structures built to house and hide U-boats when in port.
VHF	Radio frequencies between 25MHz and 190MHz. Not widely used until late in war. Most radio frequencies used by RAF were low frequency, 5MHz to 25MHz.
Wild Boar	Luftwaffe night-fighter system using single-seat fighters.

Bibliography

Title	Author
No.6 (RCAF)Group Operational Record	Chris Ward
No.617 'Dambuster' Sqn.	Alex Bateman
A Yorkshire Squadron	Bill Heron
Action Stations Vol.3	David J. Smith
Action Stations Revisited Vol.3	David W. Lee
After the Battle - Bomber Command	Roger Freeman & Winston Oliver
Bomber Command War Diaries	Martin Middlebrook & Chris Everett
Bomber Command Losses 1943/44, HCUs	Bill Chorley
Behind the Glory	Ted Barris
Behind Enemy Lines	Mary Thomas & James Moffatt
Black Night for Bomber Command	Richard Knott
Berlin Raids	Martin Middlebrook
Bomber Command	Max Hastings
Cheshire	Richard Morris
Crucible of War Vol.3	Greenhous, Harris & Johnston
Failed to Return	Bill Norman
FlyPast Magazine	Various – Key Publishing
Hamish – Story of a Pathfinder	T.G. "Hamish" Mahaddie
Halifax Second to None	Victor Bingham
Halifax – Hell to Victory & Beyond	K.A. Merrick
Halifax Special	Bruce Robertson
Lancaster Down!	Steve Darlow
Most Secret War	Prof. H.V. Jones
Over to You Over (Unpublished)	Steve Puskas
Pilgrimages of Grace – History of Croft	Alan A.B. Todd
RAF & RCAF Nose Art	Clarence Simonsen
Reap the Whirlwind	Spencer Dunmore and Bill Carter
Sixty Years of the RCAF	Larry Milberry
Sledgehammers for Tintacks	Steve Darlow
So Many	Gunson, Pierce and Golley
Straight and True (Story of RAF Leeming)	Peter Copeland
They Shall Grow Not Old (CATP Museum)	Les Allison and Harry Haywood.
Thunderbirds at War	Larry Motiuk
Wings over Linton	Peter D. Mason
Wings for Victory	Spencer Dunmore

Index

No. 1 Air Division   155
No. 1 Group   130
No. 1 RCAF Manning Depot   1, 2, 52, 57, 160
2nd Armoured Division (French)   182
No. 2 School of Air Navigation   12
No. 2 Service Flying Training School   160
No. 3 Bombing and Gunnery School   57–58
No. 3 Group   130, 132, 173
No. 4 Group   21, 130, 131–132, 135, 147
No. 4 School of Technical Training   162
No. 5 Group   130, 138, 173
No. 5 Service Flying Training School   3, 7, 9, 17
No. 6 Initial Training School   3
No. 6 (RCAF) Group   ii–iii, 19, 21, 23, 34, 52, 60, 62–63, 143, 148–149, 153, 156, 161, 166, 170–171, 173–174, 177, 179–180, 184–185
No. 6 Service Flying Training School   57
No. 6 Squadron RCAF Manning Depot   160
No. 7 Air Gunnery School   163
No. 7 Squadron   152
No. 8 Maintenance Unit   50
No. 8 (Pathfinder) Group   34, 50, 74, 127, 132–133, 138, 142, 147, 151, 153, 167, 173, 180
US 8th Air Force   73, 172
No. 9 Elementary Flying Training School   4
No. 9 Squadron   180
No. 10 Operational Training Unit   121
No. 10 Service Flying Training School   121
No. 10 Squadron   123–124, 127
13th Field Ambulance RCAMC   121
No. 14 Depot   160
No. 15 (P) Advance Flying Unit   12
16th Luftwaffe Field Division   153
No. 17 Depot   10, 160
No. 18 Advance Flying Unit   13
21st Panzer Division   153
No. 24 Operational Training Unit   13,14
No. 31 Personnel Reception Depot   10
No. 32 Maintenance Unit   162
No. 35 Squadron   121–127, 129, 131–132, 134, 136, 139
No. 61 Base   184
No. 62 Base   184
No. 63 Base   184
No. 64 Base   184
No. 76 Squadron   123, 124
No. 77 Squadron   165
No. 82 Operational Training Unit   48,60
No. 91 General Service Unit   49–50
No. 100 Squadron   73
100th Bomb Group   181
No. 106 Squadron   168
120 (Transport) Wing   154
132 Regiment of Fortress   106
No. 158 Squadron   81
392nd Bomb Group   172
No. 405 (Vancouver) Squadron   34, 60, 147–148, 152, 185
No. 408 (Moose) Squadron   155, 185
No. 415 (Swordfish) Squadron   44, 180, 185
No. 419 (Moose) Squadron   39, 62, 71, 148, 185
No. 420 (Snowy Owl) Squadron   23, 175, 180, 185
No. 424 (Tiger) Squadron   43,185
No. 425 (Alouette) Squadron   40, 45, 175, 177–178, 180, 185
No. 426 (Thunderbird) Squadron   16, 33, 35, 185
No. 427 (Lion) Squadron   46, 61–62, 72, 114, 116, 185
No. 428 (Ghost) Squadron   179, 185
No. 429 (Bison) Squadron   20–22, 36, 42, 44, 50, 67, 185
No. 431 (Iroquois) Squadron   164–168, 170–172, 174–177, 185
No. 432 (Leaside) Squadron   185
No. 433 (Porcupine) Squadron   180, 185
No. 434 (Bluenose) Squadron   165, 168, 185
No. 467 Squadron   168
No. 617 Squadron   40, 42, 122, 149
No. 619 Squadron   169
No. 622 Squadron   75, 116
No. 635 Squadron   45, 152, 179
No. 1502 Beam Approach Flight   133
No. 1531 Squadron Beam Approach Training   12
No. 1659 Heavy Conversion Unit   48, 60–61, 161, 162, 169

No. 1664 Heavy Conversion
   Unit   19, 161, 163, 166, 169, 172, 174
No. 1666 Heavy Conversion
   Unit   48, 185
No. 1667 Heavy Conversion
   Unit   169

A

Aachen   36
Abbeville   40, 45
Aberdeen   25
Abingdon   121, 132
Achères   41
Adam, Monsieur   92
Agur, P.S.   41
Aisy   46
Alameda   174
Alberta   35, 45
Aldred, Sergeant   177
Aldwych   51
Allan, Flight Lieutenant   148
Allerton Park   71–72, 149, 153–154, 173, 184
Amayé-sur-Seulles   178
Amiens   172
Anderson, Bill   41
Andes   160
Andrews, Barbara   153–154
Aquitania   154
Arbuckle, George   43
Arc de Triomphe   45
Arles   91
Arlon   77, 83
Arras   39
Artyniuk, J.   177
Asen Fjord   124
Asplin, R.J.   117
Athenia   159
Atherton (navigator)   50
Au Fèvre   36
Augsburg   73
Aulnoye   27
Autphenne, Germaine   95–97, 101, 112
Avant, Al   33, 38, 43
Avignon   84
Aylmer   116

B

Baalon   99
Baczinski, Mike   143
Baer, Russ   8, 10
Balfour, Lord   6
Bamieres   178
Barcelona   84
Barker, Lloyd   164, 173
Bastogne   112

Batad, A.   27
Batincourt   79
Battensby, Kenneth   182
Bazalgette, Ian   45, 179
Beauvoir   39
Beaujon Luftwaffe Hospital   181
Bedale   47
Belfast   160
Belgian Forestry Service   89
Belsen   152
Bennett, Don   127, 132–134, 138–139, 147, 182
Benson   41
Benz, Flight Sergeant   35
Beresford, Marjory   181
Beresford, Sam   174, 181
Berlin   22, 40, 50, 69, 72, 122, 132, 140–142, 148–151, 153, 167–168, 70–171
Biggar   143
Bilbao   84
Billancourt   124
Bingham   134
Birmingham   78
Bitz, Flying Officer   9
Blackburn   162
Blenkinsop, E.M.   152
Boczar, Steve   143
Bois de Cassan   44
Bois de Juvigny   103
Boissevain   163
Bolton, Jim   11
Bomber Command Memorial (London)   35
Bomber Command Museum (Nanton)   35
Bonn   131
Boothman, Air Commodore   26
Boscombe Down   62, 122
Boulogne   34, 39, 176
Bourg Leopold   36
Bournemouth   11, 12, 59, 67, 78, 121, 160–161
Bowen, Captain   144
Bowen, Flight Lieutenant   22
Bowles, Joan   48
Bowles, Ted   14, 19, 24–25, 27–29, 31, 42, 47–48
Boyce, Group Captain   147
Bradford   174
Brandon   143
Brantford   3, 7, 10–11, 16–17
Breadner, Lloyd   144
Bremen   131–132
Brest   123, 132
Bringloe, Warrant Officer   8–9
British Columbia   51, 120, 155
Broggi, Roger   108–109
Brook, Al   163, 173
Brookes, George   143

Brophy, John   39
Brown, Charles   129
Brunswick   148
Brussels   81, 84, 112–113, 115
Bryan, J.G.   31
Bryans, Group Captain   74
Buckley, H.   122
Burgar, Reg   143, 146
Burge, Flight Sergeant   167
Burn   164
Bury St Edmunds   74
Bushy Park   154

C

Cadogan, Warrant Officer   34
Caen   153
Calgary   45, 145
Cambrai   39
Cambridge   133, 156
Canadian Warplane Heritage   2
Cardy, Bill   61–66, 70, 112
Carere, John   143
Carron, Charlie   63
Caumont   178
Cavell, Edith   84
Chambers, Flight Sergeant   166
Champs Elysées   107
Chantilly   180–181
Cherbourg   36, 37
Cheshire, Leonard   122, 138
Child, J.S.   73
Christ Church Cathedral   120
Churchill, Winston   6, 60, 124, 130, 143, 152, 175
Clangbourne (pilot)   146
Clapham, Will   67, 77, 116
Clark, Brian   174, 176, 181
Clibbery, Flight Sergeant   70
Clichy   181
Cochrane   143
Colborne   115
Cole, Kenneth   58, 60
Colerne   136
Collyer, Eddie   163
Cologne   122, 124, 130, 132, 135, 139, 147
Cooper, T.W.   74
Collins, G.R.   117
Comet Line   84
Coquereaux   44
Corbally, Joe   64–65, 70, 77, 116
Cote, Jacques   178
Cothliff, Doreen   ii
Cothliff, Hilda   i–iii
Cothliff, Julie   iii
Cothliff, Malcolm   i–iii
Coup, N.J.   117
Couvreux   95, 112

INDEX

Craig, A.G.	165	
Craignethan Castle	177	
Cranage	12	
Cranwell	147	
Cresswell, E.K.	153	
Crewe	12	
Cribb, Peter	127	
Croft	19, 161, 163, 165, 167, 169, 171–173, 175–176, 184	
Cross, Captain	71, 112	
Crossford	177	

D

Dalton	18, 32, 166, 184
Dampicourt	92
Darlington	61, 69, 161 ,163
Darlow, Arthur	71
Dartmouth	84
Dauphin	121
Davies, Fred	161
Decarpentrie, Alice	84
Dieppe	35, 41, 176, 181
Dijon	84
Dishforth	19, 166, 169, 184
Dobson, Pilot Officer	129, 131
Domléger	39
Dorval	144, 146
Dover	176
Dow, H.	172, 174, 177
Drew, E.B.	148
Driffield	133, 147
Dunblane	41
Duisburg	131
Dunkeswell	17
Dunkirk	84
Dunlop, Gordon	149
Dunville	59
Durocher, Ken	114
Durocher, 'Rocky'	67, 114
Düsseldorf	17, 33, 50, 67, 132, 166
Duxford	156
Dyce	25

E

East Moor	21, 166, 184
Écouviez	96
Edinburgh	165
Edmonton	155
Edwards, H.	120, 146–147, 176
Eisenhower, Dwight	175
Elizabeth, Princess	46
Ellis, William	110, 112
Ellwood, Squadron Leader	152
Emden 1	31
Empress of Scotland	11
English Electric	162, 178
Éperlecques	38

Esk	164
Essen	28, 32, 124, 131, 176
Esterri d'Aneu	84
Étalle	80–82, 85, 88, 91, 94, 100

F

Fairey Aviation	162, 174
Fairfield	155
Falaise	46
Farnborough	26
Faulkner, Wilf	14–15, 17, 25, 28–31
Fauquier, Johnny	147, 149
Fayid	155
Field, Pilot Officer	129
FIDO	133
Film Board of Canada	145
Findlay, Jack	60–61, 64–66
Fishguard	60
Flensberg	133
Fletcher, Sergeant	62
Flint, Sergeant	123
Floren, Harry	148
Forêt de Nieppe	44,179
Fournier, Mrs	116
Fournier, Roger	56, 67, 69, 116
Fouss, Edmond-Pierre	91
Frankfurt	70, 74, 148, 168

G

Gainsborough	60
Galland, Adolph	123
Galt Aircraft School	160
Gamston	49
Gander	144, 146
Ganderton, V. 'Gandy'	71–72, 114
Gardiner, Flight Lieutenant	43
de Gaulle, General	106
Ghent	33–34
Gibb, Andy	17
Gibraltar	84, 123
Giles, F.A.	22–23, 27
Giot, Guy 'Emile'	95–97
Glasgow	160
Glenevon	143
Gneisenau	123
Goering, Hermann	138
Gorenflos	40
Gracie, Betty	iii
Gracie, Bill 'Scotty'	i–ii, 159–183
Gracie, Christina	i–ii, 159, 182
Gracie, David	ii, 159–160
Gracie, Jean	159
Gracie, Thomas	ii–iii
Gransden Lodge	142, 144, 147, 150, 156
Grantham	26
Graveley	133–134, 142 ,148

Greene, Lorne	145
Green Howards	18–19
Greenock	59
Green Park, London	ii
Grunenwald, James	101–102, 105–108
Guérisse, Albert	84
Guest, Flying Officer	8

H

Haines-Finnel, Charles	8–10
Halanzy	77, 79, 81, 93, 116
Halifax (Nova Scotia)	10, 59, 121, 154, 159–160
Hamber, Squadron Leader	16
Hamburg	44, 95, 122, 135, 136, 138
Hamilton	1, 9–10, 18, 31–32, 50–51
Hamilton Flying Club	2
Hammond, Sergeant	125
Hanover	63, 165
Harland and Wolff	160
Harris, Sir Arthur	22, 60, 130–132, 141, 143, 149, 171, 175
Harrison, Jim	182
Harrison, R.W.	172
Harrogate	69, 71, 173–174, 181
Hautot-sur-Mer	181
Haw Haw, Lord	11
Haxby, Sergeant	129, 135, 141
Hennequin, Lucien	106, 108–109
Henry, Flying Officer	178
Hermann, Hajo	69, 138
Hewitt, Barbara	iii
Hewitt, Ian	126
Hibbert, I.A.	179
Higgins, Flight Lieutenant	35, 42
Hill, Flight Lieutenant	172, 174
Hollywood	61
Holmes, Harry	146
Honeybourne	13–17
Hudson's Bay Company	120
Hull	70
Hull, Chester	179

I

Ile de France	59
Île de Oléron	47
Île de Ré	47
Ilkley Moor	166
Irish, Warrant Officer	44

J

James, Pilot Officer	131
Jametz	103, 109
Johnson, James 'Johnnie'	154
Johnson, Pilot Officer	180

Jones, Bill	81–83, 85–86		70–74, 78, 112, 114, 122, 147, 184	McClune, J.A.	67
de Jongh, Andrée	84	Leeder, V.V.	179	McEwen C.M. 'Black Mike'	72
de Jongh Frédéric	84	Le Havre	122	McGurty	66
		Leipzig	50, 73, 168, 171	McKenzie-King, William	6, 143
		Le Mans	36, 74, 172	McLennan, B.A.	148

K

		Lens	33, 152, 175	McLeod, D.G.	166
		Lesobre, Daniel	179	Meulan les Mureaux	172
Kammhuber, Josef	138	Leverkusen	167	Meritt, J.P.	117
Karlsruhe	33, 50, 176	Lewis, Ted	23, 175	Merville	37
Karachi	155	Liège	116	Messien, Marcel	82–83, 85
Kassel	64 ,67–68, 70–71, 166	Limoges	84	Messien, Rose	82–83, 85
Kennedy, Flight Lieutenant	17	Lincoln's Inn Fields	13, 120, 143	Metro Goldwyn Meyer	61
Kenney, Squadron Leader	26, 164	Linton-on-Ouse	iii, 16, 33, 121–122,	Metropole Hotel	112
Kiel	124, 135, 139, 141	125, 127, 153, 166, 174, 178, 184		Metz	41, 81, 155
Kildeer	164	Lister, Flight Lieutenant	168	Middlemiss, Flight Lieutenant	49
Kinder, Jim	180, 182	Little Rissington	50	Middleton St George	66, 71–72,
Kingsland, Flying Officer	44	Little Snoring	22	148, 184	
Kitchener	73	Liverpool	11–12, 21, 51, 114, 162, 183	Miller, W.C.	74
Kjarsgaard, Karl	iii, 35	Locking	13	Milliard, Gilbert	179, 180
Klein, Irwin	163–164, 173	London	18, 26, 35, 37, 40, 50–52, 91,	Moffat, David	55
Knaresborough	153, 184	113–114, 133, 156		Moffat, Elizabeth	55, 115
Koval, Richard	iii	London Aircraft Production		Moffat, Jim	ii, 55–117
Krenz, H.	170	Group	162	Moffatt, Rob	115
Krupps Works	28, 124	London (Ontario)	116, 160	Molson,	146
		London Passenger Transport	162	Moncton	10

L

		Longuyon	105–106	Mondeville	42
Lachine	51	Lorimer, George	60, 71	Montgomery, General	112–113
La Hogue	45	Lossiemouth	124–125	Montmédy	111
Laird (American army air force)	113	Louis Pastuer (SS)	51	Montreal	10, 51, 85, 144, 159, 178–179
Laird, George	60–62, 64–73,	Louvain	35, 177	Mont Royal Hotel	10
75–77, 112, 116		Lübeck	130	Montzen	152, 176
Lake Erie	57, 115	Ludwigshafen	165, 167	Morgan (flying tutor)	4
Lake Hocklingen	126	Lyons	84	Morgan J.	32
Lake Manitoba	57			Morrison, Jock	76, 117
Lake Ontario	2	## M		Mount Hope	2, 50–52
Lamontaigne	66			Muir, Jean	177
Lane, Barbara	ii	Macdonald	57, 66, 76	Munich	142
Lane, David	ii	MacIntyre, Don	123, 126–127	Murphy, Pilot Officer	46
Lane, Gerald	120	Mack, Flight Lieutenant	135, 142	Murray 'Doc'	14, 22
Lane, John	ii	Magdeburg	149, 170	Murray, Emma	162–163
Lane, Norah	120	Mala Paloma	1	Murray, John	163
Lane, Reg	i–ii, 120–156	Malton	120, 143–144, 146	Murrow, Ed	169
Lane, Susan	ii	Manchester	12, 146	Musée Gaumais	91
La Neuville	46	Mangione, John	41	Musson	93–94
Langley, Squadron Leader	152	Manitoba	57, 76, 121, 143, 163	Mynarski, Andrew	39
Laon	173	Mannheim	61, 129, 142, 148, 167		
La Rochelle	46–47	Market Drayton	60–61	## N	
Leavesden	162	Marks, Jimmy	125, 132–133		
Le Bourget	33, 174	Marlborough	12	Nanton	35
Le Clipon	36	Marham	148	Narborough	121
Lee, David	iii	Martin, Jean	107	National Steel Corporation	143
Lee, Tommy	160 ,163, 181	Martin, Sergeant	123	Naybob	56, 69
Le Bois de Chenon	99	Martincourt	99	Nekvasil, Chuck	181
Le Bois d'Ire-le-Sec	103	Marseilles	84	New Brunswick	10
Lecomte, L.H.	178	Massey, Vincent	155	Newfoundland	144
Leeds	153–154	Matherley, J.	67–68	Newson, Bill	168, 172–174, 176
Leeming	20–22, 26–27, 33–34,	Mawby, Alan	iii	New York	7, 9 ,10, 51, 115
36–38, 40, 46, 48, 52, 61–62, 64, 68,		McArter, D.M.	176	Niagara Falls	4, 5
		McCarthy (wireless operator)	50	Nîmes	84

INDEX

Noisy-le-Sec 33, 152, 174–175
Norderney 123
Norris, Gino 108
Northallerton 69
North Bay 56, 61
Northolt 146
North Weald 113
Nottingham 11–12
Nova Scotia 10, 121, 154, 159–160
Nuremberg 75, 81, 96, 130, 133, 139
Nutting, S.N. 'Clare' 148

O

Odiham 154
Oisemont 40
Okinawa 154
Olliver, Flight Sergeant 44, 47
Olsvik, D. 73
Ontario ii, 1, 7, 55, 57–58, 73, 87, 116, 143, 159–161, 163, 182
Osnabrück 61, 131
Ossington 48, 49
Ottawa 6, 115–116, 120, 144, 145
Ottawa RCAF Flyers 163
Ouston 36

P

Packard Company 143
Padgate 51
Page, H.F. 117
Paris 37, 41–42, 45, 84, 107, 124, 152, 174–175
Pat O'Leary Line 84
Pattison, J.D. 22, 33
Paul, Albert 79–83, 85, 87, 89–91, 116
Paul, Anne 80
Paul, Cecile 80–83, 86–87, 116
Paul, Christian 80
Paul, Desiré 89–92
Paul, Henrietta 92
Paul, Louis 98–100
Paul, Marie-Claire 80
Paul, Monique 83
Paul, Vital 79–80, 89, 91
Pawlack, Joseph 109
Pearson, Lester 155
Perpignan 84
Peterborough (Ontario) ii, 159, 182
Peter, King of Yugoslavia 149
Petley, D. 127
P.B. Company 26
Philbin, Gerald 163, 165–166, 168–170, 172–180, 182
Phillips, Jack 19, 20, 24–25, 29, 40, 42–43, 47–48
Phillips, Jack (Reg Lane crew) 129

Picken, E. 75, 117
Pilsen 141
Pocklington 147
Pollard, L.V. 32
Pontefract 55, 72, 92
Portal, Sir Charles 60, 152
Potter, Squadron Leader 162
Power, C.G. 145
Preston 123, 162, 178
Prestwick 144,1 46
Prinz Eugen 123
Puskas, Marie ii, 52
Puskas, Mary 9, 52
Puskas, Steve ii, 1–52

Q

Queen Mary 10, 114
Quebec 155, 163, 177
Queens Hotel, Leeds 153
Quincy 107–109, 111

R

Rachecourt 81, 116
Radlett 123, 135
Ramsbury 12
Randolet, Emile 106–109
Ravet, René 83, 86
Rawlinson, Pilot Officer 27, 36
Rawson, Barney 32
Rayson, John iii
Real St Amour 177
Reed, Ray 174, 181
Regina 159
Renescure 39
Rennes 84, 177
Reynolds, K. 129
Richie, Gordon 41
Richmond, Sergeant 131
Ringway 162
Ripon 69, 72
Riversdale, Lord 6
Roberts, B. 180
Robinson,B.V. 123, 133, 136, 141
Roche, J.I. 173
Rockliffe 115–116, 155, 163
Roe, J.R. 127
Rogerson, Jack 66
Rolls-Royce 143
Romuld, Harold 41
Rootes 21, 162
Rostock 129–130
Royal Connaught Hotel 9
Royal York Hotel 52
Ruhr Express 145–146, 148
Ryan, Sergeant 165
Ryerson Technical Institute 2–3

Ryerson University 116

S

Saarbrücken 132
Saint-Brieuc 84
Saint-Nazaire 59
Saint-Valery-en-Caux 176
Samlesbury 123, 162, 178
Sandtoft 169
Sapranov, Nikolai 94, 98–99
Sarnia 160, 163
Saskatchewan 7, 41, 143, 148, 174
Saskatoon 143
Sautrecourt 39, 40, 178
Scannell, James 135, 139–141, 148, 152
Schaerbeek 84
Scharnhorst 123
Schmidt, C.J. 117
Schweinfurt 150
Sea Island 121
Selby 164
Senantes 45, 179
Shannon, Flying Officer 70
Sharp brothers 18
Sheffield 31
Shipdam 165
Sibenaler, Lucien 101–102, 104–105, 107–110
Siracourt 42
Skipton-on-Swale 43, 64, 180, 182, 184
Skoda Works 141
Slade Farm 50
Slough 163
Smith, Flight Lieutenant 8, 19
Smith Les 67, 77, 117
Snitterfield 13
Snyder, Harry 7
Soeder, 'Red' 71–72, 76–77, 116
Sonshine, Murray 169, 171
Southport 163
Sparkes, Bill 163–164
Speer, Albert 168
Speke 21, 162–163
Spencer, Al 17
Stainton, Flight Sergeant 77
Stalag Luft 7 (Seven) 180
Stamp, Les 164, 181
St Athan 162–163
St Catherines 4, 6
Steel, James 69
Steere, Gilbert 41
Stevens, Vic 126
Stevenson, George 154
Stewart 60
St Hubert 155
Still, James 'Jasper' 14–15, 28, 30, 32, 34, 38–40, 48

St Kitts 5, 7
St Leu d'Esserent 45, 180, 182
St Maximin 181–182
Stockport 162, 174
St Omer 40
Stonefall 173
Stormy Down 163
Stratford-upon-Avon 13
Strensall 60
St Thomas 160
Stuttgart 129, 136, 139, 142, 168
Sykes, Bill 123, 126, 129

T

Tait, J.B. 122
Taylor, E.P. 145
Tergnier 152
Tetlow 141
Texel 64
Thetford 121
Thirsk 69, 161
Tholthorpe iii, 164–166, 168–169, 175, 177–178, 180, 182, 184
Thomas, Mary ii
Thorpe, Sergeant 123, 129, 131, 135, 141
Thorney Island 27, 168
Timmins 55, 67, 88, 102, 116
Tir National 84
Tirpitz 124–126
Todt, Fritz 96
Todt Organisation 96
Tomlinson, Mr 174
Topcliffe 60, 161–162, 184
Torgny 90, 99, 102
Toronto 1–3, 10, 51–52, 55, 57–58, 68, 120, 143, 145, 160, 174, 177
Toulouse 84
Trans Canada Airlines 144
Trenton 51, 57
Trenton Flyers 163
Trickett, Bob 141–142
Trimingham 136
Trondheim 124, 126–127
Trossy St Maximin 45, 179, 182
Tuddenham 36
Tullock, Sergeant 135
Turin 135, 136, 139
Turnbull, Bob 60, 65, 71–72, 115
Turnbull, John 71
Turner, Lana 61

U

United Air Lines 4
Université Libre de Bruxelles 84
University of Toronto 57

Uplands 160
Upwood 172

V

Vale of York 44, 60, 70, 121, 165
Van Adel, Pilot Officer 7, 9
Vancouver 31, 121, 145, 154
Vanderkerckhove, Pierre 61
Venn, Harry 31–33, 36, 41, 48
Victoria 120, 130, 145, 154–156
Victory Aircraft Corporation 143–144
Villeneuve St George 32, 42
Villers Bocage 178
Virton 90–91, 95

W

Wallasey i, 162, 182
Wallis, Barnes 38, 40
Walmer 136
Warion, René 109
Warnemünde 129
Warrington 51, 114
Waterbeach 61
Watford 114, 162
Watten 38
Webb, Ross 143
Webster, Flying Officer 135
Weiker, Flying Officer 73
Wendling 172
Westdale High 32
Westinghouse Electric 2, 52
Weston-super-Mare 13
Weyburn 148
Whitbread, David 182
Willey, A.E. 23
Wiley, Doug 164, 174, 176–177
Williams, Alvin 14, 29, 31, 48
Williams, Rod 48
Williams, Sergeant 122–123, 129, 131
Wilson, Sergeant 15, 36, 48
Wilson, Wilbur 16, 29, 45
Wing 70
Winnipeg 154
Wittering 172
Wizernes 40
Wombleton 184
Wood, Geoff iii
Woodbridge 41
Woodford 143, 146
Wormald Green 71
Wright, Bill 143

Y

Yardley, Warrant Officer 20

Yarmouth (Nova Scotia) 160
Yelling 148
Yenka 98–99
York 21, 52, 60, 122–123, 143, 147, 156, 164–165
Yorkshire Air Museum 155
Young, Albert 2, 4, 13–14, 23

Z

Zellen (air gunner) 11